D1757938

Warwickshire College

00500194

The book

François Baucher (1796–1863) was the centre of one of the most famous controversies in the development of modern equitation. Baucher introduced the one-tempo flying change at the canter, but in nineteenth-century France his circus performances and methods of *haute-école* training were attacked. Attempts to introduce his theories to the French cavalry were blocked, although he is now recognized as an outstanding horseman and exponent of Classical dressage. This important work combines a translation of two of Baucher's publications, *New method of horsemanship* and *Dialogues on equitation*, with a scholarly study of the arguments which surrounded them. Professor Nelson produces a fascinating insight into an important theory of horsemanship.

The author

Hilda Nelson is the Emeritus Professor of French Civilization and Literature at San Diego State University in Southern California. She is the author of several books and articles on the subject, and translated Antoine de Pluvinel's classic of horsemanship *Le Maneige Royal* for J. A. Allen. In 1983–4 she spent part of a sabbatical at St Antony's College, Oxford, and still visits England and France once or twice a year to pursue her investigations into the relationship between Classical horsemanship and Humanism, both through written works and through observation at the Ecole Nationale at Saumur. She also takes dressage lessons both in England and the United States. She lives with her husband, horses and dogs at Mount Laguna, California, in the midst of the Cleveland National Forest.

FRANÇOIS BAUCHER
THE MAN AND HIS METHOD

Baucher working his horse Capitaine at the Franconi circus in front of Commandant de Novital, with (left to right) L'Hotte, Caroline Loya and Franconi looking on. Gouache and crayon drawing by Commandant Margot. (Courtesy G. Margot)

FRANÇOIS BAUCHER
THE MAN AND HIS METHOD

Hilda Nelson

J. A. ALLEN
London

Dedication
For Burt, who lived through it all.

British Library Cataloguing in Publication Data
Nelson, Hilda
    Baucher: the man and his method.
    I. Title
    798.2092
    ISBN 0851315348

Published in Great Britain in 1992 by

J. A. Allen & Company Limited,
1 Lower Grosvenor Place, London SW1W OEL

Text editor Elizabeth O'Beirne-Ranelagh
Text designer Nancy Lawrence

Printed in Hong Kong by Dah Hua Printing

Contents

Contents

PART THREE
Dialogues on equitation by François Baucher   157

Foreword

Was François Baucher (born 1796, died 1873) the equestrian world's Leonardo da Vinci? Hilda Nelson, with a devastating impartiality backed up by equestrian scholarship, proves to this reader at least that Baucher was — and with no doubt whatsoever.

Leonardo da Vinci, with his many sensational inventions, studies, and works of art — one being his detailed study of equine locomotion which, 500 years later, is still undiscovered by scientists and equestrians alike — now seems to be complemented by the equestrian studies and inventions of Baucher in the nineteenth century. One example is Baucher's 'invention' during the early part of the nineteenth century of the one-tempo flying changes at the canter. To many experts, this is the most difficult requirement of modern competition dressage at national, international and Olympic levels. Another example is Baucher's unbelievably simple 'dismounted' method of suppling the horse — head, neck, shoulders, limbs, and hindquarters — in several days, making the most dangerous equine rogue tractable, obedient and safe to ride.

The suppling of the horse from the saddle was — and unfortunately still is — 'tradition'. Baucher's suppling of the horse from the ground without a rider calls for additional equestrian tact and subtlety from the trainer, that is deftness blended with finesse. These qualities have to be learnt and mastered by diligent practice, as each horse's character and behaviour is different. Once mastered the trainer has the 'key' to equine balance and lightness. Yet working

the horse on foot appears to be 'menial' to those who regard the horse as human carrier extraordinaire.

Two months of work, consisting of two lessons a day of a half hour each — that is to say, one hundred and twenty lessons — will be amply sufficient to bring the greenest horse to perform regularly all the preceding exercises. [These include the flying changes and piaffe. CH] I hold to two short lessons a day, one in the morning, the other in the afternoon; they are necessary to obtain good results.

We disgust a young horse by keeping him too long at exercises that fatigue him, the more so as his intelligence is less prepared to understand what we wish to demand of him. On the other hand, an interval of twenty-four hours is too long, in my opinion, for the animal to remember the next day what he had comprehended the day before. (p. 140)

These achievements Baucher demonstrated time and time again throughout his riding life, with dangerous horses destined for the slaughterhouse, and upon whom within eight to ten weeks he was giving high-school displays, night after night at the circus. These displays took place before a clamorous public with much controversy between opposing factions of nobility and military on both sides, pro-Baucheristes and anti-Baucheristes. The more famous followers of Baucher had their own permanent and private *loges* or boxes at the circus, in a manner similar to the private boxes in many Opera Houses today.

Part One of this volume is devoted to Baucher's biography, and is summarized with exemplary fair-mindedness by Hilda Nelson, who does not pass speculation off as fact, although her researches have clearly been diligent, nor does she claim to have made any sensational discoveries. Yet there emerges from this work several aspects of 'Classical horsemanship' which may well break down long-held prejudices which even now tend to stultify riding as a pure science and art!

To this reader, it is the most important equestrian – and dressage – publication of the century, which carefully develops and then brings to fruition the final break from the harsh disciplines of sixteenth to eighteenth century 'organised riding establishments with its Riding Masters, Aristocrats, Nobility, and Military equestrianism', as practised in those Classical and military riding academies which originated in the Renaissance, and which still influence horsemanship to this day, where equestrianism is fundamentally based on the precepts, principles and practices of Guérinière.

Guérinière is still generally accepted as the 'Father' of equestrian science, on whose methods the Spanish Riding School in Vienna bases its teachings. But here, for the first time in over 150 years, we are presented with the details of those 'destructive equestrian politics' which attempted to subdue and wipe out – but did not succeed, because of the support given to Baucher at the time – what fortunately for Classical horsemanship Baucher exposed with unbelievable simplicity: the many 'truths' of equestrian theory, practice, science, and art, based on Baucher's then modern precepts. Baucher demonstrated and taught throughout his life that often claimed 'mysterious quality', known by every horseman and horsewoman as 'equestrian ease, lightness, tact and obedience', defined and much discussed throughout the world of equestrianism, but seldom if ever seen. Its last great exponent – now sadly missed – and one of Baucher's most sincere disciples, was the greatly respected and brilliant Portuguese horseman, Nuño Oliveira.

For the reader who carefully reads and studies Baucher's biography in Part One, and the outcome of those jealous forces of 'equestrian politics', Hilda Nelson's presentation in Parts Two and Three of Baucher's own works is once again likely to provoke some deep thinking and meditation in the science and art of horsemanship. Baucher's opponents (and there are still two active schools of thought in France today, one for and one against, as there was when he was alive) claim that there 'is' and 'was' nothing new in his thinking, theories, and applications! Baucher's volumes presented here prove his opponents to be incorrect.

My first sentence in this Foreword posed the question, was Baucher the Leonardo da Vinci of horsemanship? Can such an emphatic statement be substantiated?

(1) There is no doubt (as the evidence exists in his writings) that Baucher was the first horseman to understand the science – and relevance – of combining the horse's centre of gravity with his centre of motion. Hence the stunning and amazing ease and lightness of his horses, which was the hallmark of his schooling and training methods. His genius, confirmed by his continued success with dangerous horse after dangerous horse, which he put on public display for about half-a-century for all to evaluate, has never been equalled or surpassed.

(2) The one-tempo flying changes at canter were unknown – and unheard of – and because his adversaries could not achieve such 'Classical horsemanship', with even one horse, they spent year after year trying to character-assassinate him. As he produced problem horse after problem horse in the flying changes at one tempo with such ease, charm, and lightness, his opponents then claimed that 'manèged' horses would be unsuitable for military manoeuvre, completely ignoring the fact that all military horses were 'heavy on the hand' and difficult to 'manoeuvre'.

(3) The 'Classical academies and riding schools' would spend years endeavouring to supple their horses in 'shoulder-in' under the rider, which is the practice of many riders today.

Baucher in his 'dismounted suppling' of his horses achieved in ten to twelve days what it took the 'Ecuyers' years to obtain, and even then many did not achieve their ultimate goal. Perhaps the reader is now beginning to appreciate the great political equestrian controversies which existed between the so-called 'Classical school' and Baucher's then 'modern Classicism'.

(4) The Spanish Riding School in Vienna bases its teachings on the principles and precepts of Guérinière. There was no 'suppling' of the rider at halt and in movement (on the lunge) in teaching the rider Classical horsemanship. So where did the lungeing of the rider originate, as carried out by the Spanish Riding School of Vienna, where its pupil-riders daily have their first lesson on the lunge without reins and stirrups, continuing for their three years of training until they become 'riders'? As the first outside 'student rider' to attend this famous riding school after the Second World War, I also had to carry out my lunge lesson each day without reins and stirrups on a 'School Stallion'. It now seems that Baucher's rider-suppling exercises — again, the first ever of their kind — were known to the Spanish Riding School, where their lungeing of the rider was developed from the new and unique rider gymnastics invented and taught by Baucher at halt and when moving on horseback.

Baucher's achievements are not helped by the lack of equestrian sensitivity and understanding of his translators. Here is a typical example taken at random: Baucher's 'imprisonment of the horse between hand and leg'. This equestrian literalism is, in the application of Classical horsemanship, no more and no less than 'containing and uniting the horse between the rider's hand and leg', yet the former implies a tendency to 'destroy', and the latter to 'aid' the horse — a subtle and very important equestrian difference and distinction!

A question sometimes posed is: Why is Baucher scientifically correct and his opposition wrong? The answer to me is simple logic. If the rider requires obedience, efficiency in posture and locomotion, combined with lightness and safety on horseback, the horse must be able to adjust his balance, to the point where he can bring his centre of gravity directly, vertically below and as close as possible to his centre of motion. When this can be achieved with the minimum tension, it is then essential that the rider's centre of gravity is situated directly over the horse's centres of gravity and motion. This is the simple mechanics of equestrian 'logical' science, the basis of true Classical horsemanship. This 'key' Baucher has given to the riding world. Such 'riding logic' is also proven day after day in hunting, steeplechasing and hurdling, eventing, etc. and can be seen in both equestrian and national press photographs. For any rider to try and find and 'perch' over the horse's continually moving centre of gravity — if he knows where it is at any given point — is undoubtedly the cause of so many riding accidents and injuries. Yet the latter is recommended and apparently taught by many national authorities throughout the riding world.

There are many other equestrian aspects contained in this impressive work written and compiled by Hilda Nelson, and for those interested in equestrian scholarship and classical horsemanship — including all dressage activists — this volume may well provide many 'missing links' to the science and art of riding, its consummate ease and beauty. In a nutshell, this volume is a unique equestrian library in its own right, forming an equestrian history of the nineteenth century studded with equestrian gems, many of which seem to have been mislaid in twentieth-century equestrian scholarship.

Charles Harris

PART ONE

François Baucher and the controversy in nineteenth-century French equitation

by Hilda Nelson

1

Introduction

A study of nineteenth-century France reveals a ferment and a multiplicity of ideas and movements, sometimes opposing each other, sometimes complementing each other. Monarchy, absolutist or constitutional, and Republicanism, democratic or oligarchic, opposed each other in the political arena. The declining nobility, and the continually ascending bourgeoisie, rivalled each other and jockeyed for supremacy. A third force soon confronted the two established groups, namely, the newly forming proletariat. Economic policies such as *laissez-faire* and utopian socialism vied with each other, each one promising the millennium. In religion and philosophy Catholicism and Protestantism locked horns with Oriental mysticism, Positivism and scepticism. In literature and art the battle raged between Classicism and Romanticism; and even within the new Romantic movement, conflicts and inconsistencies became apparent. These many-faceted conflicts and inconsistencies were also evident within individuals. Victor Hugo was first a Monarchist, then championed Republicanism and the masses. Charles Nodier, an ardent Monarchist, was, by education, overtly a proponent of Classicism, but temperamentally tended toward Romanticism and Shakespeare. These conflicts and inconsistencies began to rage in the pages of newspapers and reviews of the age, some, like *Le Drapeau Blanc, Le Journal des Débats* and *La Quotidienne*, supporting the *ancien régime* and Classicism, others such as *Le National* and *Le Globe* advocating Republicanism, socialism and Romanticism. The pro-

ponents of conservatism and Classicism were opposed to Romanticism because they saw it as the result of the subversive ideas that had emanated from Albion's shores and from beyond the Rhine. England especially, it was felt, had been largely responsible for the ideas that were not only infesting the nineteenth century, but had also influenced eighteenth-century France, the age of the *philosophes*, those believers in progress and the perfectibility of man whom the Classicists and Monarchists held responsible for the Revolution of 1789. Even the theatre of Shakespeare was considered subversive. Plays such as *Othello, Hamlet, King Lear* and even *Romeo and Juliet* were often edited and stripped of all violence, thereby making them more palatable to French sensibilities. Critic and spectator alike shuddered with horror and disgust at the thought that Mme de Staël could prefer an atrocity such as *Hamlet* to *Cinna* or *Phèdre*.

Classicism and Romanticism express different ways of looking at man and the universe. According to Kenneth Clark, Classicism belongs to a more reasonable world, a world that is consistent, symmetrical and enclosed. Romanticism longs for a world that is unbounded and infinite, continually in motion. For Charles Baudelaire, Romanticism exists 'in the way one feels' and is 'the most recent and the most modern expression of beauty ... He who says Romanticism is saying modern art — that is to say, intimacy, spirituality, colour, aspiration towards the infinite, as expressed by

One of the acts at the Franconi circus. (*The Horseman's Year* (London, 1950))

all the means that the arts contain.'[1] Indeed, Romanticism influenced and changed many aspects of life. Even in such less artistic and creative fields as, say, the garden, changes and adaptations that could be termed 'romantic' had already become evident. The eighteenth-century English garden had already made a clean break with the borrowed French style of clipped trees and straight geometric avenues. This revolution in garden design was a very English affair which, in turn, influenced the French. Another similar revolution, also emanating from England, could be detected in the field of horsemanship. The battle between Classicism and Romanticism that affected literature, art and other fields of endeavour was

also evident in the art of riding.

England of the eighteenth and nineteenth centuries was an England rich politically, socially, industrially and commercially, and it fascinated and attracted many Europeans: royalty, the nobility and the bourgeoisie alike. This holds true in literature. The gothic novels of Hugh Walpole, Anne Radcliffe and William Beckford were emulated by such writers as Charles Nodier, Balzac, Hugo and even Stendhal. The epistolary and sentimental novels of Samuel Richardson were also emulated in France by Choderlos de Laclos and Rousseau. In the domain of commerce, industry and technology, England and Scotland had developed much more fully and rapidly than

---

[1] Charles Baudelaire, *L'Art romantique* (Paris, Garnier, 1962), p. 103.

had France and other European nations. Likewise, in the field of equitation England had, for example, developed the Thoroughbred. Riding in the open air and, with it, the rising trot, was also a very English affair. Horse-racing, cross-country and the steeplechase were also of English origin. France's first covered circus with a round arena, which eventually became the 'English Amphitheatre' in Paris, was founded in 1783 by an Englishman, Philip Astley; he later associated himself with the famous Antonio Franconi, an Italian living in France and a well-known horseman. It was the Franconi family that played an important role in the further development of the circus and the presentation of *haute école* equitation in the circus.

Anglomania did, indeed, become a prevalent attitude in France. An important consequence of this Anglomania was democratization. Democratization had, to some extent, already become evident in the political, social and economic arena of French life, first during the Revolution of 1789, and then, to some extent, when Napoleon I sought to reconcile some of the achievements of the Revolution with the *ancien régime*. With the reinstatement of the Bourbons, attempts were made, especially under Charles X, to return to the old order, but they only succeeded in giving it the final death blow. Indeed, revolutions and wars always change societies and sensibilities and, despite the frequent swinging of the pendulum, the political and social revolutions of 1789 and 1830, together with the Industrial and Romantic revolutions, had an enormous impact on the institutions and thought of the age.

Democratization soon manifested itself in the life-styles of certain social classes. The nobility, consciously or unconsciously, became more bourgeois as they, albeit reluctantly, accepted the bourgeoisie into their ranks, even into their families through marriage. In turn, the bourgeoisie emulated more and more the nobility. Indeed, democratization also manifested itself in the art of riding. England had already been more democratic than France in

its development of horsemanship. While it is true that hunting had been a royal privilege and knightly activities had been banned by English kings, the right to participate in equestrian activities had very soon become a right for the English country squire and the English gentleman. One must not forget that in England there had never been a concentration of the aristocracy around the king as had existed in France, thus making democracy possible in England at a more rapid pace. While in France the nobility still dominated in the art of riding, the dandies and the *amazones* who were taking to riding were not always aristocrats; rather, rich bankers and industrialists — with or without titles — got into the equitation act; that is, equitation was now open to all who could afford this sport.

Thus in France the art of riding and the hunt, heretofore the privilege of royalty and the nobility, were taken over by the bourgeoisie. With the Restoration, and especially the Bourgeois Monarchy of 1830, *manèges* were founded in Paris, as well as in the provinces, for it had become fashionable to ride. To possess an English Thoroughbred and a hound and go riding in the Bois de Boulogne or the Bois de Saint-Germain became the thing. The Bois de Boulogne soon became a meeting place for the *jeunesse dorée*, that is, for the dandies and the *amazones* of Paris, noble and bourgeois alike. Another symbol of the age was the founding of the Jockey Club in 1833 by a group of dandies and with the blessing of Lord Seymour, an Englishman of great wealth, living in France and an ardent horseman. Likewise the circus began to attract not only the proletariat; the bourgeoisie and even royalty and the nobility came to watch circus equerries, male and female, perform *haute école* equitation. Rather than perform merely animal acts and the typical acrobatic acts on horseback, skilled horsemen and horsewomen, familiar with *haute école* techniques, became the rage and received top billing. It was in the circus that François Baucher was able to practise and exhibit his skill in horsemanship.

Count Antoine Cartier D'Aure (1799–1863).

François Baucher (1796–1873), a lithograph by
Lasalle made for Baucher's *Oeuvres complètes* in
1854.

Nineteenth-century France was lucky to have had two horsemen of great merit, François Baucher and Count Antoine Cartier d'Aure, who rekindled interest in French equitation, giving it, once again, the prestige it had had in the seventeenth and eighteenth centuries under such horsemen as Antoine de Pluvinel and François Robichon de La Guérinière and which it had lost during and after the Revolution of 1789. During this period of renown, the Classical period, France had specialized primarily in *manège* riding, also known as *savante* or Classical riding, involving *haute école*. This type of equitation was mostly a stationary and spectator-oriented kind of activity, wherein skilled horsemen exhibited the various movements such as the *passade*, the *ballotade*, the *capriole* and other airs. This *haute école* equitation had

initially been performed to prepare the horse for war; later, for self-gratification and the enjoyment of the court. During the reign of Louis XIII and, especially, the reign of Louis XIV, horse ballets, known as *caroussels*, and knightly games such as tilting the ring or the *quintaine*, were reintroduced and performed before the king and his entourage.

While *manège* riding had developed primarily in such countries as Italy, France and Spain, in England the hunt, the steeplechase, cross-country, horse-racing (and, of course, travel) were the chief activities involving equitation. This type of equitation was an outside or exterior equitation; *manège* riding, as it existed on the Continent, never took hold in England. To participate in *manège* riding, a young English nobleman had to go to the Continent, as the

Duke of Newcastle had done.[2]

When during the Restoration the attempt was made to restore the art of riding to its former glory, the masters of the re-established *Ecole de Versailles*, who taught young princes and pages to ride, and those of the *Ecole de Cavalerie* at Saumur, who taught the cavalry officers, were divided among themselves as to the type of equitation that should be taught. The Classicists and academically minded equerries at Versailles and Saumur wished a return to the academic, Classical tradition of the *manège* type of equitation of the past, an equitation that required several years of training and involved exactitude and precision at all times on the part of the horseman. The modernists wanted horsemanship to be simplified and more natural, more in keeping with the kind of equitation practised in England, that is, exterior equitation, with the hunt seat and the rising trot, as well as the military equitation practised in Prussia that stressed riding in formation, the undertaking of simple missions, and so on. While exterior and military equitation was simpler and more natural, it nevertheless demanded that the rider be more aggressive and daring. Thus for the cavalryman and the dandies and *amazones* of the *Bois*, the artificial airs, especially the high airs, had to be abandoned. The modern horseman or horsewoman had to sit deeper in the saddle with the stirrups shortened, and, most importantly, gentler bits such as the snaffle, the bridoon or the pelham, with a considerably shorter curb, had to be introduced.

These two approaches, that is, the Classical and the modernist, were epitomized in the methods of equitation of Baucher and d'Aure. Democratization and the recent stress on sports undoubtedly highlighted this controversy in that it included the press and a public from many walks of life and professions. Further-more, this controversy was not merely a conflict between two horsemen of differing techniques and methods in horsemanship. Underlying and paralleling this conflict in methods were other conflicts. Despite the democratization occurring in the art of riding, a class conflict was also evident in the clash between the aristocrat d'Aure and the *petit bourgeois*, François Baucher. In d'Aure we have the former *protégé* of Charles X, later teacher of equitation to the sons of Louis-Philippe, the Duke d'Orléans and the Duke de Nemours, equerry at the *Ecole de Versailles* until it was closed in 1830, thereafter owner and director of several fashionable *manèges* in Paris, and author of *Traité d' Equitation* (1834). Baucher was a teacher and trainer of horses in private *manèges*, first in the provinces, later, after 1834, in Paris. There he became associated with the Jules-Charles Pellier *manège* and, shortly thereafter, became a circus rider of *haute école* equitation at the Franconi circus. While Baucher, although the author of a little-known manual entitled *Dictionnaire raisonné d' Equitation* (1833), was struggling in the provinces in the early 1830s and a virtual unknown, d'Aure was recognized as an outstanding horseman, a dare-devil riding at breakneck speed, who, at the *Ecole de Versailles*, was already reacting against the formulae and routine of *manège* riding, practising exterior equitation and the rising trot, and using the English saddle.

The controversy between the two horsemen became evident in 1842 when Baucher published his *Méthode d'Equitation basée sur de nouveaux principes* wherein he presented his *nouvelle méthode* pertaining to the schooling of horses. The controversy was further expanded when the army began to show an interest in examining and, perhaps, implementing Baucher's *nouvelle méthode* in the various cavalry schools.

---

[2] It was Pignatelli, director of the famous Neapolitan Riding School, who had taught the Duke of Newcastle and Antoine de Pluvinel. Pignatelli was a disciple of Frederico Grisone, a Neapolitan nobleman, author of *Gli Ordini di Cavalcare*, published in 1550, founder and director of the Neapolitan Riding School and discoverer of Xenophon's work *On Horsemanship*.

Ecole de Cavalerie, Saumur, scenes from the *caroussel*. Jumping a fence, jumping free, saluting the officers, tilting at the ring. (Musée de Saumur)

Baucher's method, while termed *nouvelle*, remains, nevertheless, in the idiom of what is known as *manège, savante*, academic or Classical equitation. Baucher's method is almost exclusively devoted to the schooling of the horse, less to the training of the rider. (Only much later did he include a chapter dealing with the schooling of the rider.) The goal of Baucher's method is the total disposition of the horse's strength and the total submission of the horse to the will of the horseman. To accomplish this Baucher's method devotes considerable time to making the horse supple, well-balanced and light and easy to handle. The disposition of the horse's strength is accomplished by placing or, rather, compressing the horse between the hands and legs of the horseman, that is, there is an interplay of a combination of opposing forces wherein the horse is sent forward by the legs (spurs) and retained by the hands (reins). This opposition of forces is to obtain the horse's obedience by containing or immobilizing the horse through the *effets d'ensemble* (coordinated effects; see Ch. 3). One achieves this desired absence of resistance, or 'neutralization', and lightness of the horse by a long period of *assouplissement (suppling)*, that is, by the lateral flexion of the muscles of the jaws, neck and withers, as well as other muscular strengths of the horse. Exercises such as the *ramener* (flexing of the head at the poll) and the *reculer* (rein-back) contribute to this *assouplissement*. The *rassembler* (collection), 'which consists in collecting all his strength to the centre of the horse in order to lighten his two extremities, and to place them completely at the disposal of the horseman',[3] also plays an important role in the *assouplissement* of the horse and the disposition of his muscular strengths. The horse now functions only by means of the transmitted force of the horseman rather than his own instinctive or natural force. In addition, the horse's psyche or, as Baucher puts it, the horse's mental disposition is also controlled.

Despite his traditionalist and Classical training, d'Aure's equestrian art was in direct opposition to that of Baucher. Already before the closing of the doors of the *manège* of the *Ecole de Versailles* in 1830, d'Aure had foreseen and understood the need to modify the former techniques of equitation, adapt the old ones, and adopt new ones to conform to the new era and to the demands of the new horsemen and horsewomen. He was a modernist superimposed upon a traditionalist. A Classicist by training, he was a Romanticist and modernist by temperament.

D'Aure's type of equitation exemplified the new equitation, exterior equitation, and consisted primarily of forming aggressive and enterprising horsemen. In his *Traité d'Equitation*, he says that since English equitation is primarily devoted to racing and the hunt, the English consider speed 'as the most important quality' and thus, in the training of young horses, they use 'methods that are the correct ones to push them forward'.[4] D'Aure's own method can be summarized as going 'forward! always forward! and once again forward!'. This slogan is the opposite of that of Baucher. While both Baucher and d'Aure stressed balance and considered impulsion as important in the horse's rhythmical and free forward movement, Baucher's aim was total control and complete balance of the horse. D'Aure's aim was impulsion and directness, for he wanted to use the horse's natural movements and avoid any prolonged constraints on the horse. Instead of producing an artificial and total balance, d'Aure wanted to produce a natural balance. Furthermore, d'Aure's type of equitation was instinctive and personal, allowing the horseman considerable freedom to develop his own tech-

[3] François Baucher, 'Méthode d'Equitation basée sur de nouveaux principes', *Oeuvres complètes* (Paris, published by the author and Dumaine, Librairie Militaire, 1854), p. 168. A translation of this work by an unknown translator appears in Part Two of this book; the excerpts in Part One, however, are my own translations.
[4] Antoine Cartier d'Aure, *Traité d'Equitation* (Paris, Leclère, 1834), p. 49.

niques, his own improvisation and initiative. The aim was to develop a horseman skilled and capable of riding anywhere and on any horse. With respect to the schooling of a horse, it was important to channel his strength and contain him between hands and legs to permit the adequate mastery of his movements and the regulation of his paces. The aim was not to break the horse and not to extinguish everything that a horse possesses of action and energy. What d'Aure feared most was the weakening or lessening of impulsion by compressing the horse completely between the rider's hands and legs as Baucher did. He also feared too much flexion of the neck and jaw. In other words, d'Aure did not wish to dominate and overbend the horse as completely as did Baucher.

An analysis of d'Aure's *Traité* and his *Observations* reveals that simplification and modification did not mean that the achievements of the past were to be completely cast aside. While simplicity and ease in all the paces with respect to the rider, and less collection and more extension with respect to the horse, were desirable, careful training of horse and rider was still founded on Classical principles. Only when the horseman had acquired Classical and traditional training could he forsake these principles and deviate from formulae and routine. While outside equitation took precedence over *manège* or academic equitation, d'Aure saw the importance of *manège* equitation as a means of schooling horses. In short, it must be understood, 'that the *manège* is a means and not an end'.[5]

---

[5] Antoine Cartier d'Aure, *Observations sur la nouvelle méthode d'Equitation* (Paris, Leneveu, 1842), p. 21.

2

Baucher: his life and times

The Revolution of 1789 with all its ideals and enthusiasm was over. The revolutionaries had swallowed each other and the Thermidorian Revolution of July 1794 brought about the downfall and execution of Robespierre. By 1796, the year of the birth of François Baucher, the Five Sires of the Directory were, if not firmly, at least comfortably, in the saddle.[1] Napoleon Bonaparte, now a general, was leading the former Revolutionary Army against another Coalition in Italy.

Very little is known about the personal life of Baucher, because Baucher said very little about his origins, his youth, or his beginnings in the world of equitation (his treatise on the treatment of prisoners is perhaps the most intimate revelation he has made about himself). Nothing is ever mentioned about his family life, especially his wife. We know that he had an only son, Henri, who helped him experiment with his *nouvelle méthode* in the army. Through his pupil, General L'Hotte, we know that Henri and his son were present at the funeral of Baucher. There is no mention of any other family member. While everyone agrees that he was born and grew up in Versailles, some historians claim that he was born in the Rue des Boucheries, 'a stone's throw' from the former *Ecuries royales*, and that his father was a butcher. Neither of these two claims seems to be correct. A look at several old maps of Versailles going back to 1796, 1826, 1829 and 1836 reveals that there was no Rue des

Boucheries at the time of Baucher's childhood. A Rue des Porcheries near the slaughterhouse not far from the *Ecuries royales* and a Rue aux Boeufs did, indeed, exist, but not 'a stone's throw' away. An up-to-date map of Versailles shows a Rue F. Boucher (spelled with an *ou*); but the early maps consulted do not reveal the existence of any streets at all in the area where today's street is located, only open fields.

The Revolution of 1789 had closed the doors of these aristocratic establishments and almost all the men and officers involved with the *Ecole de Versailles* had gone into exile. Many had emigrated to Hamburg in 1789 to join the Army of Princes which formed the Coalition against Revolutionary France. Subalterns had taken over after the departure of most of the aristocrats. In 1793 the Revolutionary Convention had suppressed all the cavalry schools of the monarchy, creating instead militarized schools. Their function now was the rapid formation of military instructors who could develop an efficient cavalry of the Revolution. In 1796 the Directory decreed the creation of an *Ecole Nationale d' Equitation*. With the Consulate and the Empire, the *Grande Armée* of Napoleon continued to need trained cavalry officers to ward off other Coalitions formed against France. It was only with the return of the Bourbons that the *Ecole de Versailles* was re-opened in 1815. In Saumur an *Ecole d'Instruction des troupes à cheval*, by royal decree of December 1814, was opened in March 1815.

---

[1] The Directory was a short-lived conservative government which followed the extreme revolutionary government.

Despite the loss of its past glory, the Versailles of post-revolutionary days re-introduced academic, *savante* or Classical equitation, with its *airs relevés* and other equestrian practices. As a child Baucher was able to witness military equestrian exercises and parades that were daily occurring on the parade grounds in front of the buildings of the newly formed *Ecole National d'Equitation*. But his early contact with the art of riding was not limited to watching the officers of the armies of the Revolution and Napoleon's *Grande Armée* as they rode in formation or individually from the parade grounds into the countryside. One of his uncles, about whom little is known, was the individual who initiated the fourteen-year-old Baucher into his vocation and profession. How this brother of Baucher's father had acquired knowledge in the art of riding is not known. Nevertheless, during the Empire of Napoleon, Uncle Baucher was directing the stables of Prince Borghese, who had become a member of the imperial family through his marriage to Pauline Bonaparte, Napoleon's sister, and had thus been named governor of Piedmont in 1807 by the Emperor. As Governor of Milan the Prince obviously required a stable that was in accordance with his new status. It was left to his director, Baucher, to make frequent visits to France in search of appropriate mounts, carriages and personnel to bring back to the stables in Milan. It was on one of those scouting expeditions in 1810 that the uncle, returning to Milan with mounts and other equipment for the Prince's stables, also brought back with him his fourteen-year-old nephew, François. Baucher's enthusiasm for horses and the equestrian art and his lack of interest to go into his father's wine business had made it easy for his uncle to lure the young boy away from his home. The young Baucher began his professional training in the world of equitation and in life under the tutelage of his uncle in Milan. Whether Baucher had been formally initiated into the art of horsemanship in Versailles is unclear, even unlikely.[2]

In Milan, Baucher worked tirelessly and enthusiastically as an apprentice groom and learned a great deal from his uncle and other equerries of renown. At the time the art of riding in Italy was still dominated by the Neapolitan Riding School that had developed during the Renaissance under Césare Fiaschi, Frederico Grisone, Giambattista Pignatelli and others. It was in Naples, under the tutelage of Pignatelli, that such equerries as Antoine de Pluvinel (1555?–1620) and the Duke of Newcastle (1593–1676) had received their training in equitation. Both Pluvinel and Newcastle, upon their return to their respective countries, while introducing the techniques they had learned at the Neapolitan Riding School, nevertheless did much to change certain aspects of the Neapolitan School which they considered undesirable, namely the inordinately harsh bits and the overly rigorous treatment given to the horse. During Baucher's sojourn in Italy, one of Italy's great equerries, Mazuchelli, was training horses at the Academy of Milan. Mazuchelli still used the rigorous and harsh techniques developed by the Neapolitan School in the training of his horses. He lunged his horses at great length and continued to put them to the pillars to make them supple. He used excessively harsh cavessons and bits with teeth to subdue his horses, as well as the various types of whips which had already been abandoned by more progressive horsemen and equerries. Undoubtedly the observations made by Baucher as he witnessed the training of

---

[2] In an Introduction to the 1859 edition of his *Oeuvres complètes* (p. 375), Baucher reveals that as a child he had first studied manuals of equitation and then practised the equestrian art. 'I believed', he goes on to say, 'that by reading all these works I could obtain a solid instruction, and then set about the art with certitude and knowledge; well! I must admit, that after having studied these treatises, I was less capable of reasoning and even of executing the art than before.' It is revelations such as these that made it possible for his critics to accuse him of having taken up horsemanship late in life. (See, for example, the letter by Boutard to Aubert discussed in Chapter 5 below.)

Mazuchelli's horses, together with his innate astuteness and gentle disposition, must have been instrumental later on in his own humane treatment of the horse.

The downfall of Napoleon's Empire in 1814 and the return of the Monarchy brought with them the demise of those individuals Napoleon had set up in the various countries and regions occupied by the *Grande Armée*. It was also the end of Baucher's and his uncle's sojourn in Italy. Baucher's experiences and observations at the Milan stables, as well as visits to other stables in Italy, gave the young man sufficient knowledge and self-assurance to continue in his new profession. But before striking out on his own, he first returned to Versailles in 1814, a young man of eighteen. During his short stay in Versailles, he was now able to witness, with the return of the Bourbons, the re-opening of the *Ecole royale de Versailles*. He saw the return of many of the great equerries of the *ancien régime*. He greatly admired the Viscount d'Abzac and later told General L'Hotte that as a child he had watched d'Abzac as he rode on or off the parade grounds. However, Baucher could only have watched d'Abzac in this later period, since d'Abzac had retired to his estate in the Dordogne in 1781, letting his younger brother take over as *écuyer cavalcadour* and *ordinaire*.[3] Furthermore, d'Abzac left France in 1791 to participate in the campaign of the Army of Princes in 1792. He returned to Versailles in 1814, long after the decree of 1802 which gave amnesty to the *émigrés*. Back in Versailles he was, once again, in charge of the royal *manège* (taking command of the First *Manège* while his brother was in charge of the Second *Manège*). After his brother retired in 1819, the Viscount d'Abzac took charge of both *manéges*, now combined into one, which

he directed until his death in 1827. It was his favourite pupil, Count d'Aure, who took over as *écuyer cavalcadour*. His other pupils had included Louis XVI, Louis XVIII and Charles X.

However, it should be noted that while returning to the training of the king's household and pages and a return to *savante* and Classical equitation with its *haute école* airs, the Restoration never regained its lustre of the past in equitation. Aside from the fact that the king and his household no longer lived in Versailles, a new phenomenon was entering into the picture, namely exterior riding with the rising trot, shorter stirrups, and gentler bits such as the snaffle and the pelham. Also developing to a degree was military riding, which had already begun to penetrate France from the court of Frederic the Great during the eighteenth century. When, after the Seven Years' War, Choiseul[4] reorganized the *Ecole de Cavalerie* in Saumur in 1763, military equitation was very gradually and sparingly being introduced. Names such as Comte de Lubersac, Drumond de Melfort, Chabannes and, above all, d'Auvergne, who was the most influential in attempting to introduce military equitation in France, are associated with the new trend. All wanted to simplify equitation, to make it more natural and bolder, and to eliminate, if not totally, at least to some extent the artificial airs in the training of cavalry officers. With the reorganization of the *Ecole d'Instruction des troupes* in Saumur under Louis XVIII, training of horse and rider was, indeed, simplified, in the belief that it sufficed that the cavalrymen know enough to be able to ride in formation, undertake simple messages, and a few other similar missions. Its function was to train instructors, some to go on teaching mounted troops, and others, that is, the academically

---

[3] *Ecuyer cavalcadour* was a term used until 1830 to designate an equerry (Master of the Horse) who directed the stables of horses belonging to the king or princes and who also schooled these horses; *écuyer ordinaire* was used to designate equerries who served in an ordinary and regular capacity in the Royal Household.

[4] The Duke de Choiseul was a protégé of Madame de Pompadour, mistress to Louis XV. Along with the Ministry of Foreign Affairs, he also controlled the ministries of the army and the navy under Louis XV. After France's defeat and humiliation in the Seven Years' War (1755–1763), Choiseul set out to rebuild France's navy and initiated many other military changes, including changes in the cavalry schools.

Between the pillars at Saumur. (Musée de Saumur)

minded ones, to train civilian equerries. The former wore blue uniforms; the latter, in black uniforms, were known as the Cadre Noir. With the re-establishment of schools of cavalry in Saumur and Versailles, master equerries in both cities were divided as to what form of training should be given to the cavalry officers, the newer simplified methods that had already penetrated into France from Prussia during the second half of the eighteenth century, together with those that were now emanating from England, with its stress on exterior riding; or should one return to the methods of Classical and *savante* equitation, that is, *haute école* equitation. It was Comte Antoine Cartier d'Aure who was most instrumental in furthering the new kind of equitation, namely exterior equitation, in France.

It is with this background in mind that one must consider the equestrian beginnings of Baucher in France after his return from Italy. After a short period as equerry in the service of the Duke of Berry, Baucher, in 1820, went to

Le Havre where he became the equerry of a *manège* owned by a certain Monsieur de Chantillon. With money inherited from his father, Baucher bought into this *manège* and became its proprietor-director. Shortly thereafter Baucher took over the *manège* in Rouen owned by Antonio Franconi and founded by him in 1775. Baucher now directed and taught in both *manèges*. What methods in the training of horse and rider Baucher used during this period is not clear; that is, we do not know whether he taught academic and Classical equitation as taught elsewhere, using the techniques already in existence, or whether he was already using his *nouvelle méthode*. We do know, however, that he published his first work in 1833, entitled *Dictionnaire raisonné d'Equitation*, wherein the main tenets of his later controversial work of 1842 are contained. The former work indicates considerable experience, experimentation and thought, and is dedicated to his pupils. In this dedication Baucher thanks his pupils for giving him the opportunity and the necessary encouragement to pursue his research. While he does not state specifically what methods he used in the training of horse and rider, we do know that he continued to use pillars, which were still in use in Italy in the schooling of the horse. It should be noted that at that time Classical and *savante* training in horsemanship was not limited to Versailles; the provinces were also distinguishing themselves in the art of riding. Angers, the capital of Anjou, had become equally famous for its distinguished *manèges*. Englishmen such as William Pitt and Arthur Wellesly, the future Duke of Wellington, had come to study horsemanship in Angers. Of equal renown was the Academy of Lunéville.[5] It is therefore reasonable to assume that, generally speaking, Baucher continued to teach in the idiom professed by the other equestrian centres.

Despite his success as director of two *manèges* in the provinces, Baucher was not satisfied with his work and life. Restlessness, the feeling that he was out of the mainstream in his field, combined with a sense of mission in his desire to spread his methods to a wider public beyond the provinces, decided him to move to Paris towards the end of 1834. Whether his *Dictionnaire raisonné* had already preceded him to the capital is not known. However, his connection with the Franconi family made it possible for him to associate himself with the son of another illustrious family of professional equerries, Jules-Charles Pellier. With him he managed a *manège* in Paris. Baucher now began to lead a very intense and demanding life, training horses such as Partisan, Buridan, Capitaine and Neptune, giving lessons in the art of riding, and writing. Since many of Pellier's pupils had, after 1830, deserted him for d'Aure, it is quite obvious that Pellier welcomed the association of Baucher who was bringing him money and a rising reputation. However, Pellier, not satisfied with the rise in revenue due to Baucher's association and contributions, increased his

business enterprises by co-managing, with Laurent Franconi (the son of Baucher's former associate in Rouen, Antonio Franconi), a *Cirque-Manège* at Pecq, not far from Paris. It was to Pecq that Baucher, somewhat reluctantly, now moved for a while to teach and to perform.

The establishment of this circus coincided with the inauguration of the railroad in Saint-Germain. The enthusiasm of the Parisians for the newly developing railroad and their interest in the newly developing circus helped the *Cirque-Manège* prosper and bring in the cash. Indeed, interest in the circus occurred just at the moment when Baucher himself began to be associated with it. As an institution which one visited as one did the opera or theatre, the circus was of relatively recent origin. Animal acts performed in the village square, clowns, acrobats, even acrobats on horseback, had existed for centuries. But a circus under a roof to which people went and paid admission was new in 1830. At first the circus attracted primarily the *menu peuple* (lower classes), then the bourgeoisie, *petite* and *haute*. Soon members of the nobility and royalty began to frequent the circus and, before long, it even became possible to rent *loges* at the circus as had been done at the opera, ballet or theatre. However, Pecq was not Paris, and while the circus and the *manège* were doing well (riding in the woods of Saint Germain had become fashionable), Baucher yearned, once again, for Paris and its possibilities. His contact with the Pellier—Franconi team was soon to serve him well.

Indeed, Baucher's association with Laurent Franconi was a decisive factor in furthering his career. Like his famous father, Laurent Franconi had also made a name for himself as an expert in *haute école* equitation, and it was he who had introduced *haute école* equitation to the circus. For the circus had, heretofore, only known *dressages en liberté*, *exercises de voltige* and *ballets équestres*. With Laurent Franconi,

---

[5] During the Revolution of 1789 and the First Empire of Napoleon, Lunéville, like Saumur, became merely a military garrison, housing various and sundry units, including a cavalry unit.

Voltige or vaulting on horseback by one of the Franconis. Engraving by Carle Vernet. (Reproduced in Etienne Saurel, *Histoire de l'equitation* (Paris, Stock, 1971))

horsemanship took on an academic and Classical tone in the circus. In the public's mind, Franconi was, erroneously, identified with the former *Ecole de Versailles*. Actually Laurent Franconi was an outstanding horseman of Venetian origins who had come to France with his father, Antonio Franconi, and who had been trained in the tradition of the Neapolitan Riding School. Laurent was greatly impressed with the way Baucher worked with his horses, Partisan and Capitaine, and how he was able to combine his extensive Classical repertoire with the circus. As Franconi was getting along in years, he asked Baucher to devote some time to demonstrating his expertise at night in the circus to a public that was already familiar with and enthusiastic for *haute école* equitation. In 1835, a younger brother of Laurent, Adolphe Franconi, and his associate Dejean, a well-known circus owner and manager in Paris and other European cities, asked and received permission from the city of Paris to erect a tent at a section of the Champs-Elysées known as the Carré Marigny. In 1838 a wooden structure replaced the tent and in 1840 the City of Paris allowed the construction of a stone building to house the circus. It is in this newly built stone structure that Baucher began to demonstrate more fully his equestrian art and make a name for himself and for his method. It is also during this year that the Duke d'Orléans reserved for himself and his family a *loge*. Now the dandies and members of the Jockey Club, and other society people, came to the circus to watch the various equerries, male and female. Soon critics began to discuss in newspapers and reviews performances of the circus as they discussed performances of the opera or theatre. One of the important critics of the circus was the writer Jules Janin. Indeed, the circus had come of age. Although acrobatics on horseback were still fashionable, it was the *haute école* equitation as practised by Baucher, Caroline Loya and other horsewomen of great skill that the *afficianados* came to see.

Performing *haute école* equitation at the Champs-Elysées circus (which Baucher now owned in limited partnership with Franconi and Pellier), as well as in other circuses, gave Baucher the prestige for which he yearned. The appearance of other works such as *Résumé complet des principes d'Equitation* and *Dialogues sur l'Equitation* in 1835, and in 1840 *Passetemps équestres*, contributed to his prestige as his performance in the circus was contributing to his popularity.

It was precisely this prestige and popularity that, in the minds of critics and horsemen, began to juxtapose him with another contem-porary equerry of renown, the Comte d'Aure, a man completely different in birth, background, politics and personality from Baucher. It was this social difference, as well as the differences in their methods of equitation, that was the source of the controversy. But it was the publication of Baucher's *Méthode d'Equitation basée sur de nouveaux principes* and his engagement by the army to teach his method, first to a garrison in Paris, then to the cavalry schools at Saumur and Lunéville, that brought the controversy to its head.

The enthusiasm of such men as General Marquis Oudinot, former commandant of the *Ecole de Cavalerie* of Saumur between 1825 and 1830 and now aide de camp to the Duke d'Orléans (the Dauphin), and the current commandant of Saumur, de Novital, for the *nouvelle méthode* was unreserved. It was these two men, with the support of the Duke d'Orléans, who were instrumental in attempting to implement Baucher's *nouvelle méthode* in the training of men and mounts. General Oudinot wrote to Baucher on 17 March 1842 informing him that the War Minister, Marshal Soult, had approved Baucher's request to 'school remounts and those recognized as problem horses'.[6] The training was to take place in the garrisons of Paris, Saumur and Lunéville. It was this invitation to Baucher that contributed to the controversy and brought the walls of Jericho tumbling down.

In 1842 and 1843 Baucher and his son Henri placed themselves and the *nouvelle méthode* at the disposal of the army. Despite the enthusiasm of the officers and NCOs who participated in the training of their mounts with the *nouvelle méthode*, the experiment was halted with the death of the Duke d'Orléans and the succession of his younger brother, the Duke de Nemours, to his position as member of the *Comité de la Cavalerie*. By 1845 it was finally abandoned. The ideas of d'Aure, de Nemours' mentor and protégé, replaced those of Baucher at the various cavalry schools. Baucher's hopes to be more than a circus rider had come to nothing.

---

[6] Baucher, *Oeuvres complètes* (hereinafter referred to as O.C.), 1854, p. 16.

121

A view of the Cirque Napoléon, Paris. Engraving by A. Eiherincton. (E. Falkenberg archives, Berlin)

Baucher's relationship with the army had lasted from 1842 to 1845. The experimentation of his method in Paris, Lunéville and Saumur had taken place over less than two years. After this defeat, a hurt and embittered Baucher left Paris and travelled throughout Europe, performing in various circuses and continuing to demonstrate and explain his method. He returned to France shortly after Prince Louis Napoleon became Napoleon III in December 1852 by means of a *coup d'état* which established in France the Second Empire.

Baucher returned to his past activities, performing in the circus, now the Cirque Napoléon, writing, and continuing to teach the art of riding and the *nouvelle méthode*. In 1855 Baucher suffered a terrible accident. One afternoon in March, just as he was placing his foot in the stirrup, a large chandelier fell upon him. The crash frightened the mare he was schooling and she ran off, but Baucher was pinned down under the heavy chandelier. His chest and back were crushed, as were his two legs, with especially serious damage to his left leg. Luckily his head was spared. Baucher remained cool enough to be able to tell the

people who came to help him how to handle him. After this accident, Baucher never appeared in public again. He was, nevertheless, able to continue to do some riding and give lessons. The director of the circus gave him a small pension and he was allowed to keep his horses there. He was even permitted to use the circus arena for a period in the morning. Above all, he was able to meditate about an art that was his passion throughout his life. The defeat of the French armies and the fall of the Second Empire in 1870 affected him deeply, especially since he was now deprived of the pension that he had been granted after Napoleon III came to power. An even greater blow was the murder of General Clément-Thomas which deprived him of a faithful friend and supporter.

His death followed soon in 1873. A few nights before his death, General L'Hotte[7] was at his bedside. Both knew that the end was near. He died at the age of 78. It is remarkable and touching that in 1863 L'Hotte had also been at the bedside of d'Aure the night before he died. L'Hotte thus showed devotion to both his masters in death as he had during their lives.

---

[7] General L'Hotte is discussed in Chapter 8 below.

3

The nouvelle méthode *and the* deuxième manière

By 1842, when Baucher published his *Méthode d'Equitation basée sur de nouveaux principes*, the circus had become a fashionable source of entertainment for *Tout-Paris*.[1] The performances of Baucher and the charming Caroline Loya contributed to its prestige, for *haute école* equitation had begun to play an important role in the repertoire of the circus. So great was the prestige of *haute école* equitation that Baucher had the honour of performing the last number of the evening. In other words, he received top billing. As Caroline Loya was equally popular in her performance of *haute école* equitation, rather than bring about a rivalry between the two artistes, it was decided that each one perform on alternate nights, so that each one could, indeed, have the last number for him or herself.

Baucher had been performing in the circus since 1839. Behind him he had various publications: *Dictionnaire raisonné d'Equitation* (1833), *Dialogues sur l'Equitation* (1835), and in 1837 he had printed in Paris a slim deluxe brochure entitled *Résumé complet des principes d'équitation*. Neither this brochure, nor his earlier works, nor even *Passe-temps équestres* of 1840, with the exception of the group around the *manège* Pellier, made any impact on the equestrian world. Hopefully, Baucher then had all three works reprinted in a single volume. But it was principally his performances at the circus that gave him the reputation that he needed and which eventually brought about an offer from the Minister of War to consider engaging Baucher to teach the art of riding to the French Cavalry and, above all, to teach them to school their horses for total control. But it was with the publication of *Méthode d'Equitation basée sur de nouveaux principes* in 1842 that his prestige and notoriety rose astronomically, so that friend and foe alike came to see his performances at the circus. The *menu peuple*, always ready to pay their money for a thrill, enthusiastically applauded Baucher, as it did Caroline Loya. But the horsemen of repute, especially those educated and trained in the traditional manner, were hostile to Baucher. What aggravated them even more than his claim that he had introduced a *nouvelle méthode* was his declaration that no one before him had ever properly explained or defined in their writings really how to school a horse. They were shocked when, for instance, they read in Baucher's work: 'I declare loudly, that the *rassembler* has never been understood nor defined before my doing so.'[2] They were equally shocked when Baucher criticized his precursors by saying:

Unfortunately, one looks in vain at the writings on equitation of past and modern writers, I won't say for sound rational principles, but simply for the presentation of ordinary data pertaining to the strength of the horse. All have spoken well of *resistances, oppositions, lightness, equilibrium*; but no one has been able to tell us what causes these resistances, how one can combat and destroy them,

---

[1] Fashionable Paris. Comprises anybody who is anybody.

[2] Baucher, 'Méthode d'Equitation', O.C., p. 167.

'Une Amazone', probably Caroline Loya. Painting by Alfred De Dreux (1810–1860). (Reproduced in Paul Morand (ed.) *Anthologie de la litterature equestre* (Paris, Oliver Perrier, 1966))

and thus obtain this lightness, this balance which they recommend so incessantly to us. It is this serious lacuna which has brought about so much doubt and obscurity with respect to the principles of equitation; it is this lacuna which has brought this art to a standstill; it is this serious lacuna which I believe to have finally succeeded in filling.[3]

Just as aggravating was the fact that Baucher had dedicated this work to General Oudinot, 'one of them', and the man who had played a considerable role in getting him to try out his new method and demonstrate its results in Paris, Lunéville and Saumur.

Soon the public, professional and lay, took sides. Never had so much been written on the field of equitation. Pamphlet after pamphlet appeared, either defending or attacking the *nouvelle méthode* of Baucher. D'Aure became its main challenger. Writers and artists, who were horsemen of varying skill, were divided in their support of one or the other. Alphonse de Lamartine frequently visited Baucher at his *manège* in the Rue Saint-Martin. As a member of the equestrian club of Luxemburg, Alexandre Dumas sided with the traditionalists, whereas Eugène Sue and Eugène Delacroix sided with Baucher. The elite of the *faubourg* Saint-Germain, especially if they were the pupils of d'Aure, sided with their master and even began to boycott the circus. In the controversy, the dandies of the Jockey Club tried to remain neutral; however, the founder of the Club, Lord Seymour, inclined towards d'Aure. The controversy even affected the Royal family at the Tuileries. The Duke d'Orléans visited Baucher several times in the Rue Saint-Martin. When the circus was finally housed in a stone building and when Baucher's reputation rose, the Duke and his family also had a *loge* at the circus and were present at the important performance when d'Aure, Aubert, Rousselet, and other horsemen of renown attended to decide the fate of Baucher and his connection with the army. The Duke de Nemours was a *d'Auriste*.

There is no doubt that Baucher and d'Aure, each in his own way, captured the field of equitation during and after the 1840s and as late as the 1880s. Rivals during their day, and rivals after their death, each one expressed a different kind of superiority. Unfortunately some of this rivalry centred around their social backgrounds. Then, too, much was made of this rivalry by the passions and fanaticism of their disciples. Nevertheless, it is this very controversy between the methods of Baucher and d'Aure that contributed to the prestige of the two equerries and to the return of France's prestige in the field of equitation in general.

Baucher had, to some extent, already defined his methods in the training of the horse in his earlier works. But it is with the publication of the 1842 work that his method is more elaborately defined.

The horse, begins Baucher in his *Méthode d'Equitation*, is endowed with weight and strength. Both are inherent attributes. Weight fixes his mass to the ground; strength mobilizes this weight, distributes it, and transfers it from one part of the body to the other. If a horse is at rest, his body will be in a state of complete harmony, his strength distributed equally. If the horse wants to walk he transfers his weight to the legs that remain fixed to the ground. Likewise, the horse's weight will be transferred to those legs that operate at the trot and at the gallop. One must not, insists Baucher, confuse weight and strength, for strength is the determinant, weight is subordinated to it. And by placing the weight on certain extremities the horse's strength can be mobilized and, in turn, the speed at the different paces can be regulated.

When the horse determines his own strength, Baucher calls this strength *instinctive force*. If the horseman determines the horse's strength, he calls this strength *transmitted force*. In the first case, man is dominated by the horse; he becomes the victim of the horse's will and caprices. In the second instance, the horseman makes a docile instrument out of the horse and

[3] Ibid., p. 104.

submits him to all the impulsions of his will. Once a horse is mounted, he must only function in accordance with transmitted strength. The constant application of this principle determines the talent and expertise of the horseman. To succeed in totally dominating the horse, the horseman must dominate the horse's strength. (At first, Baucher said that the horseman must *destroy* this strength. After 1842, *détruites* became *réduites*, that is, reduced.)[4]

It is evident that the basis of Baucher's new method is the elimination, destruction or reduction of the *instinctive* strength of the horse and its replacement by the *transmitted* strength that emanates from the horseman. To accomplish the elimination of the horse's instinctive strength, it is necessary to introduce what Baucher calls *l'effet d'ensemble*. This 'coordinated effect' is achieved by the simultaneous use of the hands and legs, that is, those aids in opposition to each other (the propulsive and the retropulsive aids) which immobilize the natural and instinctive strength of the horse. Thus the horse, sent forward by the rapid and progressive closing of the legs (spurs), is simultaneously retained by the bridle hand; he is, so to speak, immobilized by *l'effet d'ensemble*. This immobilization or neutralization of the strength of the horse must, initially, be done gradually and gently so that the horse, especially in the case of a problem horse, is not put into a state of disorder or panic. Only gradually does the horseman then intensify *l'effet d'ensemble* to its maximum use. This immobilization of the horse is achieved and must be maintained when the horse is stationary; when he is in motion, *l'effet d'ensemble* will prevent him from modifying his pace. What Baucher is seeking is the equilibrium or balance of opposite forces. It should be noted that Baucher is generally concerned with the problem horse, the horse with a poor conformation which, in his mind, causes the poor distribution of his strength, which, in turn, hinders his balance and makes him stiff.

'It is the education of these latter horses wherein lie the real difficulties in equitation. With the others, schooling must be, so to speak, instantaneous, since all the horse's potentials are in their proper place, one has only to put them in motion; a result which always occurs with my method.'[5]

Before accomplishing the equilibrium or balance of opposite forces, Baucher proceeds separately, first to balance the forehand, then the hindquarters, for it is the harmony of the whole that Baucher seeks. (Equally important is the regulation of the direction of the horse.) Only by 'neutralizing' or 'immobilizing' the strength of the horse is the horseman in total control; the horse cannot dispose of his strength. He is contained between hands and legs, and any effort on his part to use his strength, and the ways he wants to use it, is futile. The horse cannot at any time escape these opposing aids.

At the slow paces, *l'effet d'ensemble* does not present any difficulties, for the horseman can easily control a horse by activating his leg and hand aids. At the sitting trot, however, it becomes difficult for the horseman to maintain a uniform pressure of the heels. At the rising trot (*le trot à l'anglaise*), the rising and descent of the seat allow for variations with respect to the intensity of the pressure of the foot on the stirrup; thus it is difficult to prevent these variations from varying the pressure of the heels (spurs) on the horse's flanks. As soon as the pace is increased, continues Baucher, as at the gallop, and due to the displacement of the horse's abdomen, his breathing, etc., the pressure of the heels becomes even more dispersed and brief.

Before total control and harmony of the whole is accomplished, it is of paramount importance that the horse be made flexible, light and well-balanced. The area that is the most critical is the neck, and since the jaw is intimately connected to the neck, the jaw is

---

[4] In the past, the Old School of equitation believed in the exploitation of the horse's instinctive force, not in its destruction.

[5] Baucher, 'Méthode d'Equitation', p. 108.

equally critical. It is precisely in the neck and jaw that the horse can annul all the efforts of the horseman. In the hindquarters, the horse's strength lies in his haunches. These two extremities, that is, mouth and haunches, are intimately connected, in that stiffness in the neck brings about stiffness in the haunches, and vice versa. Once one has fought one stiffness with the other, and once one has established harmony between the forehand and the hindquarters, the education of the horse is half completed. The mobility of the mouth is felt by the hands of the rider; the flexibility of the haunches is felt by the seat of the rider.

In the chapter entitled 'Assouplissements' (The Supplings), Baucher once again takes earlier equerries to task by saying that this work is 'an exposition of a method that overturns most of the former principles of equitation and that, quite obviously, I am addressing myself to men already well-versed in the art'.[6] His aim, he says, is the education of the horse; but, he quickly adds, it also includes the education of the rider, for 'this education is too intimately tied to that of the horseman, so that it is impossible for the one to progress without the other'.[7] He then explains how this education of the horse is to occur and the methods by which to accomplish this *assouplissement*. As already indicated, the first step is to establish harmony between the forehand and the hindquarters. The aim of *assouplissement* is to make the horse yield his own force to the horseman's impulsions. If the horse has been previously mistrained, *assouplissement* will instil confidence and calm in the horse, and if his conformation is poor and the cause of his resistances and poor balance, *assouplissement* will try to counteract these deficiencies. Since the neck and jaw are the areas where the horse expresses his greatest resistance, it is necessary to begin there. For the head and neck serve as the helm and compass to the horseman. Through them, the horseman directs the horse. They determine

the balance, grace and lightness of the horse. Only when they have become flexible and manageable can the horseman completely dispose of his horse. It is only now, Baucher admits, that he has recognized the tremendous influence the neck has on the entire mechanism of the horse. Once the neck of the horse has been rendered supple, all resistances disappear. And when he discovered that a slight resistance persisted, he realized that ultimately the jaw was the source of these final resistances. And once the horse's jaw had been flexed, all resistances were annulled.

But before discussing the methods by which one renders the horse supplé in neck and jaw, Baucher states a few fundamentals by way of 'subjugating the horse and making him recognize the power of man',[8] how to make the horse obey, come to one, etc. This should be done each day for a few minutes. Once this has been achieved, one should then proceed with the suppling exercises of neck and jaw of the horse, first on foot, then mounted.

The procedures by which flexion of the jaw and neck are accomplished on foot are as follows. First the horseman must approach the horse gently and talk to him in a quiet voice, flatter him and caress him with the voice and hand; all the while he must hold the riding whip in his right hand, pointing downward, then raise it to tap the chest gently several times. If the horse tries to escape backward, the horseman holds on to the bit reins tightly, while continuing to tap him gently. Should the horse try to avoid being handled and want to run forward, the horseman will try to soothe the horse by caresses and voice. At no time should he reduce the tension on the reins. Eventually the horse, trying to avoid the crop, will comply with the horseman's commands. The horseman will now begin the flexion of the jaw.

The horse is brought saddled and bridled, reins over the neck. Examination of the bit

---

[6] Ibid., p. 110.
[7] Ibid., p. 110. It is only in later editions that Baucher

discussed in greater detail the training of the rider.
[8] Ibid., p. 114.

should be made to see that it is properly placed in the mouth. A finger should be passed under the curb-chain to see whether it fits well. The horseman should look into the horse's eye with kindness, then, quietly but firmly, should start the different procedures of suppling the mouth and jaw.

The action of suppling or flexion of the jaw occurs on both sides of the jaw. The horseman takes hold of the right rein of the bit with his right hand, under the neck, six or seven inches from the cheek of the bit, and the left rein with the left hand, four inches from the cheek of the bit. An additional suppling action of the jaw occurs when pulling forwards with one rein and backwards with the other, so that one side of the mouthpiece pushes the upper jaw forwards, the other the lower jaw backwards. The same procedures should be made on the opposite side, that is, the left rein of the bit should be held with the left hand, six or seven inches from the cheek of the bit, the right rein with the right hand, four inches from the cheek of the bit, etc. The result is to produce the loosening of the mouth and suppling of the jaw. It is also hoped that the tongue will be affected. With the loosening or relaxation of the mouth, jaw and tongue, the head comes closer to the chest and perpendicularly to the ground. This results in the flexion of the head at the poll, or collection of the head, known as the *ramener*. The purpose, of course, is to make the horse yield to the slightest pressure of the bit and relax the muscles which join the head to the neck. This exercise is the first attempt to make the horse place his strength at the disposal of the horseman and should be carried out with great care.

Lowering of the neck is similar. The horseman stands near the horse's head. He takes hold of the snaffle reins with the left hand, six or seven inches from the rings, and the reins of the bit close to the cheeks with the right hand. He then gently draws the neck of the horse down with the left hand while the right hand tries to mobilize the horse's lower jaw. Only when the horse yields should the horseman

decrease the tension on the reins. The horseman must carefully follow the resistances of the horse in order to overcome them and make the horse lower his head. As soon as the horse lowers his head by his own weight, the horseman should ease all force and allow the horse to take his natural position. This exercise, repeated frequently, will soon supple the muscles which raise the neck and annul the resistances and reduce the stiffness of the horse. Should it take longer than anticipated for the horse to lower his head, the horseman should then cross the two snaffle reins, that is, he should take the left rein in the right hand, the right rein in the left hand, at six or seven inches from the horse's mouth, in order to bring about enough pressure on the chin until the horse yields.

With respect to the lateral flexion of the neck, the horseman stands at the horse's shoulder, takes the snaffle reins in both hands with equal tension and turns the head of the horse to the right, then the head is placed perpendicularly to the ground and held with equal tension, and then brought back to its normal position. The action is done conversely to the left. It is important that the horse at no time tries to initiate these movements on his own.

The horseman now attempts lateral flexions of the neck, mounted. He takes the bit rein in each hand. The left rein barely feels the tension of the bit, the right one feels a moderate tension at first, which will be gradually augmented, depending upon the resistance of the horse. Exercises similar to the ones on foot are conducted. The head is first turned to the right. The left rein will prevent the nose from passing the perpendicular line. The head is then held perpendicularly to the ground. It is important that the head of the horse be kept in this position for a while. Once accomplished, a light tension of the left rein will bring the head back to its natural position. Flexion to the left is carried out the same way. To complete the suppling of the head and the neck, it is important that the direct flexions of the head and neck, or the *ramener*, be introduced.

To accomplish this, that is, to bring the head of the horse perpendicularly to the ground, the snaffle reins and the bit reins are used and tension is placed first on the former, then on the latter. As soon as the horse yields, the right hand is raised and tension on the rein is decreased. The horse is thereby recompensed for yielding. The hand itself must only feel a force that is in proportion to the resistance of the neck. At the same time the legs are held in readiness to fix the hindquarters. And when the horse obeys the action of the snaffle reins, he will more easily yield to the action of the bit reins, whose effect is more powerful and consequently must be used with greater caution than the snaffle reins. The purpose, once again, is to bring the head of the horse perpendicular to the ground. Once this can be executed with ease and promptitude, and only a slight tension is needed to achieve the *ramener* and maintain the horse's head in the perpendicular position, then the suppling of head and neck has been accomplished. Lightness and balance in the forehand is established. In short, collection of the forehand has been accomplished, which is the aim of the *ramener*.

In order to direct the horse, the horseman must control both parts of the horse: the forehand and the hindquarters. And just as he had to supple the forehand by various means to make his horse light and well-balanced and have him under control, so must he do likewise with the hindquarters. 'A perfect relationship must always exist between these two driving powers.'[9] And just as it is necessary to render the jaw and neck supple, so is it necessary to supple the croup. With the bit reins held in the left hand, and the snaffle reins, crossed, in the right hand, the head of the horse must be brought to its perpendicular position by means of a gentle tension on the bit. If the horseman

wishes the horse to go to the right, he places his left leg behind the girth and fixes it until the horse yields to the pressure. At the same time the horseman will also put pressure on the left snaffle rein, the pressure depending upon the resistance of the horse. Thus the aim of the left rein is to combat resistances, the left leg to determine movement. The same must be executed by the right leg and the right rein. One must continue in this manner and complete *pirouettes renversées* (reversed pirouettes) to the right and to the left. As soon as the haunches yield to the pressure of the leg, the horseman must use the rein opposite to the leg being used. This is to arrive at a perfect balance of the horse.[10]

A horse, says Baucher, in his movements, cannot maintain a perfect and constant balance without the harmony of these opposing forces executed by the skilled horseman. This is why it is important, when executing a *pirouette renversée*, that when a horse has yielded to the pressure of the leg the opposite rein must be used. If one were to use the rein on the same side as the leg, one would go beyond one's goal and there would be no tension caused by the opposing forces. It should not be forgotten that during this exercise, the neck must, as always, remain supple and light, the head must be *ramené*, that is, flexed at the poll, and the jaw mobile. Once the horseman has succeeded in getting the horse to yield promptly to the pressure of his legs, he will be in total control of either mobilizing or immobilizing the horse at will.

An exercise that renders supple the haunches of the horse is the *reculer* or rein-back, that is, the retrograde mobility of the horse. A distinction should be made between the retrograde impulsion of the horse, with his croup contracted and his neck stretched and strained, that is, the *aculement*,[11] as practised by former horse-

---

[9] Ibid., p. 134.

[10] In a footnote, ibid., p. 129, Baucher explains the expression *équilibre* which, he claims, has never really been defined. Equilibrium or balance is the basis of a

horse's education upon which depends a horse's ability to adopt a pace or change direction immediately and correctly.

[11] In his *Dictionnaire raisonné*, Baucher defines *acculer* as

men, and the real *reculer*. The real *reculer* renders the horse supple and adds precision and grace to the natural movements of the horse. The primary prerequisite for the *reculer* is to keep the horse in the hand, that is to say, to keep him supple, light on the forehand, straight and totally well-balanced. The first attempts at the *reculer* on the part of the horse are usually difficult. Thus a supple neck and supple haunches will enable the horse to handle the alternating flow of his weight and initiate the necessary transference of the horse's strength and weight.

The rider must first make sure that the horse's haunches are in line with his shoulders and that the horse is light on the bit. He then brings together his legs to communicate to the hindquarters that one hind leg must be raised. The action of the rider's legs must precede that of the hand. The rider must also make sure that the horse's body yields only after the neck does. It is then that the immediate pressure on the bit, which forces the horse to regain his balance backwards, will execute the first step of the *reculer*. The rider then recompenses the horse by immediately yielding his hand to the horse. The rider must not force any further movement. One or two steps at a time, followed by an *effet d'ensemble*, should suffice at first. Should the horse's croup not remain in a straight line, the leg and the snaffle rein on the same side should be used to bring him back in line.

Baucher's horse has now been brought under the control of the rider; first his instinctive force has been immobilized by means of the suppling procedures of neck and haunches, that is, he has been collected in the forehand, and his energy has begun to be used efficiently; then by means of suppling of the hindquarters,

which is disposing of the horse's haunches and hind legs, he has been brought under further control. As the *ramener* is collection of the forehand, the *rassembler* is collection of the hindquarters. According to Baucher, to achieve the *rassembler*, one must first have 'a partial and general suppling of the neck and haunches'; secondly, 'a perfect *ramener* which is the result of these flexions'; and thirdly, 'the total absorption of the strength of the horse by the horseman, by means of the attacks'.[12] Baucher's horse can now respond to the aids of the rider and can tolerate the *effet d'ensemble*. One can definitely say that the horse has received a sound education.

It is now time, says Baucher, to proceed to the various paces of the horse. The walk, says Baucher, is the mother of all the paces and through it one can achieve the cadence, regularity and extension necessary to the other paces.

Before pushing the horse forward, it must first be verified that he is light, that is, that his head is perpendicular to the ground, his neck supple, and his croup absolutely straight. Rider and horse walk around the *manège*, briefly going through some of the suppling exercises the horseman has already practised earlier. He begins a mild opposition of hands and legs to link the forces of the forehand and the hindquarters. Cadence and speed at the walk must be regularized through the close interplay of the legs and hands of the horseman. The horseman must see to it that the horse's head is in the position of the *ramener*. Only when one has ascertained that the horse is supple, light and goes in a straight line at the walk does one begin to teach him to change direction. But should this lightness and suppleness, characterized by

---

follows: 'Movement of a horse who, after backing against a wall, remains there as though stubbornly attached to it. It is also the action of a horse who narrows the circle he must walk, despite the efforts of the horseman.' The way Baucher describes acculer in *Méthode d'Equitation*, it is a rein-back with croup contracted and neck stretched out. *Reculer* (rein-back, backing), on the other hand, is a movement designed to supple the horse's haunches.

[12] Baucher, 'Méthode d'Equitation', p. 167. Decarpentry, in his *Academic Equitation* (London, J. A. Allen, 1987), p. 88, gives this definition of *rassembler*: 'The Rassembler (collection) is the disposition of the horse's body which affects all of its parts and places each one in the best position to ensure the most efficient use of the energy produced by the efforts of the hind legs.'

Baucher as when the horse yields his jaw, dissipate, then the horseman should resort immediately to the *effet d'ensemble*.

Once lightness and suppleness have been firmly established, work at the trot should be undertaken, which the horseman will practise very moderately at first. It is at this stage, that is, at the faster paces, that the *rassembler* takes on greater importance. On the other hand, it is precisely at the faster paces that the *effet d'ensemble* experiences difficulties. In the chapter entitled 'Procedures' of his *Baucher et son Ecole*, Decarpentry analyses the difference between the *effet d'ensemble* and the *rassembler*. It is obvious that the two are not similar since the use of the hand and legs in the *effet d'ensemble* is to immobilize the horse, the *rassembler* to mobilize him and push him forward. It was only after Baucher's death that the difference between the two techniques became clear. Decarpentry believes that it was most likely Faverot de Kerbrech who elucidated a point that had remained obscure for forty years.

In the *effet d'ensemble*, the legs proceed with a continuous and persistent action, *by pressure*; in the *rassembler*, their actions are brief and intermittent, they are repeated attacks. An analogous difference also exists with respect to the actions of the hand in these two cases: they are continuous for the *effet d'ensemble*, discontinuous for the *rassembler*. Furthermore, the hand which 'held back' with the *effet d'ensemble*, merely 'contained' in the *rassembler*.[13]

It is in his discussion of the *rassembler* that Baucher declares 'that the *rassembler* has never been understood nor defined before my doing so, for one cannot execute it properly unless one has applied the principles that I have just developed for the first time'.[14] He then indicates the necessary procedures, namely, partial and general suppling of the neck and the haunches, a perfect *ramener* which is the result of these flexions, and the complete absorption of the strength of the horse by the horsemen

through attacks with legs and spurs. 'And since these prerequisites have never been defined in any treatise on equitation, I have the right to declare that the true *rassembler* has never been practised until today.'[15]

Before giving us a definition of his concept of the *rassembler*, Baucher describes the procedure as practised in the various schools of equitation which, according to him, is a matter '*of raising the hand and holding the legs in readiness*. I ask, then, what does this movement on the part of the horseman serve on an animal that has poor conformation, is contracted, and who is consigned to all the bad propensities of its own nature?' The true *rassembler*, continues Baucher, 'consists in collecting to the centre of the horse all his strength in order to lighten his two extremities . . . by bringing back the hind legs close to the centre . . . indispensable for the ease and exactitude of the different paces and the different airs of *manège*'.[16]

In his discussion of the trot, once again, Baucher emphasizes balance, a condition that is indispensable for a good trotter and enables him to change direction, slow down, accelerate, and stop with ease. It is usually the hindquarters that are responsible for any difficulties that the horse may have. And the solution, as always, is the suppling of the neck which establishes the balance between the two parts of the horse.

While emphasizing Baucher's contributions to equitation with his *nouvelle méthode*, Decarpentry, in *Baucher et son Ecole*, is at times critical of some aspects of his *nouvelle methode*. With reference to the subjugation of Baucher's horse by means of the 'destruction' of his instinctive force, Decarpentry says that 'the subjugation of the horse became much narrower'[17] and equates this subjugation to a 'micrometric' regulation of the horse's defences. Baucher, continues Decarpentry, brings to the movements of the horse 'an exactitude and a correctness that the school of the past never

[13] Decarpentry, *Baucher et son Ecole* (Paris, Lamarre, 1948), pp. 55–6.
[14] Baucher, 'Méthode d'Equitation', p. 167.
[15] Ibid., p. 168.
[16] Ibid., p. 168.
[17] Decarpentry, *Baucher et son Ecole*, p. 46.

had'.[18] This exactitude enabled Baucher to accomplish movements that previous equerries had never been able to do, for example, changes of leg at each beat of the gallop, or the *reculer* at the trot or gallop, and so on.[19] Whether one can call these innovations new art is difficult to say. Suffice it to mention that Baucher's *confrères* did not consider these movements as *haute école*; nor did they consider them graceful, for they led to awkward placement of the horse's legs. One problem that emerged from Baucher's new method was that he achieved 'not only the stylization of the paces, but also the defectiveness and even the vicious dispositions of his horses and presented them as "varieties" of the Classical airs'.[20]

Many of the horsemen of the period condemned this excessive automatization of the horse, this perpetual tension, both physical and psychological, imposed by the rider, and felt that it did not contribute to his expertise. This was especially true to the horseman who preferred exterior riding to *manège* riding.

Nevertheless, concedes Decarpentry, the power the skilled horseman had over his horse when using Baucher's method was incontestable and the results obtained by him with respect to problem horses were extraordinary, especially when one takes into consideration the speed by which he obtained these positive results. Decarpentry cites two famous examples, that of the horse Géricault, well-known throughout Paris for his stubbornness and violent behaviour and of Kléber, also known to be stubborn and a rearer and destined for the knacker. In the course of one month both these horses were able to perform before the public. These successes were witnessed by friend and foe alike, for both groups came to the circus to take a look at the phenomenon. Kléber was later ridden for several years in the circus by two *écuyères*, Pauline Cuzent and Mathilde

d'Embrun, both pupils of Baucher. Thus, by using the new method of Baucher, strength was not a necessary factor on the part of the horseman or horsewoman. And this could only be made possible by balancing the horse horizontally, that is, by making him equally supple and mobile on the forehand and on the hindquarters.

After the accident of the falling chandelier in March 1855 which crushed both his legs, Baucher, to compensate for not completely recovering the use of his legs, revised his *nouvelle méthode*. Whereas in the first period Baucher made much use of legs and spurs to get impulsion, he now recommended modification and moderation in the use of spurs as well as moderation in the horse's balance, which became known as his *deuxième manière*. It is also quite probable that this modification may have been due to his realization that, in the hands of the novice, the extreme use of legs and spurs, that is, *l'effet d'ensemble*, often led to the horse's bloody flanks and, eventually, to insensitivity.

The *deuxième manière* was already sketched in Baucher's 12th edition of his works, published in 1862, but was set down with greater detail and precision in the later edition of 1867. It is once again presented together with other aspects of equitation in a work entitled *Dressage méthodique du Cheval de Selle d'après les derniers enseignements de F. Baucher, Recueillis par un de ses élèves*, published in 1891 by General Faverot de Kerbrech, one of Baucher's pupils. The *deuxième manière* has been summed up as 'hand without legs, legs without hand'. This implies the use of only one aid at a time, either legs to bring about impulsion or the hand to regulate impulsion and indicate direction. This second manner no longer immobilized the horse so forcefully between the contrary and constant opposition of legs and

---

[18] Ibid., p. 46.
[19] 'Gallop' is used throughout the text to refer to the gait or pace now more usually known as 'canter' (after 'Canterbury gallop', the slow gallop used by the pilgrims).

The word 'galop' is still used in France today to mean 'canter', sometimes modified as 'le petit galop'.
[20] Decarpentry, *Baucher et son Ecole*, p. 77.

An *ecuyère* at the National Circus in Paris, Madame Angéle. (Reproduced in Etienne Saurel, *Histoire de l'equitation* (Paris, Stock, 1971))

hand. In a sense, as Decarpentry says, the second manner is really an evolution and an attempt to perfect the *nouvelle méthode* of 1842. In other words, Decarpentry is implying that it was not necessarily the accident of the chandelier that brought about Baucher's *deuxième manière*; rather it was a continuous evolution and refinement of method. Decarpentry also asks whether the personal experience and abilities of Faverot de Kerbrech did not contribute considerably 'to the perfection of this excellent presentation of the last thoughts of Baucher'.[21]

In the *Avant-Propos* Faverot de Kerbrech says: 'The final ideas on the equestrian art of F. Baucher are little known. This illustrious equerry, after the terrible accident which broke both his legs, could no longer ride in public. He lived, retired from public life, and, since 1861, devoted very little time to teaching.'[22] Too old and tired, almost blind, Baucher did not make his new discoveries in dressage known to the public and did not revise his works. Nevertheless, he was continually developing, making his general principles known to his loyal disciples, saying that it was up to them to apply these principles and set them down. This is precisely what Faverot de Kerbrech has done.

The work of Faverot de Kerbrech is reminiscent of Baucher's early work, his *Dictionnaire raisonné*, giving definitions of such terms as 'Action', 'Movement', 'Balance', 'Lightness', 'Resistances of weight', 'Resistances of force', the 'Half-halt', the '*Effet d'ensemble*', the '*Rassembler*', the '*Reculer*', etc. With respect to lightness, he says:

The seeking and the preservation of lightness must be the constant preoccupation of the horseman. By 'lightness of hand' one understands the ability of the horse to obey the aids without leaning on the horseman's hand and without the hand feeling the sensation of a weight that is more or less hard to displace or a force that resists its action. Lightness is thus recognized when there is no resistance to the effects of the curb or snaffle bits; the mere semi-tension of the one or of both reins must provoke the easy mobility of the lower jaw without any movement of the head and without any opening of the mouth becoming apparent; . . .[23]

A little farther on, he says that 'the consequence of the complete decontraction of the jaw becomes the *ramener*, . . . the head taking at the lightest indication of the reins a position that is close to that of the perpendicular, without the neck losing its support or its fixity'.[24]

One of the most important elements of the second manner is the *mise en main*, that is, the yielding of the jaw, to bring the horse to the *ramener* and which has now been modified. However, while modified, it nevertheless is 'a modification of the means';[25] the essential part of the method, that is, its principles and its vital spirit, has remained intact.

The lightening of the horse's forehand, sought previously only by the *ramener*, is now sought by the raising of the neck which, as with the *ramener*, provokes a transference of the horse's weight from the forehand to the hindquarters. Thus, with the neck raised, as soon as the jaw is loosened, the same degree of lightness is achieved almost without the *ramener* or, rather, with a *ramener* that is less accentuated . . .[26]

However, the *ramener* is essential if the rider wants to increase his control over the horse, either to handle a problem horse or for artistic equitation.

A second modification can be seen in the use of obtaining the *effet d'ensemble*. Now it is the hand alone that establishes the lightness of the horse. On the one hand, it is the use of the half-halt that will remedy an overload on the forehand; on the other, the use of vibrations of

[21] Ibid., p. 118.
[22] Faverot de Kerbrech, *Dressage méthodique du Cheval de Selle d'après les derniers enseignements de F. Baucher. Recueillis per un de ses élèves* (Paris, J. Rothchild, 1891), p. v.
[23] Ibid., pp. 7–8.
[24] Ibid., p. 8.
[25] Decarpentry, *Baucher et son Ecole*, p. 114.
[26] Ibid., p. 114.

the reins 'to melt' the 'muscular crispation' will also achieve this. Thus the early insistence on the simultaneous use of hand and legs to neutralize or immobilize the horse has been abandoned. Therefore the new formula: 'Hand without legs, legs without hand.' Rather than introduce a competition between hands and legs, the hand now alone assumes regulation and distribution of the action, and the legs make sure that the action is being properly fulfilled. However, the use of the *effet d' ensemble* has not been totally eliminated. Whereas heretofore it was the normal and usual method used to establish control of and ensure lightness in the horse, it is now used in problem cases, especially when the resistance and defences of the horse were of a psychological nature.

In his conclusion, Faverot de Kerbrech says that

The principle of 'legs without hand, hand without legs' must be applied as often as possible, especially at the beginning; but there is nothing absolute in this principle. One must not make a system out of it, outside of which there will only be failure. One must refrain from putting it into practice as long as there is no real reason to use it. But there comes a time in the dressage, as later in the handling of the schooled horse when, on the contrary, it will be necessary to unite the lower aids with the upper aids.[27]

In other words, if the horse does not become light, if the jaw does not mobilize immediately or resists the opposition of the bit, a weak pressure of the legs or a slight attack of the spurs, combined with the reins, is necessary, especially when wishing to perform at the various paces.

Ending his Conclusion, Faverot de Kerbrech says: 'The author wanted to present in this study *all* the procedures of dressage employed by Baucher at the end of his life ... He tried to present the reader with a comprehensive study wherein the horseman can find the solution to the various problems of dressage.[28]

---

[27] Faverot de Kerbrech, *Dressage méthodique*, pp. 190–1.   [28] Ibid., p. 195.

4

Baucher and the army

With the appearance of his *nouvelle méthode* in 1842, Baucher became even more successful. Friend and foe alike bought this work, for all were curious to see what the master had accomplished. The work was so successful that a second edition was printed three months after the initial publication. Two more editions appeared later that year. While many, especially his friends and supporters, praised his *nouvelle méthode*, many horsemen of the old school were irritated, even angered, by the work. What annoyed them most was Baucher's claim that techniques such as collection and the flexing of the horse had never really been defined by earlier teachers and writers of manuals. While at first they had merely laughed at Baucher's riding posture — the way his head drooped over his chest and his legs fell backwards behind the girth — now, with statements such as the one cited earlier, the honour of past equerries was at stake.

Professional horsemen took sides. So did the royal family. Writers and artists were equally divided. The general public, always influenced by the thrills received at the circus, and who had shuddered with delight at some of the daring steps Baucher made his horse perform, supported Baucher against 'the wigs', as they called the traditionalists. General Oudinot, as has been stated earlier, was instrumental in bringing Baucher's *nouvelle méthode* to the attention of the army and the Duke d'Orléans. The army's main concern was to improve the expertise of the cavalry officers and NCOs, which had declined considerably after the Revolution. It was their hope that Baucher's new method might accomplish this. General Oudinot was himself an outstanding horseman. During his campaigns in Algeria he had become keenly aware of the limitations of the training in equitation which the military was receiving. Classical or *savante* equitation with its low and high airs, it was felt, was too cumbersome and too time consuming in the training of men and mounts. While military equitation had been in existence in Prussia since the eighteenth century, and some equerries had attempted to introduce it into France, it had not yet become accepted by the French cavalry. In fact, many innovations such as the rising trot had been forbidden at Saumur.[1] However, men such as Oudinot and others still wanted to convince, if not themselves, at least the sceptics of the value of Baucher's *nouvelle méthode* in the schooling of horses, especially problem horses (and the army had plenty of horses that had to be retrained). In order to conquer the sceptics and those with reservations, proof was necessary. Lord Seymour and one of his horses named Géricault was to

---

[1] While the army frowned upon the use of the rising or English trot, d'Aure had his regiment execute it when riding in formation. Once his commanding officer and a general were at Headquarters when the arrival of a regiment on horseback was heard. The general commented that this was undoubtedly d'Aure's regiment, for what was lacking was the terrible clatter of swords.

serve that purpose.

Géricault was a strong-willed, even violent horse whom nobody could ride. Lord Seymour proposed that whosoever could succeed in riding Géricault for a short time around the Bois de Boulogne without being dismounted could own the horse. This proposition of Lord Seymour's caused great discussions in the equestrian world and excited even further the rivalry between the two camps, the *Bauchéristes* and the *d'Auristes*. A *d'Auriste*, the Viscount de Tournon, tried first and failed. Then came a *Bauchériste*, Count de Lancosme-Brèves, well-known equerry and writer on horsemanship, who, by means of a little trickery, succeeded. When he mounted Géricault, friends and disciples of Baucher surrounded the horse so tightly that he was unable to use his usual defences. The *d'Auristes* further claimed that Lancosme-Brèves had until recently belonged to the traditionalists and had been converted to the *nouvelle méthode* only recently, thereby making his modest success due to the *nouvelle méthode* even more questionable. Lancosme-Brèves, despite his questionable victory, was given the horse by Lord Seymour. He then gave the horse to his mentor, Baucher. This was the chance Baucher had been waiting for to prove not only to the opposition forces, but especially to the army, the validity and success of his *nouvelle méthode* in the training of the horse.

Baucher's habit was to work with his horses early in the morning with no one present. This led his critics to generate all sorts of rumours: that Baucher was hypnotizing Géricault, that he was giving him soporific drugs, and even that he was depriving the horse of food, water and sleep to render him docile. Baucher let them talk. At the end of the third week of Géricault's dressage, it was learned by word of mouth and through the pages of *Le National* that Baucher would present Géricault on the Friday of the following week. It was to be a gala performance. Tongues wagged and heads shook. Baucher's disciples, sure of their master's success, began to celebrate in advance. The opponents, of course, hoped for failure.

That Friday towards the end of the year 1842 the circus was filled to capacity by the faithful. Count de Lancosme-Brèves was naturally present, as was Baucher's dedicated disciple and friend Louis Rul. Baron Le Cornieu, well-known horseman and hippologue and equally well known for his salient remarks, was filling the artistes entrance with his witticisms. General Oudinot looked worried. Writers and artists were also present. Got, a well-known actor of the *Comédie Française* (critics of Baucher have claimed that Got revised and edited much of Baucher's written work), Eugène Sue and Delacroix were present. Théophile Gautier was also present, considerably fatter but wearing nevertheless the famous red waistcoat that he had worn at the *Hernani* performance in 1830. Also present were the opponents: all those connected with the former *Ecole de Versailles* and the *Manège Royal de Paris*. D'Aure was heard talking to his friend Aubert in his clear Garonne accent. Next to him stood the Viscount de Tournon, still visibly in pain from his fall from the back of Géricault. In the royal *loge* the Duchess and her two sons were already visible, although the Duke d'Orléans was still absent. While applauding politely the various artistes who were occupying the ring with their performances, the audience eagerly awaited the Duke and the performance of Baucher on Géricault. Just as the last act was coming to an end, the Duke entered his loge discreetly and quickly, quietly asking the public not to applaud his arrival. Some of Baucher's supporters, who had expressed concern at the Duke's absence, now began to show happier faces, while the expressions of some of Baucher's opponents darkened.

There was a marked silence when Baucher made his entrance into the ring. The costume he was wearing was similar to that of an officer in the National Guard. At his side he wore a sabre, the sabre of the cavalry. Géricault advanced to the centre of the ring with a measured

A view of the Franconi's Cirque Olympique. Painting by Jean Demosthene Dugourc. (Bibliothèque Nationale, Arts du Spectacle, Coll. Rondel)

but rapid step. Baucher held him there quietly and greeted the public with his two-cornered plumed hat. When Baucher faced Géricault towards the royal *loge*, he sat there bowing deeply for a lengthy time.

According to the many eye-witnesses, Géricault behaved exceptionally well, somewhat taken aback rather than frightened by the music and the applause. He executed the paces Baucher had taught him correctly and precisely, showing neither reluctance nor resistance. He was not even disturbed by the noise Baucher's sabre was making as it rattled against the spurs. He trotted, galloped, did half-halts, pirouetted, and executed a few changes of hand. When Géricault and Baucher finally stopped in the centre of the ring, Baucher saluted (with greater self-assurance than he had done at the outset). The applause was deafening. The supporters were delirious; the sceptics were now convinced that the method was, indeed, working. But the opponents were unconvinced and unrelenting.

One of the most important defenders of Baucher's *nouvelle méthode* was Jacques-Léonard Clément Thomas,[2] an army man who, under the name of Clément-Thomas, wrote a series of articles in the *National* dated 6, 10, 16 and 23 September 1845 (and reprinted in pamphlet form in 1846) shortly after the special *Comité de la Cavalerie* decided, as Baucher puts it in his 'Préface', 'that my system of equitation would

---

[2] Clément-Thomas later became a general in the National Guard and was shot by the Communards in 1871 in France's civil war between the Communards (revolutionary forces in Paris) and the Versaillais (Government forces in Versailles) which followed the Franco-Prussian War of 1870.

cease to be applied in the army'.[3] It was, indeed, a very surprised Baucher, as he points out in this same 'Préface', who discovered that the Minister of War had decided not to use his system but to continue the use of the flexions of the neck. It was a remarkable decision when one remembers that Baucher's system was based on flexions of the neck.

Clément-Thomas begins his articles by discussing the state of the equestrian art in France. While France's cavalrymen are known for their courage and loyalty and behave in an exemplary and worthy manner in this battle against Europe, he said, what they lack is the dexterity and limberness of the Athlete in general and, more specifically, equestrian ability, without which one cannot really be a true horseman. To remain in the saddle, to gallop, does not suffice. One must have complete mastery of one's courser, show intelligence and good judgement in handling him, and be able, without effort, to push him forward, direct him, halt him, use the aids properly, and know his physical defects. Military strategies as used by the cavalry today are different from those used in the past. No longer does one charge and fight *en masse*. Now each horseman works individually as rifleman or as forager. When there is a charge, one mingles and each horseman is on his own. Woe to the man who cannot guide his horse and finds himself paralysed, incapable of using his aids. It has been said that the simple foot-soldier has nothing to fear of the cavalryman in a battle. This is only true if the latter is inept. But if he is a knowledgeable horseman and can manage his horse well, then the horseman has the advantage over the foot-soldier.

Of all the arts, he continues, that of equitation is the most difficult. The painter, the sculptor, the architect, etc. are in total control of their art. They follow certain prescribed rules, but, in essence, they use inert materials. If they do not succeed, they alone are to blame

for their lack of skill, intelligence and imagination. All the resources lie within them. The horseman, on the other hand, must contend with a creature which has motion, physical power far superior to man's, and a will of his own; which can express anger and stubbornness, and which can carry his rider off to dangerous waters. Everyone knows that the basic way to control a horse fully and combat his defences and resistances and make him easy and even is to inculcate lightness, limberness and balance into the horse. All the great equerries of the past knew this. But what they lacked was the ability to define these resistances and to state succinctly how one should go about combating them.

Clément-Thomas first deals with Frederico Grisone, the famous equerry of the Renaissance, credited with the re-discovery of Xenophon, and teacher of Pignatelli who, in turn, taught Antoine de Pluvinel and the Duke of Newcastle. In his treatise *Gli Ordini Di Cavalcare*, Grisone also discusses the suppling of horses. To accomplish this, he prescribes that they be worked in a circular ditch, and that one be harsh with those who are sensitive and have a big heart, and to hit them on the head between the ears. Clément-Thomas then discusses the procedures recommended by Pluvinel, namely that the horse be attached to a lunge, and 'invents this enormous whip called a *chambrière* which makes the poor animal trot and gallop by giving him blows'.[4] He then gets to Newcastle who, in turn, ties the horse to a pillar by one of the reins of the cavesson, and a helper, taking hold of the other rein, is armed with a puncheon, another armed with a switch, and the three of them, 'having thus *the philosopher's stone*, school with perfection all horses'. And, continues Clément-Thomas, 'one can also read in La Guérinière, in Montfaucon, and others, similar principles that are equally rational. But one should not think that experience and good sense

[3] Baucher, O.C., p. 86.
[4] Jacques-Léonard Clément Thomas, *De L'Equitation militaire de l'ancienne et de la nouvelle école* (Paris, 1846), p. 10.

Gallerie. du. Louvre.

M.le Grand.

M. de Belleuille.

Figure. 5. 1.partie:

Page. de. l'Escurie.

Antoine de Pluvinel's method of lunging with the horse attached to the pillar and the *chambrière* urging him on. (Pluvinel, *The Maneige Royal*, translated by Hilda Nelson (J. A. Allen, 1989), with engravings from the original edition)

have today eliminated methods that are not as savage and absurd as those just heard.'[5] In fact, continues Clément-Thomas, a well-known contemporary equerry recommends that if a horseman has damaged the right bar of the horse's mouth, he should then do the same on the left bar so that he will be forced to execute a particular movement.[6]

However, says Clément-Thomas, one should not judge these men by all the techniques they have advocated. These men were all distinguished equerries, the most distinguished and the most skilled in their day. Yet, despite their skills and their successes, they were incapable of overcoming and defining a number of the difficulties that beset the art of riding, and were, in fact, unable to understand them. While these peculiarities contained in their manuals explain their contradictions, their vagueness, and so on, these men still demonstrate considerable equestrian skill and personal aptitude.

Thus with all these contradictions, this vagueness, this labyrinth of correct and erroneous principles, what could military commissions do but winnow and sift and apply those principles that were the most useful, the simplest, and the least dangerous to the cavalry, and compose its own manual, albeit imperfect, yet the most serviceable for instruction in the army?

This composite of principles was also responsible for causing the army to turn in a circle that was monotonous and lacked innovation. But the army, instead of going to equerries and professors of equitation imbued with the precepts of former masters, decided to choose an equerry who was intelligent and bold and who proclaimed that he had discovered a new method of equitation in the flexing of a horse's neck, jaw, haunches, and so on. This man is M. Baucher, declares Clément-Thomas.

Clément-Thomas is unstinting in his assessment of the importance of Baucher's work and his *nouvelle méthode*.

What strikes us at the outset in this exposé, what makes it a felicitous contrast with the many undigested and confused compilations published formerly on the same subject, is its clarity, its logical sequence of the definitions that this new master develops. He tackles directly and boldly all those difficulties that the old school left vague or avoided, due to lack of comprehension; he explains in clear and concise terms, the origin of the horse's resistances, their causes, their effects; and in order to combat and vanquish them, he indicates procedures of a totally thematic application, the veracity and efficacy of which each individual can easily verify.[7]

This is precisely the point made repeatedly by Baucher himself.

Clément-Thomas is especially impressed by the section in which Baucher discusses the difference between the strength and weight of a horse, their definitions and their functions. 'One does not, at first glance, capture the significance of this simple and natural definition; but as one follows the consequences, one sees, indeed, how important it is to establish a distinction in the organization of the horse between the functions of strength and weight, since it is in the interaction between these two elements that all true equitation rests.'[8] No good equitation is possible unless the movements of the horse are sustained and facilitated by a constant and regular balance between the horse's diverse parts. Indeed, the horse's balance depends upon the distribution of the horse's weight which, in turn, is distributed by the driving power. It follows that the art of the horseman is constantly to use the strength of his steed judiciously.

It has always been said, Clément-Thomas goes on, that the best way to master a horse's

---

[5] Ibid., p. 10.
[6] This refers to a rumour that was spread with respect to d'Aure and his schooling of horses. D'Aure, in his *Observations*, objected vehemently to this rumour at-

tributed to him. For a discussion, see Chapter 5 below.
[7] Clément-Thomas, *De l'Equitation militaire*, p. 12.
[8] Ibid., p. 13.

strength, to control his resistances, and to make him pleasant, easy and regular, is to make supple every part of his structure. At all periods it has been attempted to give the horse these qualities. But all too often recourse has been had to dangerous procedures, or if not that, to ineffectual measures. And if use is no longer made of Grisone's circular ditch, or of the puncheon of Newcastle, a horse is still made to walk at all paces in a circle for a long time in order to make him supple.

The former masters wrote volumes discussing the use of mouthpieces and bits, the position and function of legs and hands; but when, asks Clément-Thomas, did they ever give us a single rational precept so that we could make use of these important aids? They claim to have taught us how to dominate the strength of a horse; yet the horse still remains master of his instincts. Moreover, the schools of the past gave little credence to the idea that physical problems could be the cause of a horse's resistances and defences. Likewise, while sustaining the idea that in the schooling of a horse, his moral disposition was often the cause of his resistances and defences, one nevertheless gets the impression that, in many instances, the efforts of equerries often came to nothing.

The ancients also recognized that the perpendicular position of the horse's head was the most favourable one with respect to the bit and its position on the bars of the mouth. They also believed that this position depended solely upon the conformation of the horse. But they were unaware of the veritable causes for a horse being light or heavy on the hand and attributed this to an illusionary sensitivity of the horse's mouth, rather than to stiff muscles of the jaw and neck. They then set about inventing all sorts of instruments of torture in order to cope with the situation.

In general, says Clément-Thomas, the ancients relied primarily on rare and privileged horses, those favoured by nature and whose schooling is usually successful. As for those horses less favoured by nature, with much patience, time and violence they obtained a sort of mechanical obedience, but they were never able to make them do anything out of the ordinary without coming across the horses' resistances and defences.

In this respect Baucher's new method is much more logical and intelligent. Baucher, when he says that almost all of equitation consists of dominating the strength of the horse by the horseman, actually does more. He tells us how to accomplish this and tries to prove it, giving us sure, positive and really scientific methods. Then, too, he does away with all the old heresies accepted and disseminated for so long by the former masters, and which now are causing so much discussion.

You claim, asks Clément-Thomas (as Baucher had done before him), that the disposition or temperament of the horse is often the cause of his resistances and defences? Wrong! These resistances and defences have as their origin only a physical cause. They become moral or psychological only when one tries to combat these physical problems by irritating the horse rather than correcting the problem. You say that one cannot correct a horse's attempt to avoid the bit by pushing his head forward? Wrong again! All horses can be made to hold their heads perpendicular to the ground (*ramener*). You also say that a horse born with a tender or hard mouth is more or less sensitive to the bit and that the only way to remedy this is by means of *very active* instruments which can control the horse? Wrong! All horses have the same sensitivity which has nothing to do with the thickness of the membrane that covers the bones of the bars. Rather it is due to the contraction and stiffness of the muscles of the jaw and the neck, compounded by stiffness of the hindquarters. Eliminate these problems and the so-called hardness of your horse's mouth will also disappear. In every instance, it is the skill of the horseman and his ability to over-come the physical imperfections of the horse. By creating a harmonious whole he can bring about harmony in the horse's movements.

Clément-Thomas now proceeds to give an

analysis of how Baucher attempts to dominate the strength of a horse and combat successfully his resistances and defences. It is, he says, by means of what Baucher has called *l'effet d'ensemble*, that is, the legs that establish impulsion working together, but in opposition to the hands that direct and regulate this impulsion. You know, yourself, that it is this dual action that acts upon the neck and the haunches which makes the horse contract. It is not by making the horse trot eternally in a circle that will flex the neck and haunches of the horse; rather it will be this play with hands and legs that will accomplish it. And as the neck and head of the horse is the helm and compass of the horseman, it is thereby that he directs and contains impulsion. It is through them also that he can vanquish a horse's resistances.

While Clément-Thomas does not indicate specifically that he is voicing the thoughts and recommendations of Baucher, it is clear that he is concurring fully with him. His suggestions and advice are clearly those Baucher expressed in his *nouvelle méthode*. Use simple and gentle bits and reject those terrible implements of torture. With the aid of the bit and the reins flex the muscles of the jaw and neck. This is to be done on foot and mounted. The result will be the perpendicular position of the head which will now give easily to the tension of the hand on the reins. Similarly, the hindquarters are to be flexed. Its goal is to bring about the *ramener*, that is, the action of distributing equally the weight of the horse, which will result in regularity at the walk and the trot. It is different at the gallop where the movement is executed by strides from the forehand to the hindquarters, each part of which is alternatively raised or resting on the ground. It is a continual flux and reflux of the distribution of the weight. For the horse to function with regularity at the gallop it is important that the strength of the horse be brought together (the *ramener*) at the centre of the horse's body. This will facilitate the regu-larity and cadence of these movements. Thus the horse will learn how to retain at the walk, at the trot, at a change of direction, that certain lightness and balance, without which a horse will automatically fall into his old defences. Work at the gallop requires further disposal of the horse's strength, namely, the *attacks* (of legs and, by extension, spurs). But, warns Clément-Thomas, it should be noted that he means by this *the reasonable use of the spurs*. For when Baucher and Clément-Thomas refer to attacks, they do not mean a stupid, dangerous punishment which could only make the horse desperate; rather they are a means of education.

Once the *ramener* has been accomplished by judicious use of the legs and spurs, by means of a little more pressure we can achieve the *rassembler* (collection, that is, all the forces of the horse are reunited at the centre of the horse's body). Thus by means of the *ramener* and the *rassembler* we now are the master of our horse. Not only can we make him execute with ease all the exercises performed in the *manège*, but we also perfect nature.

Here, says Clément-Thomas, is the succinct, albeit incomplete analysis of Baucher's method. However, it is in the works of Baucher, or better still, at his school, that one can learn and appreciate this method in all its details.

After having analysed and defended Baucher's *nouvelle méthode*, Clément-Thomas discusses the social conflict that affected this controversy. 'One can well imagine', he says:

how the publication of a system that is so new and so positive could produce an effect on the men who are concerned with equitation. Six editions of the method went out of print in rapid succession in France, and one was quickly published in each of the principal languages of Europe. Such a major success was bound to give rise to numerous criticisms, which were readily forthcoming to M. Baucher, and one can divide these opponents into three categories.[9]

---

[9] Ibid., p. 20.

In the first category, Clément-Thomas places the 'solemn and impartial men who doubted the soundness of the system for lack of interpreting it properly but who, once enlightened, approved of it, for the most part, unreservedly'.[10] In the second category, he places 'a host of *gentlemen*, so-called *riders*, little gentlemen who wear yellow gloves, are amberscented and conceited, and who found it impertinent that a simple artiste, a man who had never frequented the *turf* and who was not a member of any jockey club, dared consider himself an authority on equitation'.[11] In the third category of adversaries, Clément-Thomas places the professors of civilian equitation, colleagues of M. Baucher, who attacked more the rival in Baucher than the innovator. Some of these professors had even published their criticisms; but in them one can find only passion, ill-will, even anger, but not a single one gives a good argument in their condemnation of the system. 'Better still: we have noticed that the majority of these *Aristarques* did not even understand what they were attacking, and one of them, pushing frankness to the limit, even went so far as to say in all honesty that he had not bothered to study it.'[12]

Clément-Thomas ends the second part of his series of articles, in which he discusses the reactions of civilians, by saying that Baucher has answered and refuted the criticisms of his most weighty opponents. It is obvious that Clément-Thomas, without saying so, is thinking of d'Aure and his *Observations*.

In the third part, Clément-Thomas comes to the crux of his articles, namely Baucher's *nouvelle méthode* and its application in the army. When the Minister of War heard that a new system of equitation existed that was innovative and original, he wanted to know whether it was something that could be applied to the army. He thus commissioned Lt. General Oudinot, a judicious and bold horseman, as well as a responsible and dutiful officer, to investigate the matter. This Oudinot

did by immediately contacting Baucher who, at the request of Oudinot, explained his method to him in great detail. (Oudinot had also attended the famous gala performance of Baucher on Géricault.) To get practical experience as well, Oudinot became once again a pupil. This convinced Oudinot that Baucher's system had merit. He shared this thought with the Minister who decided that Sens would serve as a theatre of operations; he also decided to set up a committee, the *Comité de la Cavalerie*, composed of General Marquis Oudinot, President Carrelet, Colonel of the Municipal Guard, de Novital (squadron chief at Saumur where he commanded the *manège* of the *Ecole de Saumur*), and two captain-instructors of the 5th Cuirassiers and the 3rd Lancers respectively.

Much of what Clément-Thomas now relates and quotes to substantiate his point is material taken from the documents published by Baucher. These documents reveal Baucher's two-year relationship with the army. The first document is dated Paris, 14 January 1842, written by Lt. Col. Champmontant of the General Staff and Secretary of the *Comité de la Cavalerie*. In this letter to Baucher, Champmontant states that the *Comité*, before deliberating, would like to discuss the matter with Baucher. The members of the *Comité* hope that 19 January would be agreeable for him to present himself.

A few days later Baucher received an important letter from General Oudinot wherein Baucher is advised that his Excellency, the Minister of War, 'has decided that there will take place in Paris a series of experiments with respect to your method which would school mounts known to be problem horses. Consequently, one hundred horses taken from the cavalry regiments garrisoned in Paris will be schooled in accordance with your system.'[13] Baucher is then asked to meet with Oudinot and members of the *Comité* the following day.

---

[10] Ibid., p. 20.   [11] Ibid., p. 20.   [12] Ibid., p. 21.   [13] Baucher, O.C. p. 16.

Important also is the report prepared by the Commandant of the *Ecole de Cavalerie* of Saumur, de Novital, and quoted briefly by Clément-Thomas, which gives a daily account of the experiment begun 21 March 1842 at Sens. This report praises the first attempt by Baucher to introduce his method in the schooling of undisciplined mounts and untrained men.

These officers, NCOs and horsemen, after a succinct, to the point and rational explanation given by M. Baucher, pertaining to the foundation of his method, on the various causes of the defences of the horse and on the simple but efficient means of combating them, these officers and NCOs, I say, after a demonstration of a few minutes, put themselves to the task and almost instantaneously obtained results with respect to these wild and rebellious natures. At the end of half an hour, each horse understood the aids and put himself, so to speak, with good grace, to following all the demands of the horseman, first on the ground, then mounted.[14]

After giving a full account of the daily events, de Novital specifically praises Baucher's method:

Here, then, are the results accomplished after thirteen days and even less for some horses. The facts speak for themselves; they are conclusive. To obtain in thirteen days what one usually accomplishes in six months or a year is an immense advantage which the cavalry will take pleasure in recognizing. To make of each horseman, whoever he may be, the instructor of his own mount, is another no less important accomplishment. To spread the taste of equitation by the attraction it has for all those who practise it is also one of the benefits that the method of M. Baucher will achieve.[15]

Further on, de Novital concludes:

The method of M. Baucher must take the lead because it is based on principles that are true, fixed, rational and motivated; everything presented is mathematical and can be proven by numbers [mathematically]. To him belongs the new era which is beginning, to him belongs the glory of having placed the horse completely under the control of the horseman by paralysing all his resistances, his will, and by replacing the instinctive strength by the transmitted strength.[16]

Clément-Thomas in his analysis of this document praises both de Novital and Baucher's method, pointing out that this daily exposure to the *nouvelle méthode* resulted in the elimination of the horses' resistances. It is important to note that General Oudinot, in his report to the Minister of War, Maréchal Soult, was also speaking for the members of the *Comité*.

After receiving all these excellent reports, the Minister of War wanted to witness the results of the experiment for himself and visited Sens. He came, he saw, and he was won over. However, to convince himself even further and make doubly sure that the experiment should be put into practice in the army, and upon the advice of Oudinot, Soult decided that further experiments should be conducted with a larger number of men in Paris under the direction of Baucher, and in Lunéville under the direction of Baucher's son, Henri. In Saumur, those officers who had already studied the method with Baucher could conduct their own experiment.

In Paris, twenty-six officers, under Squadron Chief Grenier of the 9th Curassiers, were initiated into Baucher's system. All these officers were already seasoned horsemen who had studied horsemanship under various masters. Now they were being directed by a civilian and taught a new method. This was a rather problematical situation, but one from which, according to Clément-Thomas, Baucher extricated himself quite well. Whatever scepticism and disdain may have existed initially on the part of seasoned officers for a civilian dissipated rapidly as the experiment progressed. In fact, says Clément-Thomas, the officers demonstrated courtesy, frankness and even a certain amount of self-effacement. Discussions between Baucher and the officers were often quite animated, even brilliant. The enthusiastic re-

---

[14] Ibid., p. 17.   [15] Ibid., p. 20.   [16] Ibid., p. 20.

Experimenting with the *nouvelle méthode* in the Paris garrison. (Lithograph from Count de Lancosme-Brèves, *Guide de l'ami du cheval*)

ports of the twenty-six officers attest to the success of Baucher and his method. A certain captain-instructor, sceptical at first and wanting to put Baucher's method to a test, admits in his report that he had brought along with him a hack of heavy proportions, with a heavy neck and head and defective hocks, who leaned on the bit and constantly resisted his attempts at controlling him. But lo and behold, this ungainly creature became light and balanced. He became a saddle horse who could now be *ramené* and *rassemblé*, and could even *piaffe*. The squadron commander, A. Grenier, speaking for the twenty-six officers, says: 'Little by little confidence emerged, opposition disappeared, but it was only at the end of the first month, after about twenty-five lessons, that all the officers, without exception, understood and recognized the superiority of the principles of M. Baucher over those known by us.'[17]

De Novital, pleased with the results, selected some of the more advanced instructors to apply the new method on a number of unschooled and problem horses. In his letter to the Minister of War, he once again states that the new system has proven considerably useful to the cavalry in that it guarantees the health and preservation of the horse, develops his faculties, and increases harmony and balance. 'Baucher's system must be considered as eminently worthy of preserving as a dressage that is well graduated and well devised, and which cannot have any ill effect on the physical aspect of the horse.'[18] Finally, the *Comité* made clear that after having weighed the advantages of the new system, it 'remains convinced that it can render the greatest service to the cavalry'.[19]

In the fourth part of his articles Clément-Thomas gives his own conclusion. With all these testimonies, the Minister of War could

---

[17] Ibid., p. 32.   [18] Ibid., p. 29.   [19] Ibid., p. 30.

no longer hesitate. Yet hesitate he did. He ordered all the instructor-captains and lieutenants who had not previously participated in the experimental course with either Baucher or his son to meet at the headquarters of the *Ecole de Cavalerie* of Saumur to take, for two months, a course from Baucher and his son. Baucher came to Saumur with his son to begin work on 16 February 1843. It was a somewhat tense situation for Baucher. In the 1854 edition of his book he says that he was fully aware that he had men facing him who were already skilled in the equestrian art. But he was ready for them. He had already experienced a similar situation in Sens and had emerged from it victoriously.

According to Clément-Thomas, it was obvious that the influence of those antagonistic towards Baucher's new method was working behind the scenes. Hence the delays. It was a question of who would have the greatest influence, the military world or the civilian world of equitation? The battle between the two groups was already raging in the newspapers, civilian and military alike. Captain-Instructor Auguste Delard of the 9th Curassier wrote a brilliant defence of the new method in the *Spectateur militaire* of 15 April and 15 October 1843.[20] But the damage was already beginning to be felt by Baucher.

The course was to be given under the direction of Lt. General de Sparre whom Baucher had already met earlier in Paris and who had given Baucher no specific instructions at that time. The first overtly negative act came in the form of a *communiqué* by de Sparre in which Baucher was ordered to use in his course a sort of manual for the schooling of the horse, based on his method, but considerably abbreviated and changed. When Baucher examined this manual he had difficulty recognizing the method it represented as his own. To use his method in such a truncated form made it totally useless.

Baucher was especially hurt by the fact that there had been no prior discussion about these changes. When Baucher finally was able to discuss the matter with General de Sparre, the latter said to him: 'We do, indeed, want your method, but we don't want any equitation.'[21] To this statement, Baucher quipped: 'One must, before going any further, explain the value of words, or else await the publication of a new dictionary.'[22] That both Baucher and his defender, Clément-Thomas, were astonished by this strange request is understandable. Equally astonishing was a request by the general as reported by Baucher: '"Do one thing" said the general to me, "and we will be in accord; do not mention legs in your course."'[23] This, explains Clément-Thomas in his articles, was uttered by a man who was supposed to direct an experiment dealing with the field of equitation, and who 'wants equestrian aptitude without equitation, and proposes seriously that one not mention the legs of a horseman in the presentation of an art that rests, to a large degree, on the judicious use of these important and indispensable motors'.[24] Baucher explains that he terminated this strange discussion by insisting that as far as he was concerned, it was all or nothing.

When de Sparre became aware that Baucher would rather abandon the lessons than comply with these strange orders, he gave Baucher free rein to proceed without interference. 'I believed it to be my right to expect to be treated with consideration',[25] says Baucher. Seventy-two officer-instructors, skilled in horsemanship, came from various locations to assemble in Saumur. According to Clément-Thomas, what was especially disturbing was the fact that they had been privy to the conversation between Baucher and de Sparre, which did nothing to enhance Baucher's authority with men who were already skilled horsemen, who had been

---

[20] See footnote in ibid., pp. 60–1.
[21] Ibid., p. 64. Baucher published this conversation in the 1854 edition of his O.C.
[22] Ibid., p. 64.
[23] Ibid., p. 65.
[24] Clément-Thomas, *De l'Equitation militaire*, pp. 33–4.
[25] Baucher, O.C., p. 63.

uprooted from their routine lives, who were sceptical, and whose scepticism and negative disposition was increased by the verbal battle between General de Sparre and the civilian Baucher.

But matters seemed to improve as the course proceeded. As had occurred in Sens and in Paris, the officers soon showed a willingness to participate, and even expressed enthusiasm. When the course was over, the officers were asked to submit a report. The reports of the seventy-two participants, save three, were favourably disposed to the new method and expressed their approval by urging its adoption. They even went so far as to criticize the fact that the manual Baucher was using was a truncated version of his method.

Then, asks Clément-Thomas, why did things go wrong? Why did the army eventually cancel the teaching of the new method? Clément-Thomas gives a number of reasons. Many of the instructors at the *Ecole de Cavalerie* who had been asked to experiment with the new method were only imperfectly versed in it and their attempt to teach it to others caused a certain amount of dissatisfaction. Some were quick to blame the problems on the method itself. To compound matters, General de Sparre, who had been asked to supervise the course, disappeared after two or three meetings, only to return to order the cancellation of the programme. It is obvious, says Clément-Thomas, that de Sparre was listening to certain voices, for the general was far from being an expert in the field of equitation, something he himself stated later in a letter. Nevertheless, while the Minister of War now ordered that the new method be introduced provisionally into all the cavalry regiments in France, things continued to deteriorate. While the previous reports made by the officer-instructors who had participated initially in the experiment in Paris, Lunéville and Saumur had been favourably disposed to the new method, the successive reports of the captain-instructors were far from

expressing enthusiasm and were far from being unanimous. Clément-Thomas explains that many of the officer-instructors were too old or simply had not gone through the training of the new method themselves and, unfamiliar with it, could hardly be expected to teach it to others. Yet, despite these problems, of the 102 officer-instructors, eighty-three accepted the method without any modification. Even the *Comité*, composed of seven generals including de Sparre and Oudinot, with the exception of two members, approved the new system of Baucher. Clément-Thomas explains that the two members who had rejected the method had done so because they had not taken the trouble of enlightening themselves. Thus for approximately two years the report of the officer-instructors, while not unanimous or enthusiastic, nevertheless expressed approval. So did the members of the *Comité*. A letter written by General de Sparre, dated 25 March 1843, while obliquely admonishing Baucher for having made use of his method, and admitting that he knew little, or nothing, of this very method, nevertheless says at the end, '*I still recognize*, Sir, *that the results you obtained in schooling the young horses at Saumur were, in general, satisfactory, and I take pleasure in telling you this.*'[26] Then why the final rejection of Baucher and his method?

According to both Baucher and Clément-Thomas, the fly in the ointment was the Duke de Nemours who, at the death of the Duke d'Orléans, had replaced the Dauphin as a member of the *Comité* and as heir to the throne of France. While d'Orléans had always shown enthusiasm for Baucher and had frequently attended Baucher's performances at the circus, his brother, when dutifully attending some of the experiments executed by Baucher in Paris, Lunéville, and Saumur, had always shown a studied indifference with respect to the lessons that were in session. He had, in fact, made it a point never to study the new method. This attitude on the part of the Duke de Nemours

---

[26] Ibid., p. 67.

was especially evident at Lunéville when a group of young horses, schooled in the new method for only twenty-six days, executed a *caroussel* to the enthusiasm of everybody else present. 'It is he, he alone,' cries out Clément-Thomas, 'who deprived the army of an innovation that was as useful as it was profitable.'[27] De Nemours had been a pupil of d'Aure and d'Aure's influence on him was well known. When asked why he opposed Baucher's new method, he answered: 'I do not want a system that depends upon the impulsion of horses.'[28] A strange statement, indeed, when one remembers that a good part of d'Aure's own system of equitation was based on impulsion. Moreover, it is an indication of de Nemours' lack of skill as a horseman. Neither does it indicate that he was an independent thinker. This is precisely what Baucher is implying when he writes:

What could possibly have been the obstacle against which my efforts were smashed? Jealousy, the bad faith of an equerry/instructor or the Duke de Nemours. This equerry did not hesitate to use his influence which his position gave him with respect to his pupil and, incredibly, knew how to make use of his title as Prince of the Blood, and impose his will on certain members of the *Comité* set up to judge in the last resort ... Ah, Sire, you aspire to be regent of the realm, and yet you let yourself be influenced to the point of hiding the light under the bushel in order to please one of your domestics? That you should be grateful to one of your teachers is commendable; that you should give him decorations and positions, that is how it should be, for their devotion merits this. But you ought also to have been, above all, a man of progress, and when it was a matter of an innovation that was in the general interest, your personal interest should have been silenced and you should have thought only of your country.[29]

Thus in July 1845, Baucher received a letter from the *Comité* informing him of the cancellation of the course and expressing the following reasons for the cancellation.

1. That the new system was not compatible with military training, as there was insufficient time for the men to become well-versed in the system, which thus contributed to the impossibility of making them understand the system and apply it without endangering themselves and their mounts.
2. That Baucher's method was more in keeping with *manège* equitation, rather than the training of military horses, in that it would make the military horses too refined and delicate to withstand the pressure of formation riding.
3. That this excessive refinement and sensitivity would be detrimental to a military horse.

Clément-Thomas considers the letter addressed to Baucher as expressing the mind of a bureaucrat, especially one who had never sat on a horse. How can one, asks Clément-Thomas, make a distinction between a 'system of dressage' on the part of an equerry and a 'method of equitation?' And how can a system that is so simple and clear, as everyone seemed to believe, suddenly become incomprehensible to officers? And to say that Baucher's method will render the cavalry horses too refined and sensitive is utterly ludicrous. 'But here are these wonderful considerations this superior commission claims to have used, that is to say, the Duke de Nemours used, in order to oppose the immense majority of cavalry officers.'[30] Justice, says Clément-Thomas, has been violated. Baucher has been condemned for social reasons, not for his system.

Had he emerged from a more elevated rank, his renown would not have lacked voices to celebrate his merit; but his status is obscure and for this he was shown disdain. The envious ones, believing him fallen from grace, went on to consider him an impostor; they had the audacity to say and write that his system, already condemned by all the competent judges, was now finally being rejected by

---

[27] Clément-Thomas, *De l'Equitation militaire*, p. 39.
[28] Ibid., p. 40.
[29] Baucher, O.C., pp. vii, viii.
[30] Clément-Thomas, *De l'Equitation militaire*, p. 43.

the army because it was absurd and filled with errors. This is why I have taken up his defence. It shall not be said that in a country in which equality reigns, where discussion is free as it is in France, that talent, no matter what it is, could only flourish if supported by influence and fortune, or that envy could be stifled with impunity.[31]

Clément-Thomas says he is also taking up the gauntlet because his fellow officers have been insulted, in that, although consulted, their support of and enthusiasm for the new method was finally rejected not because the method was inadequate, but for political and personal reasons.

---

[31] Ibid., p. 45.

5

Baucher and his critics d'Aure and Aubert

Shortly after Baucher published the work in which he defined his *nouvelle méthode*, and after the famous performance on Géricault, he finally received the attention he had so much desired. It was these accomplishments and the army's decision to allow Baucher to demonstrate for them his *nouvelle méthode* in the retraining of men and mounts that led d'Aure to publish his *Observations sur la nouvelle méthode d' Equitation* and P.-A. Aubert to publish his *Quelques Observations sur le système de M. Baucher pour dresser les chevaux.*

D'Aure begins his *Observations* with the matter-of-fact statement that the use and especially the riding of the horse, and the means of controlling the horse, are all too well known for anyone to declare that they have discovered a new method. The use of the horse does not, after all, begin with the year 1840. D'Aure, like other horsemen such as Aubert, Rousselet and others, that is, the remaining few with Classical training, were, in fact, not very impressed with Baucher's new movements and his *tours de force* at the circus; neither were they impressed with his seat. Above all, they were disconcerted with the way Baucher's horses were imprisoned between hands and legs.

D'Aure gives the reader a credible analysis as to why the uninitiated opted for Baucher. The real practitioners, he says, of Classical or *savante* equitation were gradually disappearing from the scene, and those who could distinguish between pure Classical equitation and the equitation that was currently being presented in the circus under the guise of *haute école* equitation were few and far between. 'This kind of equitation, once lost, and no standards of comparison existing any more, everything could appear as new and good to those who had seen nothing else.'[1] D'Aure goes on to say that people are confusing the equitation they are witnessing today with the equitation as it was practised before the doors of the *Ecole de Versailles* were closed. Furthermore, he points out, the government is chiefly to blame for this state of affairs for not supporting the art of equitation and its traditions and not keeping them alive. Unfortunately, when the various techniques of the schools of men such as Newcastle, Grisone, Pluvinel and others were taken up again, it was principally to train horses to perform in the circus. And when someone comes along and begins to talk about and exhibit such things as the *ramener* and the *rassembler*, people assume that they are hearing and seeing something original and new.

While d'Aure compares Baucher's type of riding to *manège* equitation, nevertheless, d'Aure claims, in the past the function of the *manège* was still to prepare the horseman for active and exterior riding. Baucher's type of equitation, d'Aure implies, may today be appropriate for the circus, as it tends to restrict the paces of the horse and make him perform in a small area. But tastes have changed. Now horses are trained to carry their heads free in

---

[1] D'Aure, *Observations sur la nouvelle méthode*, p. 20.

D'Aure practising exterior equitation. (Painting by Philippe Ledieu, Musée de Saumur)

the wind, that is, they are not collected. They push forward and carry their weight on the forehand and not on the hindquarters.

The main goal in the schooling of a young horse is 'to render him free and straightforward, to be able to turn him easily to the right or to the left, to keep him straight, to regularize his paces and his movements, so that he can be useful for the longest period of time. This will develop his strength, widen his paces, and make him honest.'[2] As to the posture of the rider, it must be such that he can always remain the same without getting tired, and thus be able to preserve at all times his ability

to keep the horse under control by means of the aids. Since the sensitivity of the horse is the result of his total make-up, it does not depend upon the horseman to increase or to decrease it; at the most, he can modify it. French equitation, d'Aure continues, demands that

the horse be contained between the hand and the legs so that the horseman can adequately be master of the movements of the horse and regularize his paces. It does not mean that the horse be broken, nor does it mean that everything that a horse has of action and energy be extinguished . . . While controlling the horse, he should, nevertheless, be given

---

[2] Ibid., p. 5.

the necessary freedom to allow him to develop his paces; for real talent lies in the ability to put the horse in the position of doing things of his own accord, rather than imposing upon him work that is often beyond his ability and strength. It is necessary, under certain circumstances, to make the proper concessions to conserve the horse's strength. It is equally necessary to have a rapport with him because often he can indicate how much he can give and of what he is capable far better than can the horseman. Our equitation at no time upholds the idea that all horses are equally susceptible and thus must be placed under the same rules; neither does it believe, as does M. Baucher, that all horses have the same *impressionability* and the same energy.[3]

In his criticism of Baucher's method, d'Aure states that for someone to interpret equitation the way Baucher does, he must never have really made use of a horse other than in a *manège* or in a circus situation, which is quite different from active or exterior equitation. In the former situation, the movements of the horse are unnatural and thus it is necessary to control the horse completely and at all times, and to capture his attention constantly. A moment of relaxation could bring about the deterioration of any brilliant performance. In active or exterior equitation, a horseman can allow the horse to use his own initiative and intelligence. How often, be it during travel, the hunt, or in war, has the horse not shown intelligence and courage. Furthermore, the difference between the two types of equitation can also be seen in the health, energy and carriage of the horse.

D'Aure then proceeds to discuss the basis of Baucher's *nouvelle méthode*, namely, flexion of the neck and the jaw.[4] If, continues d'Aure, a rigid neck is bothersome, then too much flexibility in the neck is worse, especially if one wishes to get out of the shortened paces. To submit a horse to too much flexion, even if reason and caution are used, to demand too

much of him, are ways of making him unsure of himself and may arouse his defences. It is usually man's misuse of the horse that brings about a horse's defences. It is only when he has been made sure of himself and has been rendered free and straightforward that his schooling can begin.

Furthermore, the idea of flexion is not new. Placing the head of a horse is not unknown to horsemen and equerries. Newcastle had already discussed this technique in his *Nouvelle méthode d'Equitation* published in 1660. In the seventeenth and eighteenth centuries horsemen had already attempted to put the horse to shortened paces, but they did so in a much more intelligent manner, namely, when the horse was in motion. We, continues d'Aure, of the *Ecole de Versailles* also proceeded in this manner, but we were much more sober in the flexion of the horse. The same holds true when it comes to the *ramener*, that is, the placement of the horse's head and closing the angle between the head and the neck. Here, too, objects d'Aure, Baucher is implying that no one until now knew how to place the head of a horse. D'Aure criticizes Baucher's technique of the *ramener*, which, according to him, is to hold the animal prisoner, to prevent him from developing, and to enclose him in such a manner that 'he can only function in a small space'.[5] For d'Aure, however, the *ramener* is not to hold the head of the horse perpendicularly to the ground; rather its function is to place the head of the horse in such a way that the bit can find the correct contact on the bars which will enable the rider to stop the horse, maintain him in his paces and speed, and direct him. In his natural state, the horse's head is positioned slightly diagonally, with his nose thrust forward. But when a horse is held back by the reins and excited by the spurs, the horse is prevented from going either forward or backward; all he can do is *piaffe*.

---

[3] Ibid., p. 6. To substantiate his point, in a footnote (p. 6) d'Aure discusses the ideas of the distinguished veterinarian Legros.
[4] Ibid. In another footnote (p. 10) d'Aure quotes once again the veterinarian Legros who 'by means of anatomy

shows how Baucher is in error for, instead of considering, as he does, the forehand and the hindquarters as antagonistic, should, rather, consider them as complementary'.
[5] Ibid., p. 15.

Another criticism levelled against Baucher on the part of d'Aure is Baucher's system of *les attaques des éperons*, a technique considered new by Baucher, but, according to d'Aure, something that had always been used in equitation. Every horseman, says d'Aure, knows that the legs have the function of pushing the horse forward, but they also have the additional function of straightening out the haunches, of making them supple and able to support the hindquarters whenever the bit acts in such a way as to want to make the horse go backward. A horse is well seated only when his hindquarters are supple and when the haunches have been controlled. Only the rider's legs have this function. This has been known since time immemorial. A horse is schooled only when he moves himself straight and freely forward by the *attaques des éperons*. It is an aid that must be used soberly in order for the horseman to conserve all his power. Too many horses tend to ignore the spur and to push themselves above it. It is wrong to get them used to feeling the spur all the time, especially with little kicks, as the new method suggests. Indeed, each attack of the spur, followed by stopping with the hand, will of course lead to the *ramener*, but these continual annoyances, so tiring and disturbing to a horse, can only serve to shorten his movements and break his paces. A horse continually subjected to such restrictions loses his natural energy very quickly. Equitation does not consist in making each and every horse *piaffe* (which, according to d'Aure, is what Baucher's continual use of the *ramener* will do), but in making a horse useful for other things. 'I, for one', adds d'Aure, 'prefer horses who do not *piaffe*; and I esteem even more men who try to prevent horses from *piaffing*.'[6]

D'Aure now turns to criticizing Baucher's posture. What can be said about this new posture of Baucher, asks d'Aure, which places the horseman on the fork, torso leaning forward, legs bent towards the flanks? 'Is this not the posture used in the Middle Ages, when men wore armour from head to toe, and when they presented themselves in the lists during a tourney, either to give or to receive a blow? Usually they were standing in the stirrups. Since then, the horse has been used for other activities and it has been necessary to rectify the posture to adapt oneself to the uses of the present . . .'[7]

It should be noted, insists d'Aure:

that the *manège* is a means, not an end; that one must know how to use it with discretion; that if one does not know how to combine outside equitation with inside equitation, the schooling of the horse will be imperfect; that each and every horse made to submit solely to the rules of the *manège*, once he is suppled and broken, can, perhaps, do some very pretty things inside, but will be hopelessly inadequate on the outside. I apologize to those who have provoked this reaction of mine, but in accepting as good the prestige of the circus, can these people give proof of discernment? I rather believe that partiality played a role in this, for if one really wanted to ameliorate the instruction of our cavalry troops, would they not have consulted specialists? France still possesses some. Is it necessary for the pupils of d'Abzac, of Coupé, of Jardin, to engage someone from the circus?[8]

D'Aure then goes on to point out that it is understandable that young officers with no experience have been seduced by an equitation which they hoped would make them shine, and believed that from now on horses would function on their own, that harsh paces would automatically become gentle, that good qualities would eradicate poor ones, and so on. Furthermore, making an indomitable horse 'change hands, hold a leg in the air, dance and valse – activities that seem unusual and new today – had already been exploited by such men as Astley, Ducrow, Franconi and all the other organizers of fairs, and even by Monsieur de Pluvinel in his famous *caroussel* prepared in 1609 for the festivities of the marriage of Marie de Médicis, wife of Henry IV'.[9] However, d'Aure continues, these men used the *caroussel*

---

[6] Ibid., p. 19.   [7] Ibid., pp. 19–20.   [8] Ibid., p. 21.   [9] Ibid., p. 22.

and horse ballets as a secondary concern, not as their goal. Most importantly, the *Ecole de Saumur*, in its reorganization, ignored the precepts of the *Ecole de Versailles*. Had they not done so, they would today have schooled equerries imbued with the pure and exact principles of French equitation which could have been transmitted to future generations. D'Aure repeats once again his concern for modern equitation and the consequences that arose with the closing of the doors of the *Ecole de Versailles*. He repeats his former admonishment that with no comparison to be made with the past, everything new is good to those who know nothing else, regardless of whether it is a repetition of the past or a poor imitation of the past. And now that the army finds it desirous to teach horsemanship to its cavalry, it ignores the past and goes to the circus for inspiration and training.

D'Aure recognizes that, despite the enthusiasm of some people for this *nouvelle méthode*, those same people have deemed it necessary to simplify greatly the flexion of the neck and jaw, and have developed an equitation which places the horseman more deeply and more comfortably in the saddle, with the legs hanging straight down rather than being bent at the horse's flanks, and eliminates the eternal use of spurs. With all these rectifications, why all this fuss, asks d'Aure? It only gives added credence to the notion that Baucher's method is a personal matter. For all the fuss has accomplished little. It has only succeeded in hurting the feelings of some people and created a schism in the field of equitation.

D'Aure goes on to say that he only hopes that this conflict will bring about a reaction out of which truth will emerge. This truth is what he desires in the interest of an art whose utility has, for a long time, been misunderstood and misused.

Far from attaching to my statement anything personal, I have all my life envisaged the horse and his education as something too elevated to place any importance whatsoever to similar pettiness; and I would have been disposed to accept the application of these new means, had I considered them good ... It is true that I make little case of what one considers today a well-schooled horse, when this schooling is based upon *manège* exercises, and when the horse is of no use for anything else. I want my *manège* horse of winter to become my pleasure horse in summer, and my hunter in autumn.[10]

D'Aure concludes his *Observations* by saying that he, too, has ridden horses schooled in the new method and that he has never seen or ridden any that were worse. 'Broken in their paces, uncertain in their movement, stamping instead of walking, always ready to turn their head towards the boot of the horseman, offering no certitude and assurance when one pushes them forward; nothing is left of the paces of a horse.'[11] Ever since the introduction of the *nouvelle méthode* one only hears speak of indomitable horses, as though there is nothing else but this type of horse. Partisan, ridden previously by a woman and by a twelve-year-old child, now becomes indomitable; Capitaine, after having been a hunter and a pleasure horse becomes indomitable; Buridan, first a saddle horse, then a carriage horse, is now indomitable. If all these dangerous horses have made the reputation of a horseman, that is wonderful. But in the past, horsemen were content to school horses without bragging about it or giving value to their reputation by saying that the horse they have schooled had been poorly schooled by a previous equerry.

P.-A. Aubert was a professor of equitation, an equerry of the *Ecole Royale d'Application*, and author of several works (one on the equitation of women). *Quelques Observations sur le système de M. Baucher pour dresser les chevaux* (*Some Observations on the System of M. Baucher for Schooling Horses*) is divided into seven observations, and asks the questions whether the *nouvelle méthode* of Baucher should, indeed, be

---

[10] Ibid., p. 24.   [11] Ibid., p. 25.

adopted by the cavalry troops of the French army.

In his 'First Observation', Aubert points out that M. Baucher did not invent the suppling of the neck and withers, that is, as Aubert puts it, the suppling of the vertebrae of the neck or cervical vertebrae; he merely imitated the methods of certain Neapolitan equerries of the past. All the geometrical figures since the fifteenth century — the *volte*, the *demi-volte*, *voltes renversées*, *serpentaux*, *spirales*, *sarabandes* etc. — are attempts to supple the neck, the shoulders, and the hindquarters of the horse. However, unlike Baucher, who wishes to supple the horse while he is stationary by pulling him back, former equerries like Pignatelli, de la Broue, de Pluvinel, and Newcastle, who were writing when the art of riding was still in its infancy, wished to supple the horse 'while pushing him forward in order not to *l'aculer sur lui-même*'.[12] Aubert had already made a compilation of the methods of flexion used by the Neapolitan equerries and discussed them in his own *Traité d'Equitation* published in 1836. These methods consisted in tiring the horse out on the lunge so that all its resistances were overcome. Once the horse was exhausted, flexion of the horse, while stationary, began. The aim was to push the horse's head as close to the neck as possible, then between the forelegs, and, finally, to break some nerves in the neck. Is this not the system that Baucher is using in his attempts to flex the neck and withers of the horse? Other points made by Aubert in this 'First Observation' are that Baucher is teaching his method to horsemen who have already had training by other equerries, and that his method attempts to accomplish flexion of the horse in the shortest amount of time by means of great play or attacks with the spurs, of halts, and of attacks working simultaneously. All this aims at overcoming the horse's resistances. Thus the most vigorous horse, with the best conformation, will be reduced within a few months to the state of an ambulatory cadaver. This, says Aubert, is the secret that Baucher is willing to impart to us.

In footnotes to the 'First Observation', Aubert refers to the fact that a horse resembles an 'ambulatory cadaver' after he has been subjected to Baucher's *nouvelle méthode*, Aubert makes a personal statement about how, during the latter part of 1839, he had been asked to attend a performance of Baucher on Partisan and that he found that Baucher's posture was even worse than he had anticipated. Nevertheless, he had tried not to let Baucher's poor seat influence his assessment of Baucher's training of the horse and, as he had promised, he observed the movements of the horse with the most scrupulous attention. Aubert goes on to say that he had felt a tremendous personal triumph because he now had proof that what he had written earlier, namely, that one could do spectacular things with a *manège* horse given the right music, was vindicated. He remembered how M. Laurent Franconi, about fifteen years ago, after having given up acrobatics on horseback (stunts known as *voltiger*) had taken up *haute école* equitation in the circus, and that while his horse was inferior to Partisan in his movements, he had done something similar and that the right kind of music had contributed to the tremendous theatricality of the performance. Aubert then compares the manner in which Franconi and Baucher held the reins when they moved to the right or to the left on two tracks, and the problems that arose when holding the reins in the left or the right hand. Aubert criticizes Baucher who, he claims, held the reins 'continuously stretched like the strings of violins'.[13] However, when it came to changes of hand executed by Partisan in the air, these were, despite Baucher's poor seat, exemplary. Aubert condemns the constant attack with the spurs on the flanks of the horse who laboured so hard as to get out of breath and seemed to

---

12 P.-A. Aubert, *Quelques Observations sur le système de M. Baucher pour dresser les chevaux* (Paris, Leneveu, 1842), p. 4.
13 Ibid.; see footnote, p. 3.

have lost all sensitivity into the bargain. 'I find a mournful sadness in the very regular movements of *Partisan*, something vaguely sepulchral.'[14] When his friend urged him to comment on the performance of Baucher on Partisan, Aubert answered: 'Upon my word, I find that in his line this horse works very regularly. If it is a mechanical horse, one must admit that he imitates nature perfectly; but if it is a natural horse, one must also admit that he resembles greatly a mechanical horse; he reminds me of an ambulatory cadaver.'[15] Aubert ridicules the audience whose tremendous applause reverberated throughout the circus when *Partisan* held his leg up in the air. 'But since I cannot see the utility of this, I cannot call it progress in equitation ... in my youth ... I saw a learned little horse do the same thing. His master, who exhibited him on the Pont Neuf, called it imitating the horse of Henry IV. In Italy I saw things that were even more astonishing.'[16]

Aside from the fact that flexions of the neck and jaw were common practice in the past, the question that Aubert posed in his 'Second Observation' is whether too much flexion, that is, too much of a bend or fold in the neck, obtained by flexing the horse while stationary, is not harmful to the horse in that it flexes the other vertebrae of the spinal column, and whether this excessive flexing of the neck does not contribute to a horse's use of defences. Of course, a horse going to the right in a *manège* must hold his head turned somewhat to the right; but if the horse turns his head too much to the right, the result will be that more of his weight will fall on his left shoulder, his balance will be compromised, and the points of contact badly distributed. Thus, with the horse's head and neck forced to the right, should one wish to turn squarely to the right, his haunches will be stopped on the left by the wall, and it will be necessary to close the outside leg, instead of giving support with the inside leg. This is necessary in order to re-establish, by means of the movement of the haunches, the balance

that has been lost in the shoulders due to the forced bend made in the neck. And, insists Aubert, an inexperienced rider could be in greater danger with a horse schooled *à la Baucher* than had he ridden his horse as he received him from the seller. A horse trained *à la Baucher*, whose neck is flexed and who is hardened by the incessant 'attacks with the spurs', will want to defend himself by pushing his haunches to the left, if you fix his head to the rider's boot on the right, and vice versa; and if you want to push his haunches to the right by closing the left leg, this horse will not respond because he has become insensitive through the attacks with the spurs; neither will he respond to both legs. It should be noted that it would be less dangerous if the horse should use his defences in the *manège* than during a hack.

In his 'Third Observation', Aubert says that not all defences or resistances on the part of a horse are due to a stiffness of the neck. In this, as in other instances, Baucher is in error. He speaks like a man who has come to the art of equitation at a late age and as one who has not ridden many horses, and has ridden mostly in the *manège*. Above all, he has belittled horsemen who have had a great deal of experience and ridden horses for hunting, in the army, in the snows of Russia and in the sands of Spain, before the Revolution of 1830 and the closing of the doors of the *Ecole de Versailles*. Aubert questions the claims made by Baucher and his disciples, namely, that Baucher has had more success on Partisan than all the equerries of the past put together. Can a man who has ridden, at the most, thirty horses during his lifetime, be more competent than those who have ridden thousands of horses, and under all sorts of conditions? Thus it is strange that the government, deaf to all entreaties made by well-known equerries such as the Marquis de Chabannes and the Viscount d'Aure, and other equerries of repute, should suddenly decide to reorganize the school of equitation in France

---

[14] Ibid., p. 6.   [15] Ibid., p. 6.   [16] Ibid., p. 7.

and engage for this purpose Baucher and his *nouvelle méthode*.

Aubert then asks Baucher some rhetorical questions, all pertaining to the stiffness of the neck and the results that ensue. When a horse buckjumps (*fait le dos de carpe*) with the result that the rider is sitting as though on a ball, and then jumps forward and tries to bite the legs of the rider, is this due to a stiffness of the neck? Or if he turns his head to the right to touch his tail, in order to flee to the left with his haunches, is this due to the stiffness of the neck? And if he bucks, turning his neck first to the right then to the left, is it because his neck is stiff? And if the horse, despite the fact that his head and neck are well placed, has poor *contretemps* at the gallop, is this due to stiffness of the neck? It is with a resounding 'no' that Aubert answers these questions.

In the 'Fourth Observation', Aubert states that Baucher's system is a very personal one, based on his own by experience, the opposite of the fundamental principles established by past horsemen. Actually, there is no modification of general principles in Baucher's system; rather, his system is an amplification of the old Neapolitan method. If M. Baucher had wanted to 'generalize a principle'[17] in the schooling of a horse, he could have done so without wanting to stress his opposition to all the equerries of the past and present. He could have simply stated that 'all resistances and defences on the part of a horse who is ridden are almost always preceded by a halt that is more or less sudden and has not involved the hand of the horseman'.[18] No one would have gainsaid him. Furthermore, he would have been forced to recognize that to ward off resistances and defences, both of a young unschooled horse and of an old horse become sour, he must push the horse forward. But M. Baucher's manner of equitation is quite personal and eccentric and is in accord with none of the French schools of equitation. It is for that reason that M. Baucher has adopted a posture that is his very own and which would be sheer torture were we forced to adopt it, especially at the trot. It should be noted, continues Aubert, that the posture M. Baucher has selected is the least effective in the development of a vigorous horse; rather, it excites a vigorous and sensitive horse to impatience and resistance. A horseman with this type of seat is naturally forced to use and adopt methods that are energetic and prompt in order to neutralize, even destroy, the natural strength of a horse, that is, to destroy his most precious resources. He is forced to take such measures simply to stay on the horse, for this posture of his violates the laws of gravity and balance. It is for this reason that M. Baucher takes the opposite position of those equerries who say 'Push your horse forward'; for he says 'Keep your horse stationary, rein back indefinitely.'[19]

Aubert wards off possible criticisms levelled against him, namely that he has only seen Baucher perform once, by saying that he has read the works of Baucher. He attacks in particular Baucher's *Dictionnaire raisonné* (1833), saying that the ideas that are valid in this work he had already observed in the works of La Guérinière. Everything else Aubert considers incomprehensible, especially when Baucher writes that to overcome the forces and resistances of a horse, one must oppose them with other forces. What resistances? asks Aubert. He has ridden several thousand horses and has found few resistances. Furthermore, all horsemen agree that to combat force with force is the worst thing one can do and is doomed to failure. To understand real resistances of a horse one must have ridden horses from Aleçon and areas of Normandy or wild ones from Russia, and not the well-behaved horses imported from England who are easy to train, who go forward readily, and are the kind that

---

[17] In a footnote, ibid., p. 15, Aubert explains that 'to generalize a principle' means to make a principle the basis of a whole system of learning.

[18] Ibid., p. 16.
[19] Ibid., p. 19.

Caricature of Baucher by Lorentz: the riding master. (Musée Philipon)

Baucher has trained. Aubert ends his 'Fourth Observation' by addressing Baucher directly: 'The resistances that you experience from your horses are the natural and inevitable consequences, first, of your seat, secondly, of your personal system of schooling.'[20] Aubert believes that he and Baucher have little in common with respect to the schooling of a horse; where he finds in the horse a child easy to school, Baucher sees in the horse a dangerous enemy, difficult to overcome and whose strength must be destroyed. What Baucher achieves through force and pain, Aubert and his *confrères* obtain through correct posture, a feat, according to Aubert, which Baucher will never accomplish because he began to ride so late.

In the 'Fifth Observation' Aubert compares the civilian and military schools of equitation from the time of Louis XIV to the present with the methods of Baucher as set down in his publication of 1833. Once again Aubert tries to isolate Baucher by comparing his own back-

---

[20] Ibid., p. 22.

ground and that of most equerries with the background of Baucher. All *our* masters, he states, have told us

to sit absolutely straight and relaxed on the horse, for instability of the seat and stiffness result from a poor posture, for they destroy the use of the aids and *excite the horse to defend himself*. And squeezing your thighs or your knees will not achieve a proper seat if your body is not straight on its base. If your seat is good, your aids will work well; if you are poorly seated, your aids will be ineffective. In the first hypothesis your horses will obey without effort; in the second one, *they will resist* more or less, depending whether they are sensitive or *suffering*. With a proper and relaxed posture, you will be tied and united with all the leg movements that the horse makes on the ground, *the walk, the trot, and the gallop* . . . [21]

Whereas the above recommendation is followed by all good horsemen, Baucher, according to Aubert, does just the opposite. Instead of being well seated and relaxed, M. Baucher is seated on the fork, torso pushed forward and not in the least in line with his base. He therefore cannot resist the simplest movements of his horse unless he continuously squeezes with his thighs and knees. Consequently he can only be rigid and his aids can be neither relaxed nor correct. Far from being linked to and united with the movements of his horse, 'M. Baucher, despite the strength he uses with his thighs and knees, *detaches himself quite visibly from his saddle with each tempo of the trot;* . . . neither can he feel *the tempo of the gallop*. Moreover, he does not understand that one can *feel the movement of each and every extremity at the walk*. (See *Dictionnaire* of M. Baucher, page 151.)'[22] Even more serious, continues Aubert, is Baucher's statement in the same work that the equerries 'who claim to profit from this feeling to push their horse forward at the gallop on the right leg and on the left leg, give impractical data, which are only QUACKERY and TRICKERY. (See Baucher's *Dictionnaire*, page 151.)'[23]

Thus, repeats Aubert, speaking directly to Baucher,

it is your poor seat and your lack of unity with your horse that prevents you from feeling your horse. It is this first and foremost infraction of the principles of good and proper schooling that gives you the crazy pretention to want to reform the field; and it is this first and foremost infraction that *causes the resistances* of the horses that you claim to school in your manner. All the masters of the past were familiar with these resistances, and knew them better, but they tried to learn how *to avoid* them. Whereas you *provoke these resistances* so that you may have the glory of *combating* them in accordance with your own method.[24]

Another criticism levelled against Baucher is the question of halting. Referring to the masters and quoting from them, Aubert says that they do not want the halts to be prolonged by using the rein for too long a period. Rather, give and take up several times. This will not jar the horse's hocks. Baucher and his disciples, on the other hand, halt firmly and for a considerable length of time, without giving the reins to the horse but, rather, keeping them continuously taut. And since the poor animal wishes to preserve himself and keep his balance, and has difficulty knowing where to place his legs, and his breathing becomes difficult, the result is a battle between horse and rider.

Another source of contention is the position of the legs of the rider. Once again Aubert quotes from the masters to make his point. 'Let your legs fall naturally on the stirrups, which should be longer than shorter . . . If you hold your legs constantly closed you despair the sensitive horses and harden the cold ones. And if you render insensitive the latter kind, you compensate by making use of those painful spurs.'[25] Aubert then describes once more how Baucher sits on the horse with shortened stirrups, legs tight and thrown backward. While Aubert equally deplores it if the legs are thrust forward too much, he prefers this ungainly sight rather than Baucher's equally ungainly,

---

[21] Ibid., pp. 23–4.   [22] Ibid., p. 24.   [23] Ibid., p. 24.   [24] Ibid., p. 25.   [25] Ibid., p. 27.

Caricature of Baucher by Lorentz: the writer. (Musée Philipon)

but dangerous and exasperating posture — dangerous to the horseman and exasperating to the horse. Baucher may call the exasperation of a sensitive horse the *resistances* and *defences* of a horse, but it is usually the rider's poor posture and his faulty aids that make a horse resist. Once again, Aubert alludes to the masters of the past, namely, that the rider should, at all costs, refrain from constraining the horse too much between the aids. He also quotes a former equerry, the learned Dupaty de Clam, who, in determining the ideal position of the horse's head and neck, wants the triangle between head and neck to be wider, rather than narrow, as determined by Baucher, which places the head perpendicularly to the ground. De Clam attributes this constraint and resulting pain to the long curbs used during the fifteenth and sixteenth centuries. But even the former masters understood why horses resisted and thus suggested that gentler and simpler bits be used. While Baucher, in his *Dictionnaire raisonné*, also recommends gentle and simple bits, Aubert feels that he contradicts himself when he recommends that the horse's head be placed perpendicularly to the ground, which, according to Aubert, gives the impression that the horse is wearing a hood. And while Baucher does not use a bit with long curbs, the curb-chain he uses is so taut that one could not place one's fingers through it. Aubert also accuses Baucher of not understanding the use of the different kinds of snaffles or bridoons or a martingale, which Baucher rejects as being too severe on the horse. But, says Aubert, Baucher's use of the *ramener*, the result of the powerful leverage of the curbs, is more painful to the mouth and hocks of the horse than the use of a martingale. Equally painful for the horse are the attacks on the same spot, indefinitely prolonged, which bring about the *ramener*.[26]

Aubert takes Baucher further to task for only giving in his *Dictionnaire raisonné* the initials rather than the full names of authors he is refuting. Who are the M. W., or M. G. or M. R. you have exhumed from cheap books, he asks Baucher, challenging him directly? They are not the names of important equerries. Furthermore, your so-called universal system of mouthpieces and your taut curb-chain prove that you have not studied that aspect of equitation; and yet you have attacked past masters who have discussed this subject. And above all, he continues, 'as the masters say: Be sober in your corrections, and, especially, in the matter of spurs. *Nothing sours a horse as much as spurs used too often and applied poorly.*'[27] And, adds Aubert, Baucher neutralizes the pain the horse experiences on the bars through the bit and curb-chain by causing an even worse pain through the *attaques sur place* (attacks on one place) of the spurs. These attacks with the spurs are

not a *gentle pinching with the spur* as suggested by La Guérinière, *but massive kicks with the spurs* which produce a dull sound, when the horse is kept stationary by the extreme tension caused by the left bridle hand placed below the horse's loin on that side, and the right hand holding the bridoon below the loin on the right side. And, for this lesson to be

correct, the horse must remain immobile while he receives the kicks of the spurs, and the animal manifests the pain he feels only by a sort of moaning or belch that those initiated in this method indicate by voice imitation. This they call *giving in.*[28]

Aubert calls these stationary attacks a monstrosity which would have adverse effects if introduced into the army. In the final analysis, says Aubert, it is not what a horse does in the circus by which one can judge him, but what he does outside at the fast paces, as he goes up and down hills or jumps over obstacles.

At the end of the 'Sixth Observation', Aubert discusses Baucher's flexion of the jaw when the rider, on foot, takes hold of the lower part of the curb and puts pressure on the mouthpiece of the bit by means of a seesaw movement, first on the right bar, by pulling up on the left side, then on the left bar, by pulling up on the right side, so that each bar of the horse is alternately compressed, and the horse, to allay the pain that is produced, also rotates his upper jaw. This action, says Aubert, is what Baucher calls *action of strength or scissors*. Not only does Aubert condemn this exercise, but in a footnote he quotes La Guérinière, who also condemns the *action of strength* and who deplores this motion on the part of the horse, that is, when the horse continually moves his lower jaw from left to right and vice versa, for he considers it 'a defect common to weak mouths'.[29] Baucher, adds Aubert in this same footnote, is confusing two different kinds of motion on the part of the horse, one that is the simple movement of the horse's mouth, the other, when the open mouth crosses over from one side to the other.

In this 'Sixth Observation' Aubert also asks whether it is advisable that such a personal method, as is Baucher's, should replace those methods based on the principles of the civilian and military schools that existed from the

---

[26] In a footnote, ibid., p. 31, Aubert says that as he writes this there is a horse in the *manège* of M. D'Aure which belongs to Caroline Loya and on whom one can see pronounced marks caused by the bit and a tight curb-

chain which undoubtedly gave constant pain to the horse.
[27] Ibid., p. 33.
[28] Ibid., pp. 33–4.
[29] Ibid., p. 35.

reign of Louis XIV to the present? But before attempting to answer this question, Aubert states his belief that these *Observations* refuting Baucher's method were written without malice or jealousy, but simply out of love for the art of riding which he wants to defend from a system which, if adopted by French cavalry schools, will have dire consequences for the horseman as well as for the horse. Furthermore, a ministry that adopts such a method should be called a foreign ministry.

Aubert now proceeds to ward off any criticism that may emanate from Baucher's disciples: that he is not competent to judge military equitation; that he has not been in the army; that he has not been to war, and so on. Aubert believes that he can answer these questions by saying that neither have the challengers had these experiences and that while he has no knowledge pertaining to matters of cavalry, he does have knowledge when it comes to equitation in general. He would then ask those officers who have studied the course based on the Baucher method and given by the *Ecole de Cavalerie* of Saumur whether this method of Baucher agrees *in toto* or in part with the theories taught at Saumur in the past. No, answers Aubert, no more than do the principles expounded by Chabannes, Cordier and Rousselet. And, by adopting for the army the seat of Baucher and that of his disciples, can the horseman, who is not sitting straight on his horse, manage the necessary offensive and defensive techniques? And when one takes into consideration the pack that the troops have to carry, will this not cause a problem when, as Baucher's method demands in order to execute the *ramener*, the hand is placed lower than the belt? And would not the legs turned towards the flanks of the horse, feet out, and the spurs turned more or less near the flanks (according to the height of the horseman) cause disorder within the ranks? There are more questions which Aubert will ask several competent judges to resolve.

In fact, says Aubert, it is known that some disciples of Baucher's method who use it *with*

modification have already spread the news that if and when the army adopts Baucher's method, they will reject his position on the horse as well as the way he uses the aids. This is, indeed, a strange way of arranging matters, that is, to introduce Baucher's system of dressage without adopting his seat and his *effect of the aids*. Aubert stresses once more the fact that if the cavalry instructors use Baucher's method to school their horses, these horses will begin to defend themselves and become spoiled, and the men who will have to use them will become sullen. And once this has happened how will the situation be remedied? To whom will one address oneself? Who will be to blame? The officer who initially favoured the new system? He will say that he was the dupe of those in high position who imposed the system on him. The instructors? Neither will they accept any blame. The author of the new system? He will say that his system failed because it was not used correctly.

Aubert ends this 'Observation' by pointing out some of the the dangers that can ensue during a battle as related by officers; namely, that if a horse is given the spurs too much, he can become dangerous, and the horseman, losing control of his horse, may suddenly find himself within the ranks of the enemy and unable to get out. This, of course, is an additional criticism of Baucher's frequent *attaques des éperons* which his method prescribes.

In his 'Seventh Observation', Aubert discusses the danger of choosing a personal system of equitation in the army which will not only cost a great deal of money, but which will instil discouragement and disgust in a great number of officers and NCOs.

But, says Aubert, if we were to admit that Baucher's system is superior to those whose works have been diligently consulted in the cavalry schools since 1778, and if we were to admit that the training and the manuals used at Saumur are inferior, should we nevertheless adopt, without reservations, Baucher's system? Other problems will arise. First of all, it will be necessary to change the bits presently in use, replacing them with bits that use a very taut curb-chain. It will be necessary to replace the present saddles with those *à la Baucher*, the kind once used by Condé and Louis XIV. And there are other problems that could be mentioned.

But above all, admonishes Aubert, no government that is a constitutional government has the right to protect the industry, interest, principles and self-esteem of one individual at the expense and prejudice of the industry, interest, principles and self-esteem of all. 'In other words, to reestablish privileges.'[30]

Aubert then imagines the reaction of those who already see the transformation of a Baucher in the circus of the Champs-Elysées to a Baucher at the *Ecole de Saumur*.

Were one to give the position of first equerry at the Ecole de Saumur to Baucher and give him the right to replace the equestrian theories of the Schools by his own, it would not simply be the granting of a privilege, nor of offending those who are meritorious, it would be justice done to someone whose merit is superior to all other merits ... Well [concludes Aubert], *I believe in a miracle.*[31]

At the end of his 'Seventh Observation', Aubert asks what if there should be living in the provinces someone who, like M. Baucher, is a self-taught individual and who is instilled with a talent greater than all the equerries put together, what then? Would M. Baucher give up his position in the army and give it to the newcomer 'as justice rendered to a recognized merit that is superior to all other merits'?[32] No, adds Aubert, he, himself, would recommend keeping M. Baucher, considering all the expenses incurred which would once again be incurred by exchanging him for another. He would keep M. Baucher, who, after all, has cost the army a considerable amount.

In his 'Conclusion' Aubert asks whether it would not be reasonable for the French cavalry, which has always done well and has great prestige without having to adopt the *personal system* of M. Baucher, to retain its former

training in the art of riding and do as well as it has done in the past? Would it not be better to allow the equestrian art in Saumur to continue to pursue the principles of a Chabannes, a Rousselet and a Cordier, all men of experience and learning, rather than subject it to the personal system of M. Baucher?

And so, concludes Aubert:

By leaving M. Baucher to the *Franconi-Circus*, cradle of his glory and scene of his triumphs, his admirers will be able to continue enjoying the pleasures he gives them and shower upon him millions of crowns without anyone finding his equitation to be poor. In Saumur, he would no longer have any *controlled music* to follow the movements of his horse step by step, nor any other glories even more powerful to maintain the thrills of his equestrian genius. And were one to give him huge epaulettes and scintillating decorations, he could still find more than a single miscalculation, more than a single disgust, and more than a single regret. He might also find RESISTANCES more obstinate and more difficult to combat than all those with which his horses opposed him until now.[33]

At the end of his essay, Aubert includes three letters written in support of his *Observations*. All three writers had received manuscripts of the *Observations*. The letters are written by Parisian directors of *manèges* and professors of equitation. The first one is from a M. Boutard, a former pupil of the *Manège de Versailles*. He is particularly offended by Baucher's introduction in which Baucher discusses his background and qualifications and claims that he had learned about equitation by reading the books of past masters and that he had later learned how to ride.

That is to say, I tried to learn how to ride from books; which is not to say that I learned to ride in such and such a *manège* or with such and such an equerry. I set out to study these authors and to judge them only after emerging out of my ignorance and after I had ridden many horses according to their principles, good or bad ... I believed that by reading all these works I could obtain a solid instruc-

[30] Ibid., p. 42.   [31] Ibid., p. 42.   [32] Ibid., p. 42.   [33] Ibid., p. 44.

BAUCHER

1950

François Baucher as drawn by Commandant Margot of Saumur for General Decarpentry. (Courtesy G. Margot)

tion, and then set about the art with certitude and knowledge; well! I must admit, that after having studied these treatises, I was less capable of reasoning and even of executing the art than before.[34]

Boutard uses this introductory statement of Baucher to accuse him of having begun to ride late in life, making it impossible for him to succeed in an art which demands a limber and tough body. It is obvious that men who wish to judge others and lack the skill and knowledge themselves can only *talk*.

The second letter is written by M. Thirion, former pupil of Chabannes, Cordier and Rousselet at the *Ecole de Saumur*, former officer of the cavalry, *écuyer aux gardes du corps* of *Monsieur* [the king's brother], presently equerry at the *Manège de Luxembourg*. After thanking Aubert for letting him read the manuscript, Thirion, in agreement with Aubert, states his belief that Baucher's method is so full of errors and contradictions that it is not worth the effort of refuting it. He then proceeds to refute certain aspects of Baucher's method, especially the statement made by Baucher that he cannot understand how one can feel through one's seat 'the movement of each one of the extremities at the walk'.[35] More importantly, as a former military officer who is familiar with war, he believes that it is impossible to apply Baucher's system to horses in cavalry regiments as he is certain that the method would ruin many horses and shorten their paces, which is detrimental to cavalry horses who need to be free, forward-going and determined. Furthermore, a dragoneer or a cuirasser, placed on his horse as is Baucher, would very likely not only receive sabre blows but be incapable of giving any, which, he adds, would be a revolting thought to any man who has the honour of wearing a French uniform.

The third letter is from Lecornué, pupil of the *Ecole Impériale de Saint-Germain* and the *Ecole Royale de Saumur*, proprietor and director of the *Manège de Luxembourg*. Lecornué repeats Thirion's criticism that Baucher regards those who claim to feel the movement of each one of the extremities at the walk as quacks and tricksters. He praises Aubert's own treatise which is one of the few that presents correctly the theories of de la Guérinière, Deputy de Clam, de Bohan, Thiroux, de Chabannes and others. He also admires the judicious and quiet tone Aubert uses in his *Observations*.

In fact, Aubert's tone in the *Observations* is far from quiet. He criticizes Baucher's method, which, as a horseman and educator, is his right. But he also spends a great deal of time criticizing Baucher personally, his poor seat, his social and professional background, his supposedly late arrival in the field of equitation, the mechanical and mournful appearance of his horses, and so on. At times he is quite vitriolic. Frequently he either pretends to misunderstand Baucher or, in fact, does not understand him.

D'Aure, on the other hand, never ridicules Baucher personally. D'Aure usually limits his criticism to the dangers that may ensue from Baucher's method in the training of horse and horseman, especially modern horsemanship, that is exterior and/or military equitation. 'It is proper to point out', says Decarpentry, 'that in his attacks against the *nouvelle méthode*, d'Aure wisely refrains from criticizing Baucher's talent of performance and the artistic value of his work. It is the absolute validity of the method for the use of the horse in exterior riding that he contests.'[36]

---

[34] Ibid., p. 45.   [35] Ibid., p. 46.   [36] Decarpentry, *Baucher et son Ecole*, p. 66.

6

Baucher answers his critics

As we have seen, the main criticism levelled against Baucher and his *nouvelle méthode* is that his system is far from new. Horsemen of the past, the critics claimed, were already familiar with the notions of flexion and the exercises that contributed to the suppling of the horse's forehand, that is, his jaw, neck and poll, and with the flexion of the hindquarters, and that they had already executed the necessary exercises to accomplish this. It is primarily to this kind of criticism that Baucher responds in his 'Introduction' to the 1854 publication of the *Oeuvres complètes*.

I know well that several of my rivals have claimed that my method, the fruit of twenty-five years of conscientious research, was already known in Germany, Russia and Italy long before I saw the light of day. These excellent patriots, rather than recognize that a reform useful to their country is the work of one of their own citizens, would prefer, no doubt, that it be the work of a foreign source. *It is only proper that one denounce those who plagiarize*, but before blighting their hopes, one should at first make sure of their bad faith. Here, far from seeking the truth, my adversaries have brought forth in their attacks neither certitude nor good faith. Everything was pure invention on their part. Envy slanders so very easily.[1]

And, continues Baucher, 'If my method was known before me, then why did they not practise it in all its expanse? There is not a single equerry who would not prefer to obtain results in one day than in a month, nor obtain results in a month than in a year.'[2]

Baucher decries the fact that

after having spent my life and intelligence in the search of a useful truth, I now have to spend my time thwarting jealous rivalries and putting forward my own authority more than it is necessary to do ... and when I spoke of attacks and pointed out their usefulness as a means of schooling a horse, they replied that M. de la Guérinière had already said something about a *delicate pinching with the spurs*. If I then asked how I am to execute this delicate pinching, at what moment, for what purpose, what must the effect of the hand be to second it, everyone remained silent like M. de La Guérinière himself. They claimed that each person must interpret as best he can this silence which he probably kept not without good reason.[3]

The same held true with respect to flexions and their usefulness. There, too, the critics said that the work had already been done long ago. Neither was the *ramener*, the *rassembler*, and so on new at all. All these definitions, the critics claimed, had already been used and explained.

And all the past authors also spoke of strike off at the gallop. But who has given any rational principles on this subject? And what about the influence of the horse's conformation on the disposition of his strength, and what I said, repeatedly, about the need to combat this instinctive strength, to annul it, and to put it at the disposal of the horseman so that he can distribute it as he wishes and thereby compensate for the effects of the physical vices of the animal? They either did not understand me or

---

[1] Baucher, O.C., p. 3.   [2] Ibid., pp. 3–4.   [3] Ibid., pp. 4–5.

pretended not to, because they could not find the proper words that corresponded to this kind of work in any manuals of the past.[4]

Baucher also answers those who want to know whether one can use his new method on horses which are still green. 'My answer has always been a negative one.'[5] People also challenged, continues Baucher, his claim that he could annul the horse's resistances by opposite and contrary forces and were amazed when they saw that the horse performed easily and lightly. But they were equally surprised, Baucher adds, when this same horse, who had appeared so well schooled, suddenly refuses to execute the simplest movements when mounted by another rider. This is an indication that the rider is not very skilled and the horse, sensing this, takes the initiative.

Baucher states that his method, while it accelerates a man's knowledge of horsemanship, also teaches him to perform well. The method is

defined, graded, reasoned; everything follows everything else and hangs together; each movement is the consequence of a specific position which, in turn, is produced by a transmitted force. Thus it is never the animal who is to blame, it is the rider; and then it is the crop or the whip that is used to castigate what one considers the disobedience or the hostile behaviour of the horse ... I uphold that the horse is never to blame ... If he has the freedom to use his strength, he will be master of his movements and will do as he pleases despite the rider's wishes ... Then why punish the horse for resisting and using his defences which are the natural consequence of the position in which one places him. One must first get him out of it, which becomes easy once the rider has suppled the horse sufficiently to enable him to dominate his strength and always to place him in the proper position.[6]

Baucher then attempts to answer those who attacked him for showing himself to the public for the price of a franc, rather than working, as others do, in a *manège*. But, says Baucher, the position of equerry in a *manège* is not very

remunerative; it is the least thankful and requires a substantial layout. Furthermore, equerries are no longer given subvention by heads of state. Thus it is necessary for him to perform in a circus. It is precisely his work in the circus that brought him to the attention of certain groups. Without these public performances on Partisan, Neptune, Capitaine, Géricault, Buridan and so many others, he would still be buried and unknown, in one of those *manèges* in the capital. Besides, working in a circus does not deny him his dignity. 'I like and honour all respectable professions, especially those that serve to enlighten and entertain the public.'[7] He ends this Introduction by comparing himself to Molière and Shakespeare who also 'sank so low' as to perform, in public, in their own works. All he is doing is following in their footsteps.

While Baucher answers his critics throughout much of his work, he does so specifically at the end of the 1854 edition of his *Oeuvres complètes* in an essay entitled *Réponse aux Observations de M. D'Aure sur la Nouvelle Méthode d'Equitation*. In this 'Réponse' to d'Aure he reiterates the importance of his method and suggests to d'Aure that he should read his treatise without prejudice, for then and only then will he be able to understand his use of *suppling* and what he means by *attacks* with the spurs. In his 'Réponse', he attempts to show how erudite, incomprehensible and erroneous d'Aure is in his own *Traité d'Equitation* and quotes frequently from this work to do so. But what is especially interesting in this 'Réponse' is his appendix where he shows how d'Aure has departed from his original ideas as stated in his 1834 edition. 'Since the appearance of my brochure, M. d'Aure has rushed to publish a new edition of his *Traité d'Equitation* in order to palliate the heresies contained in his first edition.'[8] Baucher is, of course, saying quite explicitly that d'Aure changed some of his ideas in the new edition after Baucher published

---

[4] Ibid., p. 6.   [5] Ibid., p. 6.   [6] Ibid., pp. 8–9.   [7] Ibid., p. 12.
[8] Baucher, 'Réponse aux Observations de M. d'Aure sur la méthode nouvelle d'équitation', O.C., p. 624.

his *nouvelle méthode*, and because of the criticisms levelled against him.

In a short 'Préface' Baucher explains why he attempted to answer d'Aure's *Observations*.

I could have absolved myself from adding this brochure to the writings contained in this volume; but I decided to bring this tract to light because it contains some principles of great importance held by my learned antagonist. This courtesy towards M. d'Aure has as a goal to teach the future generations that he has written a treatise on equitation. If he is not angry with me, I believe that posterity will take this into consideration.[9]

He starts out by saying that he is surprised that such an equestrian celebrity should deign to enter the fight. What perplexed him was the statement d'Aure made at the end of his *Observations* wherein he reproached Baucher for having said '*that horses that I have schooled had formerly been unsuccessful with him*'.[10] A glance at this essay by d'Aure does, indeed, reveal that d'Aure was accusing Baucher of having made this statement. D'Aure then adds that if the commandant of the stables of the king had deemed it necessary to send horses to be trained in the *nouvelle méthode*, it had nothing to do with him, since he had not been involved with this institution since 1830. Furthermore, in all his years as equerry he has never failed in the schooling of a horse. Baucher claims that d'Aure's reproach is not valid since he had never made such a statement, neither in writing nor verbally. Baucher also accuses d'Aure of resorting to little lies about him and his horses. This applies especially to Partisan who, d'Aure had claimed, was a very gentle horse and had been ridden by women and children, and was not at all the problem horse Baucher had made him out to be and had transformed, by using his system, into a capable and obedient horse. It is unfortunate that both d'Aure and Baucher resort to petty attacks rather than to keeping the controversy on a methodological level. For

example, Baucher becomes personal in his attack when he says that 'difficulties are not to the taste of M. d'Aure; this becomes easily understandable when one discovers that M. d'Aure does not like to ride and does so rarely'.[11] In a footnote he adds: 'At least that is what he led me to believe each time we met.'[12] Both these statements are incorrect. D'Aure enjoyed riding and rode frequently and exceedingly well. He was known to have an excellent seat, strong, well-placed legs and a light hand. Secondly, Baucher and d'Aure met only once, when d'Aure wanted to sell him one of his mares.[13]

Baucher challenges several ideas and expressions presented by d'Aure. For example, d'Aure brings up the term *parader un cheval* (to put a horse through its paces) which he uses to criticize Baucher's method as it is demonstrated when performing in the circus. In the process, d'Aure, as usual, criticizes the foundation of Baucher's method, namely, the disposition of the horse's strength. This gives Baucher once again the opportunity to repeat the importance flexion plays in order to achieve the kind of resilience which gives the horse its radiance and brilliance when performing even the simplest paces.

Baucher repeats once again the correlation between a horse's conformation and his irritability (which he distinguishes from a horse's sensitivity). Destroy the horse's irritability and you give it a positive sensitivity. This, Baucher repeats, he can achieve by suppling the horse's neck which is the principal seat of a horse's resistances. Rendering the jaw of the horse supple is another prerequisite, according to Baucher. But once again Baucher becomes personal when he says that suppling is an idea that was also prevalent in the old days 'of which M. d'Aure is a worthy representative'.[14] He is, of course, using d'Aure's own argument, namely the historical one, and mocks d'Aure's old-fashioned type of equitation. While it is true

---

[9] Ibid., p. 582. [10] Ibid., p. 584.
[11] Ibid., p. 586. [12] Ibid., p. 586.
[13] This meeting occurred in the *manège* of the Rue Duphot managed by d'Aure when d'Aure had heard that

Baucher was looking for a school horse and offered to sell him one of his mares. L'Hotte relates this lengthy and amusing episode in his *Souvenirs*.
[14] Baucher, 'Réponse', p. 587.

that d'Aure was trained in Classical or *savante* equitation as it had been practised at the *Ecole de Versailles*, we know that his temperament had pushed him towards the new equitation which was taking hold in France, namely English equitation or exterior equitation, with the rising trot, the English saddle and shorter stirrups.

Baucher also repeats the justification of his practice of *les attaques des éperons* which he uses in opposition to the aids of the hands. If d'Aure had read the section dealing with these *attacks*, he says, he would have noticed that he had defined them as gentle progressive attacks and that their aim was to contain, and thereby control, the horse between the two opposing aids, that is, between the legs and the hands; this would distribute the horse's strength and balance him. But it is not to throw forward, in an abrupt manner, the horse's mass. 'The basis of my system, M. d'Aure, consists in the balance of the horse, not in the kind of balance that prevents him from falling, but in the kind wherein the forces counter-balance each other, where they show up advantageously.'[15] One of the differences between d'Aure and Baucher, the latter points out, is that d'Aure uses these attacks to increase the speed of the paces, whereas he makes use of them to change the positions of the horse that serve to regulate the paces and to increase the speed. Balance, especially horizontal balance — that is, when the weight of the horse is equally distributed between forehand and hindquarters — is of paramount importance to Baucher. 'One single position brings about lightness in the horse; balance obviously summarizes the whole of equitation. I understand by balance this special position when, without having recourse to the reins, the horse keeps his head in a perpendicular position; outside of this position there is resistance.'[16]

While Baucher is attempting to respond to d'Aure's criticism of his method, that is, the placing of the head of the horse perpendicularly to the ground, namely the *ramener*, and thus bringing about lightness and suppleness, Baucher, in turn, accuses d'Aure of making an error when he states that to halt a horse one 'has only to place the head in such a way that the bit finds on the bars the necessary *appui* [contact] which enables one to halt the horse'.[17] And, asks Baucher, 'What is this position? For I have already said it, that other than the perpendicular, the horse will always resist, will be stiff, and consequently, ungainly.'[18]

It is interesting to note that Baucher catches d'Aure in a serious contradiction. As we know, d'Aure attacked Baucher for stating that one important method of controlling the horse is to place his head perpendicular to the ground. He subsequently discovers that d'Aure, in his *Traité*, made the following declaration: '"The more the head is placed PERPENDICULARLY, the better is the horse in contact with the bit." Well, one will remember that in his brochure directed against my method ... he attacked this very position, *because* I had described it.'[19]

With respect to d'Aure's statement that he has little liking for horses who *piaffe* which, he feels, is what Baucher's horses all eventually do due to Baucher's rigid system, Baucher retorts that d'Aure is inconsistent. On the one hand he makes himself the champion of the writers of the past and then with one stroke of the pen, he condemns them when he condemns the *piaffe*. After all, says Baucher, 'M. de la Guérinière liked very much to make his horse *piaffe*'.[20] Then too, Baucher continues, it looks as though M. d'Aure does not really understand what actually constitutes the *piaffe*. But, unfortunately, to achieve the piaffe one must supple the horse, one must teach him the *ramener*, the *rassembler*: 'but I forget, these notables do not understand or *do not want to* understand the *ramener* and have vowed to despise all this *silliness* of the art'.[21]

---

[15] Ibid., p. 590.   [16] Ibid., p. 592.   [17] Ibid., p. 592.   [18] Ibid., p. 592.   [19] Ibid., p. 605.
[20] Ibid., p. 597.   [21] Ibid., p. 593.

Another discussion between the two equerries centres around the schooling of the young horse. In his *Observations* d'Aure said that 'the best way to school a young horse is to accustom him to go forward by pulling on the snaffle bridle. The first condition is to render him free and straightforward; this, I believe, is the only thing which must preoccupy one in his early schooling.'[22] Fine, says Baucher, but if this idea were put into practice without taking into account the action of the horse and the posture of its body and neck, then nothing very satisfactory would be achieved. 'There we have once again the enigmatic and ambiguous style of the old school: give constantly, as a general rule, principles that are only practical under special conditions.'[23] He then adds with a certain amount of irony: 'I beg your pardon, M. d'Aure, but the *parader of the circus* will compensate for the stubborn silence in which *the great equerry* has enveloped himself with such obstinacy, and serve his cause.'[24] Becoming serious once again, Baucher then states that if one wishes to guide a horse, to make his movements easy, regular and graceful, one needs *action* and *position*. Action gives impulsion, and

the hand must take over this impulsion for the benefit of the position, which, in turn, determines and regulates movement. If the action is too strong and the impulsion too forceful, then the horse, unbeknownst to the horseman, will take a position which will enable him to do whatever he wishes or will fight to his advantage. And if there is a lack of action, then the impulsion will be slow and difficult, and as there is no position without force, there will be no position at all. It is important that these two extremes should be avoided, whether they derive from the horseman or from the horse.[25]

M. d'Aure, says Baucher, claims that his criticism of the *nouvelle méthode* is in no way a personal attack; rather it is his concern for the schooling of the horse that made him take up his pen. Baucher, however, questions d'Aure's

motives. Why did he never attend any of the experiments that took place in Paris? And if the reason is not a personal one and not out of jealousy, then it can only be a result of this recent mania for polemics.

After having taken d'Aure to task for his many criticisms of the *nouvelle méthode* in his *Observations*, in this same 'Réponse' Baucher criticizes d'Aure's *Traité d'Equitation*, published in 1834. He says:

I believe it is necessary, in order to complete this response, to add some observations on the principles M. d'Aure published in 1834. I urge the reader to follow attentively the passages in quotation marks which have been extracted literally from the work. Many refute each other; others— But let us leave it to the reader to judge for himself.[26]

D'Aure's *Traité* is divided into 'Basse école', which is brief, and 'Haute école' which takes up the major part of the manual. D'Aure explains that 'Work done in the *basse école* stage consists of fixing the rider's posture, knowing how to guide the horse straight in front of one, and acquiring solidity.'[27] Acquiring confidence is the first aim of the pupil at this stage. When the pupil has achieved this, he will automatically acquire a good posture. Thus for d'Aure '*la tenue*' (posture) is of the utmost importance and in the succeeding pages he gives a description of what he considers good posture: 'Posture is the result of two kinds of strength, balance and the pressure of the thighs and knees.'[28]

But it is d'Aure's reference to the position of the rider's hand that once again gives rise to Baucher's criticism. Baucher criticizes d'Aure for teaching that when one wishes to halt, one raises the hand in front of one until the horse stops and that one must not use one's legs. To go backward, one raises the hand until the horse moves backward. As soon as he has done so, the effect of the bit must be diminished by lowering the hand. But before answering this

---

[22] D'Aure, *Traité d'Equitation*, p. 16.   [23] Baucher, 'Réponse', p. 594.   [24] Ibid., p. 594.   [25] Ibid., p. 594.
[26] Ibid., p. 599.   [27] D'Aure, *Traité d'Equitation*, p. 9.   [28] Ibid., p. 11.

principle, Baucher makes light of d'Aure's remarks: 'Undoubtedly, it is from *a point of view that is too elevated*' (sometimes puns are lost in translation; *élevé* means raised both physically and socially), 'and it is due to his disdain for *the miseries of the art* that we owe such a principle'.[29] Then, becoming less ironic, he continues:

It is, on the contrary, the general rule that one must not halt a horse nor make him go backward without the use of the legs. All the reasonable authors have, at least, added (without any explanation, it is true) that the legs ought to accompany the hand. But this does not suffice. It is necessary, and I have proved it, that in all retrograde movements, the use of the legs precedes the hand.[30]

In the section entitled 'Haute école', Baucher says that d'Aure tackles this problem with great simplicity and he quotes from him: 'The work of *haute école* must impart, precisely and in detail, the means employed to know, demand with discernment and obtain from a schooled horse what is required for his conservation and, at the same time, the safety of the rider.' This, adds Baucher, 'is what is most salient on pages 17 and 18'.[31] Instead of saying that it is *haute école* that indicates the means, he could have been more explicit to the pupil and '*indicated the means* needed for *haute école*'.[32] According to Baucher, d'Aure did not consider it necessary to explain this, undoubtedly because he felt that the 'General Principles' given later would do so. And when Baucher quotes d'Aure's statement that 'If one puts a stronger pressure on one bar than on the other, the horse, to avoid the strongest pressure, will give in and go backward, crosswise', he is at his most ironic. 'This seems to be an admirable discovery. Is it the result of chance or of reasoning?'[33] he quickly asks.

With respect to the concept of action, Baucher says that the author takes a great deal of trouble to review its definition again:

'The action of the hand is completely opposed to that of the legs, since the hand serves to halt or go backward, just as the legs carry the horse forward, whereas the separate pressure of the legs exerts upon the aids a sensation similar to the tension of the reins on the neck and the curbs of the bit.' I ought not to have reproduced this part of the text [Baucher concludes ironically], but it is only proper for the reader to know everything that so famous a name can produce.[34]

In the first lesson of d'Aure's three divisions, Baucher, paraphrasing him, says that the author claims that the horse turns to the right due to the pressure of the right rein made with the right hand. Then, continues Baucher, d'Aure, in attempting to explain *appui* says that 'the *opening* of the rein will give a sense of opposition on the right bar, and so on'. 'I cannot go on', says Baucher, 'as I am tired of hearing young equerries repeat these seductive principles to pupils who try in vain to understand them.'[35] When discussing d'Aure's second lesson wherein he deals with the opening of the rein, then of two reins which, operating together '"provoke in the mouth of the horse a movement which makes him taste the bit and renders the sensation less agreeable"', Baucher admits that he 'cannot discuss such gibberish'.[36]

When d'Aure mentions in his *Traité* that the more a horse is on his haunches, the better his mouth will be, and the more his legs will be activated; and the more he is on his shoulders, the more the point of tension will be felt in the hand; and then goes on to say that this explanation may seem odd because it has never been demonstrated, one can almost hear Baucher shout as he says: 'I will observe to M. d'Aure that my *Dictionnaire raisonné d'Equitation* appeared a year [1833] before his quarto [1834]. Suffice it to say to him that what he claims to be his, belongs to me. The reader will find in my dictionary the discussions stressing this principle.'[37] And when Baucher quotes from d'Aure's 'Résume', which repeats the idea that

---

[29] Baucher, 'Réponse', p. 600. [30] Ibid., p. 600. [31] Ibid., p. 602. [32] Ibid., p. 602. [33] Ibid., p. 602.
[34] Ibid., p. 603. [35] Ibid., p. 603. [36] Ibid., p. 603. [37] Ibid., p. 605.

when a horse leans too heavily on the forehand, he is on his shoulders, and when he leans more on the hindquarters, he is too much on his haunches, Baucher says:

One may think that I am only choosing insignificant fragments, that it is not possible that the author never gives precepts of any sort, and that he does not limit himself in this manner when he says that it is the hand that brings the forehand on the haunches and the legs that bring the horse on the shoulders. Indeed, nothing is truer, and whoever takes the trouble of reading the *Traité d'Equitation* of M. d'Aure will find nowhere any indication giving a cause, a demonstration, or an explanation of an effect.[38]

Then, too, when d'Aure discusses the causes that, for example, place the horse on the forehand, or the position of the head when the horse is on the forehand, nowhere does Baucher find any explanations given by d'Aure. D'Aure, says Baucher, is as vague as ever. 'The illustrious equerry has *too vast* a sense of equitation to stoop down to such minutiae.'[39]

D'Aure's discussion of the paces gives Baucher the opportunity to poke further fun at d'Aure. ' "The paces are subject to augmentation and diminution" (M. d'Aure makes us pass from surprise to surprise). "Thus one can walk, trot, or gallop, upright or on the haunches, or too much on the shoulders." That is all the horse can do; readers, use him without fear, take advantage of the *vast* way the author sees things, and do not ask further.'[40] And, again, ' "The walk is the slowest of the paces." Oh, M. de la Palisse! your shadow must have quivered with ease when you heard this astonishing verity proclaimed.'[41] And when d'Aure describes the trot, Baucher quips: 'We must now

remain necessarily convinced that the horse goes faster at the trot than at the walk!'[42]

D'Aure then talks about the correlation between extended paces and a horse leaning more heavily on the forehand, and shortened (collected) paces and leaning more on the hindquarters. To this Baucher retorts that

If M. d'Aure really knew what constitutes a balanced horse, he would understand that this horse can take up a fast trot without weighing on the forehand, and that one can for that reason decrease the speed of the pace without his being on the hindquarters. I can show him horses who go backwards at a walk and even at a trot, with an elevation of the hind legs that is equal to the elevation of the forelegs; which proves the balance of the horse, but balance the way I understand it.[43]

The many quotes, the remarks, the quips on the part of Baucher are too numerous to select them all. When d'Aure talks about the means of putting the horse to the walk or the trot, Baucher retorts that d'Aure never discusses the way one actually puts a horse to the walk or the trot. 'All the paces, like all the changes in direction, must be the result of a specific position given by the horseman, etc. That is equitation; but d'Aure is determined not to say a word about this in his treatise.'[44] When reference is made to putting the horse to the gallop, Baucher says that d'Aure is not only vague but in error. For when d'Aure explains that to put the horse to the gallop one must use the hand and the leg on the side with which one wishes the horse to start out, and when he then underscores that 'the raising of the hand to bring the weight of the shoulders to the hindquarters and bring the haunches under the horse', Baucher contends that the gallop 're-

[38] Ibid., p. 606. [39] Ibid., p. 606.
[40] Ibid., p. 608. [41] Ibid.; p. 608.
[42] Ibid., p. 608. La Palisse or La Palice was a French officer killed at the Battle of Pavia in 1525 (where François I was beaten and made prisoner by the Spaniards). La Palisse's soldiers, upon his death, composed a song in his honour which contains these lines:

A quarter of an hour before his death
He was still alive.

At the time of the composition of this song, these lines meant that just before his death he had fought valiantly. However, little by little, these two lines took on a more naïve and sarcastic meaning. The expression 'a verity of La Palice' now means a blatantly obvious truth (or, as the French say, 'a truth that jumps one in the face').
[43] Baucher, 'Réponse', pp. 609–10.
[44] Ibid., p. 610.

quires more force and the movement is only the result of this force, therefore it is necessary that the legs precede the hand in order to increase the impulsion and to give the proper position *which makes the horse take on the gallop*'.[45]

References are also made to d'Aure's discussion of changes of hand, work in circles at the walk and the gallop, then at the trot, strike off at the gallop, changes of hand in the air, how one prevents a horse from bucking or rearing, the causes that introduce the horse's defences, and so on. It is in d'Aure's explanation of the horse's defences that Baucher becomes quite critical of d'Aure and replaces the latter's explanation by his own pertaining to the causes of defences and their remedies, that is, flexions of neck, jaw, poll, haunches, and so on, the only actions which will ultimately produce a well-balanced horse. The final advice given by d'Aure and attacked by Baucher cannot be omitted. After discussing the schooling of the young horse, d'Aure concludes that 'It often happens that many horses defend themselves out of weakness, and *the surest way of schooling them* is good food and rest.'[46] One can almost see Baucher shake with laughter (or anger?) when he retorts, 'Indeed, here we have once again a profound and ingenious precept *on equitation*.'[47] Nonetheless, it was a sound piece of advice on the part of d'Aure with respect to horse management.

The 'Appendix' that follows Baucher's *Réponse aux Observations de M. d'Aure* was written several years after d'Aure had published a new edition of his *Traité* in 1843.

Since the appearance of the pamphlet printed above, M. d'Aure made haste to publish a new edition of his *Traité d'Equitation* in order to mitigate the heresies of the first one. It is good that one should do one's utmost to do less harm; but why insult me, why treat me as slanderer? That is unbelievable. Why, I simply transcribed word for word a passage from the *principles* found in the *Traité*

d'Equitation of M. d'Aure and for this I am considered dishonest. Oh! Sir Count, if you often take advantage of your birth, confine yourself to that. To go any further would be an indiscretion which could have the most dire consequences rather for others than for me . . .[48]

Baucher has, indeed, done a sound, if partial, analysis of the two texts. And Baucher even admits that this second edition

is without question less monstrous than the first one; there is, without doubt, a beginning and an end. It is good that one recognizes and tries to amend one's errors. If M. d'Aure had confined himself to doing so, I would have had nothing to say, I would have merely wished that the conversion of the sinner would have been more complete. But no! while amending the end of the paragraph presented above (obviously because of the criticism I made), M. d'Aure, in a note added to the new corrections in the 1843 edition (page 111), flies into a violent rage against me, without, however, making any reference to me. I am placed in that category of mentalities who are *jealous* and *unfortunate* persons with whom calumny is a habit and that I attribute to M. d'Aure *absurd principles* which, repeated, *as though coming from him*, could make him lose whatever influence he has due to his former position, etc. etc.[49]

The footnote of d'Aure's *Traité*, does, indeed, state that:

as a former equerry of the king and of the *manège* of Versailles, he must necessarily be included in all these idiocies. It thus became necessary to attribute to me absurd principles which were repeated, as emanating from me, by men to whom I have never spoken or who have never seen me, and which could make me lose the kind of influence I have due to my former position. Thus, with respect to the means I have just indicated to prevent a horse from swerving or shying, it was hawked throughout Paris and in all the army that I had established, as a general principle, the idea that when a horse had a bar that was sensitive or damaged, one had to damage the other one. I never said anything other than what I have just quoted.[50]

[45] Ibid., p. 611.   [46] Ibid., p. 623.   [47] Ibid., p. 623.   [48] Ibid., p. 624.
[49] Ibid., p. 625.   [50] D'Aure, *Traité d'Equitation*, p. 11.

The argument in question centres around the means to be used when a horse tries to defend himself by swerving or shying. It was rumoured that d'Aure had suggested that to cope with this problem one must irritate the bar on the side opposite to the one in which the horse swerves or shies. The footnote, as quoted by Baucher, is, indeed, taken somewhat out of context and does not state clearly what d'Aure had actually said.

Baucher's overall explanation is that all he did was to examine the two texts of d'Aure side by side, in order to let the reader see the changes made, and how he, Baucher, had merely pointed out some of the inconsistencies and aberrations existing in the work. Furthermore, Baucher explains, he did not have the gift of prophecy to enable him to know that d'Aure, like a new equestrian Saint Peter, would deny his own words and amend them in a new edition 'thus mitigating his errors which I [Baucher] had pointed out'.[51]

This brief (and only) quote comparing the 1834 and 1843 editions serves as a point of departure for Baucher to discuss other aspects of d'Aure's treatise, for example the idea of flexions and the *ramener*. 'In the first edition of the *Traité d'Equitation* of M. d'Aure', declares Baucher,

there is no mention of flexions nor of the *ramener*. In the new one, M. d'Aure has begun to *play* with the reins in order to bring the head of the horse to the right and to the left. He recommends, several times, the *mise en main*, but he is careful not to admit that he has been converted to my precepts. He declares in a footnote that it is, of course, not I who invented the concept of flexion and suppling. Only now, instead of accusing me of having borrowed it from contemporary German equerries, as M. d'Aure had previously claimed, I have now, in this respect, merely plagiarized the idea from one of our most ancient equestrian authors. Soon it will be said that I took the idea of flexion and suppling from an equerry contemporary of Noah who is supposed to have exported them from the Ark immediately after the deluge.[52]

Baucher then goes on to say that d'Aure, despite his conversion, persists in believing

that an excessively suppled neck destroys the speed of the paces, renders the horse flagellant in his movements, that he loses his dash, his energy, etc. etc. If judicious suppling [retorts Baucher] produces this kind of results in a horse, one must then conclude, by a rigorous analogy, that a dancer has less strength, grace and agility in the legs because he has to exercise these parts a great deal. The same applies to the arm used by the master of arms, the fingers by the pianist, etc. etc. And one would, as a consequence, become incapable and idiotic by exercising judiciously one's intelligence. This, indeed, is where the logic of M. d'Aure would lead us.[53]

To avoid the possibility of the consequences warned of by d'Aure, Baucher recommends that not only isolated parts of the horse be exercised, but the total horse, *l'ensemble du cheval*.

Baucher takes this opportunity to accuse d'Aure of exhibiting the patience of a Benedictine monk, when he buries himself in the dust of libraries 'to try and discover proof that the principles that make up the basis of my *nouvelle méthode* were already familiar and have been practised before me'.[54] But Baucher states that he can show how d'Aure's research has come to nothing and proceeds to criticize d'Aure's introduction to his *Traité* which details historically some of the methods introduced and used by equerries of the past.

With the exception of the single quotation which compares d'Aure's two editions, much of the 'Appendix' is an attack on d'Aure which is a repetition and continuation of the polemics between the two men. It is primarily an attack on d'Aure's 'Introduction' which gives a history of equitation. It is interesting to note that here Baucher is not so much criticizing d'Aure, as criticizing men like Grisone, Pluvinel, Newcastle and La Guérinière. And if he criticizes d'Aure, which he does, it is to point out that d'Aure is merely discussing the methods of past

---

[51] Baucher, 'Réponse', p. 625.   [52] Ibid., p. 626.   [53] Ibid., pp. 626–7.   [54] Ibid., p. 627.

equerries in order to show that Baucher's claim to have discovered a new method in the schooling of the horse is really not that new.

Baucher concludes the 'Appendix' by mentioning the publication of d'Aure's new book, *Cours d'Equitation*, published in 1853, which, he maintains, is more a manual geared to the equitation of the cavalry. He accuses d'Aure of having taken some of the ideas presented in his new book from his own *nouvelle méthode*. Nevertheless, the principles the book contains are 'made with the same flour as the ones he has just pointed out to the reader; I will say no more out of respect for the *Comité* that has sanctioned this precious *Cours d'Equitation*.'[55]

At the very end of the 1854 edition of his *Oeuvres complètes*, Baucher has added a two-page statement entitled 'Sin acknowledged is sin forgiven'. It is an appeal to criticism (and his critics) which, 'this time, will not forgive me for having gone beyond the limits that are already too extended to allow me to make an incursion into the domain that belongs to the country's important men of ability. What temerity!'[56] It is a pitiful cry on the part of a man who feels that society has robbed him of his dignity, his prestige, even his miserable pension, and everything that he held dear. He implies that society has done this because the men he attacked belonged to a social class considerably higher than the one to which he belonged. Referring to himself, he says:

Poor equerry, speak as well as you can, of bridles, saddles, crops and whips, spurs, horse, etc.; but do not go any further if you do not want to see your outbursts [in equitation the word also means sudden swerves of the horse] well and duly flagellated. Criticism lost! vain advice! Who can stop a man from giving birth to an idea? ... Regrets, I don't doubt, will soon follow the printing of my last word; but the die is cast and I will pass the Rubicon! ... Criticism, you who will soon prepare for me your most bloody traits, what will you do were I to give you as nourishment, all my more or less indigestible lucubrations on the *causes* and *effects* and which I entitled Intelligence, Arts, Crafts, Agriculture, Sorrow, Pleasure and Money, Government, Freedom of the Press, Instruction and Education, etc.; all subjects treated from a novel point of view, and for which you would not have a sufficient voice to throw the blame on their author? But no, poor lamb, I bleat softly, quite softly, out of fear of attracting the wolves.[57]

---

[55] Ibid., p. 631.   [56] Ibid., p. 719.   [57] Ibid., p. 720.

7

Baucher the humanist

Throughout his work, Baucher reveals himself as a sensitive and affectionate man when dealing with those who have shown and given him affection. This is especially evident in his relationship with his friend and disciple, General L'Hotte. General L'Hotte has described this relationship in his *Souvenirs*. Baucher revealed a similar sensitivity and affection for the equine quadruped. In his *Dialogues sur l'Equitation*, which are dialogues between the Great Hippo-Théo, God of the Quadrupeds, a Horseman, and a Horse, published in 1835, Baucher expresses his love of and concern for the welfare of the horse. Towards the latter part of his life Baucher wrote an essay entitled *Système pénitentiaire* (*Penal System*) which he included in the 1859 (eleventh) publication of his *Oeuvres complètes*. This essay deals with the social disorders and the penal system of his time. It is primarily these two works, which stress his concern for man, especially for the underdog, the pariah, and for God's other creature, the horse, that permits one to consider Baucher a humanist.[1]

As early as the Introduction to his *Méthode d'Equitation*, Baucher discusses man's relationship to the horse as a relationship between one intelligent creature and another. And if, by chance, as men seem to believe, God has given man an intelligence superior to that of creatures less privileged, then it behoves this superior intelligence to behave with decency and honour when dealing with those who serve him or serve him as instruments. The Old Testament, says Baucher, recommends the following: 'With the horse employ the whip, the muzzle with the donkey, and with the ignorant use the rod.'[2] And how, asks Baucher, can one understand this maxim except to consider it apocryphal, for if one took it literally its meaning would be unworthy of divine justice. The horse would then merely be a machine with no memory, no discernment and no instinct. And even if this were so, there is still a mechanism whose gear work must be perfectly harmonized if it is to function with regularity and as a whole. But is

---

[1] The expressions 'humanism' and 'humanist' first appeared during the Italian Renaissance and were very soon adopted by France and other European countries. The humanist was an individual who could lead a meditative life as well as an active life, the active life of a citizen of his city or his country. The Renaissance man, and thus the humanist, was a well-rounded individual who could handle the sword or the dagger, the pen, the paintbrush, and the compass with equal ease. Horsemanship was also considered a necessary accomplishment for young gentlemen; Rabelais, in his *Gargantua et Pantagruel*, mentions the importance of horsemanship as part of the education of a philosopher-king. The Renaissance man was interested in the universe, in man, in man's place in the universe, and in man's relationship to man. He was interested in knowledge, every kind of knowledge, not necessarily for the greater glory of God, but for knowledge's sake. He wished to know all, to absorb all. Names like Shakespeare, Erasmus of Rotterdam, François Rabelais, Montaigne, Michelangelo and Leonardo da Vinci are but a few that come to mind. François Baucher, in a more restricted sense, can be called a humanist in his ability to combine the meditative life with the active life, his interest in knowledge, and his concern for man, especially the pariah, and for the equine quadruped.

[2] Baucher, O.C., p. 1.

it with the *whip* that one can accomplish this when one is merely dealing with a machine? Certainly not.

And were one to allow the horse his intellectual due which is his right, if we were to acknowledge that the horse is capable of appreciation and discernment, that he possesses sensation, memory, and the ability to make comparisons, we must then deduce that he is subject to all the rules common to sensitive and intelligent beings; and thus, while making an effort to avoid giving him pain, one must try to give him pleasure ... It is obvious that the precept of the Holy Book can only have the meaning one is inclined to give it; for whether machine, automaton or intelligent being, it is by means of science and reason, and not the whip, that one must guide and school a horse. I say this primarily to those who, in accordance with the principle given above, or any other person lacking logic, feel that all that is necessary is to pay a large sum and to hit hard and they will then possess good horses and know how to guide them. Rather, how much time, how much study must be spent in order to understand fully this noble animal! An entire life does not suffice if one wishes to practise equitation conscientiously, with discernment and love. But what compensation does one not receive in the work itself! What joyful satisfactions, what delicious moments for the equerry! What a noble interpreter does he not find in this interesting friend of man! What an intimacy full of charm! What pleasant conversations, interesting and instructive! Ask all those who have tasted similar pleasures if it is true that the horse is only an intelligent machine![3]

His affection for the horse is further revealed in his *Dialogues*. Hippo-Théo, God of the Quadrupeds, begins by saying that there is an underlying war going on between the human species and the equine quadrupeds. To give both sides, that is, the horseman and the horse, the right to present their arguments, the God of the Quadrupeds has given the horse the ability to use the human tongue — French, to be exact.

The horseman starts out first to present his case because, as he says, he is 'the one most ancient in the use of speech'. He is full of complaints at the way the horse behaves with him, how it takes him a full five minutes to place his foot in the stirrup, how despite his whoas and sharp jerks of the bridle to convey to the horse that he is anything but docile, the latter pays no attention, and several times maliciously almost broke his leg by bucking and kicking.[4]

When Hippo-Théo asks the horse to defend himself against these accusations, the latter refers to the very nature the god had given him, namely action, which he should obviously make use of. His present horseman, declares the horse, is completely different from his previous master who, with agility, mounted him, got him to caracole, and who then, with a tug at the reins, got him to gallop off. He could easily have refused, but he complied with pleasure, although at times the sudden pressure on the bit gave him pain. But his present master is impatient and never takes the trouble of making himself clear to the horse. When Hippo-Théo asks what he should have done differently, Baucher gives the horse the opportunity to discuss the technique of mounting a horse; first, one must approach and look at the horse with kindness, caress him, talk kindly to him, while placing one's foot in the stirrup, and then gently put pressure on the horse's flanks.

The horseman is somewhat taken aback at the horse's complaint, saying: 'I was unaware that such procedures were necessary with an animal whose condition in life is servitude, and whose lack of intelligence forces him to submit to all our whims.'[5] Hippo-Théo immediately challenges this assumption and points out that it is man's vanity that prevents him from perceiving that the horse is endowed with intelligence. When the horseman then describes

---

[3] Ibid., pp. 1–3.
[4] Baucher, 'Dialogues sur l'Equitation', O.C. (Paris, Published by the author and Dumaine, 1859), p. 330. A translation of this work appears as Part Three below.
[5] Ibid., p. 332.

other intemperate behaviour on the part of the horse, the horse again appeals to the fact that the god gave the horse such a sensitive nature that he can immediately feel a rider's awkward and jerky behaviour, as well as his uncertain seat which immediately disturbs the paces. 'Am I wrong', the horse appeals to the god, 'in wishing to make known to him that I do not like to be ill-treated and that he must learn the rules of an art before putting it into practice?'[6] The horseman now loses his patience: 'Fiddlesticks! Why should I, civilized man, have to learn what primitive peoples practise so well of their own accord and without following any principles? If I am rich, am I not able to buy a horse appropriate to my needs and thereby exempt myself from playing the role of artist? I state once more that the horse is shaking too much the yoke to which he is bound by the laws of nature.'[7]

Hippo-Théo immediately attacks this 'arrogant outburst'. First of all, 'when it comes to his physical strength, primitive man is superior to civilized man. And as money means nothing to him, he has to find other means of providing for himself and, in order to succeed, is forced to spend entire days mounted on his beloved companion. Since childhood, he has devoted himself to perilous journeys which make him into a sound horseman.'[8]

The horseman then challenges the so-called nobility of the horse. When he tries to go for a ride in the many well-frequented areas so that he can show off his grace and skill, there is a continual battle going on between him and the horse, and often he is forced to complete the promenade on foot instead of on horseback as he had set out to do. Is this nobility? 'My answer is simple and easy', replies the horse. 'As your means of transmitting your commands to me are so ambiguous, lack energy, and constrain me so painfully without making me understand your wishes, you must not hold it against me when I freely dispose of my own

strength and try to avoid that which is painful to me.'[9] 'But why', asks the horseman, 'if my means of execution are always the same, are you obstinate only from time to time? Does this not denote caprice or ill-will?'[10] 'No', the horse quickly replies,

it is proof of my lack of spite. I promptly forget what your ignorance has produced and often return to the basic good nature of a horse. But then your movements exasperate me so much that, despite myself, I abandon a ride that would have been pleasant and useful to me. I prefer to remain pinioned in your unhealthy stable and suffer the harsh treatment of your groom; for as in other things, like master, like servant.[11]

Hippo-Théo does not accept any of the horseman's arguments and excuses. 'I hope . . . that your complaints rest on more solid foundations',[12] he says.

Much of the dialogue now centres around particular instances when the horseman gives a specific order which the horse disobeys and, instead, does something else. The horse explains that he has two choices to make: 'Either I can dispose of my strength and I am free to do as I please, and can use this freedom as does any other thinking being; or you contain my voluntary movement and I must submit myself. In the latter instance you have to know what my natural movements are so that they can be consistent with your directions.'[13]

The discussion then turns to the trot which, according to the horseman, comes naturally to the horse. The horseman wants to know why he can make the horse neither slow down nor accelerate at will, why the horse is subject to buckling at the knees and why his shoes come together, a sound that is 'most shocking to the ear of a gentleman who appreciates the horseman only by the qualities of his horse. Is it out of malice or ill-will that you succeed in making me appear pitiful in the eyes of all the amateur riders who mistake you for a hack?'[14] In answer to the horseman's first question, the horse says

---

[6] Ibid., p. 333.   [7] Ibid., p. 333.   [8] Ibid., pp. 333–4.   [9] Ibid., p. 335.   [10] Ibid., p. 335.   [11] Ibid., p. 335.   [12] Ibid., p. 335.   [13] Ibid., p. 336.   [14] Ibid., p. 338.

that the fact that the horseman cannot co-ordinate his hands and his legs is responsible for the uncontrollable trot, and, for that matter, the walk. What is needed is the 'opposition between these two forces' (which Baucher will later call the *effet d'ensemble*). Good balance on the part of the horseman is also essential, says the horse. After all, it is good balance that permits a weak human being to direct a mass of equine proportions. If the position of the body is poor, then this cannot be done. And, adds the horse, as far as cost is concerned, that has nothing to do with him. That is a matter of fraud and horses are strangers to such niceties possessed by the civilized species. As far as the buckling at the knee and the clicking of metal brought about by over-reaching, both may be due to certain vices, or because the horseman is incapable of guiding or directing the horse.

Once again Baucher makes a derogatory remark about the human species and their inability to admit when they are wrong. 'Remember', Hippo-Théo says to the horseman, 'that to admit not to know something is knowing something. We are here together to give each other advice ... Retracting a false notion and yielding to evidence denotes a man of honour.'[15] The horseman's response to this is that the god would find it inexcusable were he to accept the reasoning of others without being himself convinced of the argument. Too many learned men support doctrines so different from each other and give such marvellous reasoning and so subtle a logic in their defence, that they all seem correct. Baucher is making an oblique reference here to his belief that it is mainly the good or poor conformation of the horse that determines the successful or unsuccessful schooling of a horse, and that there is no such thing as a malicious horse. 'Horses', insists the horse, 'have nothing in them to engender vice. They know neither vanity, nor pride, nor greed, nor hypocrisy, nor meanness, nor avarice, nor ambition, nor egoism, etc. On

what would they base their viciousness, which would not exist even among humans were it not for these vices, which are products of civilization?'[16] Why should the horse, so much stronger and with a superior construction than that of man for walking, not carry the rider with pride, even gaiety, for if his weight is well distributed, it would not cost him any more effort than it costs the rider to be part of his movements. 'We cannot be naturally evil, since everything that gives rise to evil is unknown to us; only your poor methods, your ignorance, can give us this defect.'[17] Thus a horse who has all the physical and moral accomplishments (a sacred fire that constantly renews itself) as can be found among the English horses (the horse now reveals that although he had been sold as an English horse, he is really from Mellerault (Merlerault?), and while coming from a respectable lineage, one must recognize that horses from across the Channel are superior), a horse that is well-balanced and with good proportions, can be easily schooled and the horseman will have little or no trouble with him. The horse then explains why he causes problems to his rider. He has, indeed, some of those defects mentioned earlier. Then, too, he was ridden too early, when he was four years old. Furthermore, 'until we have reached the age of four, we must not be abandoned in a pasture at the mercy of a brutal guardian who instils in us disgust and antipathy for all that man represents'. Neither should he be sold before he is four years of age. And one should not ask hard work of a horse before he is seven years old. Should these rules be violated, and should one be treated brutally, is it not understandable that horses use whatever means at their disposal to defend themselves?

Thus, continues the horse, moral problems, brought about by the ignorance and the brutality of humans, compound the problems of conformation. No two horses are alike, physically and mentally. That is why one can succeed

---

15 Ibid., p. 339.
16 It seems as though we have in François Baucher a

disciple of J.-J. Rousseau.
17 Baucher, 'Dialogues sur l'Equitation', pp. 342–3.

with some horses and not with others. Baucher is once again implying here, as he has done in his other works, that conformation affects the success or failure of the schooling of a horse.

Now Baucher, through the intermediary of the horse, introduces the positive aspects of horse management. Early training, that is at the age of three, should occur in the stable, little by little, and by people who are gentle and patient. Gradual tasks should be given, in proportion to the strength of the horse. The horse should slowly become familiar with the ways and manners of man; and soon he will become man's best friend.

The discussion then centres around the questions as to why England has such good breeds whereas France does not. 'The fact that you ask this question . . .', says Hippo-Théo, 'does not speak favourably with respect to your knowledge in equine matters. Do you ignore the fact that your country was once the best endowed with good breeds, and that your lack of interest in these animals, and your lack of national pride, are responsible for allowing these breeds to degenerate?'[18] And, adds, Hippo-Théo, he has indeed reproached himself several times for having made mistakes in the choice of favoured countries. He then mentions that Henry VIII had used very violent means to keep the equine breed pure by having mares who were unsatisfactory killed; and that the English, at great sacrifice and cost, imported Arab stallions. Indeed, many English lords put their horses to difficult tests. On the other hand, there is not a single mistress who receives better care and attention than do the lords' horses when they enter their beautiful and salubrious stable. And a groom devotes himself exclusively to a horse. He dries him with a linen towel when the horse is in a sweat, and then rubs and brushes him until his hair is as smooth as silk. He also washes his nose and mouth with a mixture of water and vinegar. Good management goes into the horse's diet

and the care of the stall. The temperature of the stall is always measured so that the temperature inside compensates for that of the outside.

The French, on the other hand, continues Hippo-Théo, do not show much interest in horses and when they have a horse do not take good care of him. When the horse returns from an outing sweaty and hot, no one bothers about him; perhaps a light blanket is placed upon his back, that is all. The groom, a Jack-of-all-trades, is very likely occupied with the preparation of the meal and leaves his poor quadruped alone, facing his flake of hay. He never bothers to remove the mud from his legs and belly and shows no concern for stopped perspiration or inflammation of the chest. And, continues the horse, this kind of concern will destroy the qualities of the best horse and is more perfidious than the plague and the famine.

In the end, the horseman promises, not, as did Boileau, to uphold the idea 'that the most stupid animal is man; but that his inexperience can make him commit all sorts of blunders, and that he often finds himself to be inferior to the animal he is handling'.[19] He also promises to take lessons in equitation and hopes that Hippo-Théo will grant him a second audience. Before departing, Hippo-Théo gives the horseman good advice with respect to the suppling of his own thighs and back, how to obtain a good seat and mobility of arms and legs, and, eventually, acquire sound coordination. He tells him never to be impatient, unjust or violent, for the horse will respond in kind. '*Know yourself first!*', said a philosopher of antiquity. Or, 'as a profound moralist said: "*How many defects do we not attribute to others that really belong to us!*" How many vices do we not attribute to these interesting creatures, which are really the result of the ineptness or brusqueness on the part of the horseman?'[20]

The *Second Dialogue* assembles the same characters. Hippo-Théo has kept his promise

[18] Ibid., p. 346.
[19] Ibid., p. 352. Boileau was a writer of the French Classical period in the seventeenth century.
[20] Ibid., p. 355.

to meet once more with the horseman and the horse. The horseman comes up with an interesting revelation, namely, that most often the mistakes made by horsemen towards their horses are due to the ineptness of teachers of equitation, whose systems are founded on principles derived haphazardly and then imparted to their pupils to the detriment of their mounts. Between the First and the Second Dialogues, the horseman has taken lessons from the most renowned teachers of equitation. He attended their lessons with great expectations and religiously paid attention to all their demonstrations, all to no avail. No progress crowned his efforts. He was confused, and his movements continued to be awkward and without a goal. After two months of useless work, he became disgusted and almost abandoned teachers, horses and equitation.

Hippo-Théo says that while he was familiar with the decadence that exists in the equestrian art, he never realized the extent to which the teaching of this art had degenerated. The horseman goes on to say that he had even tried to find *manèges* where the teaching was supposed to be superior; but they, too, were lacking in excellence. 'Everywhere I found ignorance, repetition and contradiction. Occasionally some rays of light shone through, though too few to reveal the truth.'[21] But the horseman, now motivated, refused to give up. Finally, in France itself, he found a few French equerries who were skilful, and whose principles were in accord with those mentioned previously by Hippo-Théo: to do gymnastics to limber his limbs so that he could sit naturally and easily in the saddle. At last he was able to sit straight in the saddle and with it came ease and regularity in his movements. New principles were taught him and the ability of his teachers made it possible for him not to confuse old principles with new ones. He now realizes how important a good seat is and that the horse will execute movements only if the horseman is well placed. He is now able to coordinate the action of his aids. Suddenly a kind of magnetic harmony developed between the horseman and his mount.

The horse suggests that the horseman etch in his mind two words which contain all the principles of equitation, namely 'suppling' and 'position', and that from then on all the horseman's wishes will become his own. Hippo-Théo, too, is convinced that this principle will eventually become an axiom. He points out that the horseman's ability to learn how to demand certain movements from his horse nevertheless depended to some extent on the intelligence of his horse. The horseman now has the proper posture which determines the movement the horse must execute. The horse obeys, not because the horseman employs excessive force, but because he understands the horseman's intentions.

The horse is in agreement. He defends the equine race once more. 'Were we not intelligent, how could we know that we have to move forward when an unskilled and awkward horseman jerks the bridle sharply when he wants to get us to move? How could we finish the movements begun when the legs and hands of the horseman are in flagrant contradiction to his commands?'[22] Now that the horseman has been put on the right track by his new teachers, the horse executes, without hesitation, every movement that the horseman wishes, because they are demanded without hesitation and always in conformity with the laws which govern a horse's organism.

Harmony now exists between the horseman and the horse, each one granting the intelligence and good will of the other. This is due to the three weeks when the horseman assiduously persevered in the lessons in equitation with his teacher placed him properly and naturally on the horse, and to the limbering exercises and so on which enabled him to determine his own position and that of the horse. 'A magnetic relationship of some sort was established between my organism and that

---

[21] Ibid., p. 359   [22] Ibid., p. 362.

of my mount.'[23] For not only did the horseman's teachers fashion him physically, but they also fashioned his intelligence and the use of sound judgement. Their clear explanations and their readiness to answer his questions, made things easy. He also realized that his inability to understand the ancients when they said: 'Movements determine the horse. Some horses have hard mouths', was because the ancients lacked clarity. Only when his teachers somewhat rephrased the dictum to: 'The actions of the horseman determine that the horse take the position appropriate to the movement. Some horses are heavy in the hand',[24] did he finally understand the importance of the horseman's position and movements in determining the horse's position and movements, which, in turn, depends upon the proper distribution of his weight. All these obstacles can be eliminated through the new method.

The horseman wants to know how one can recognize a 'hard mouth'? Obviously, declares Hippo-Théo, by the degree of resistance the horse uses to oppose the action of the bit. Only superficial observers believe that the insensitivity of the bars cause this resistance. And so these people invented all sorts of instruments, one more cruel than the other, to triumph over the bars. The results were zero; disillusionment and disgust soon followed, and the equerry condemned his horses without trying to discover why his efforts had come to nothing.

Neither Hippo-Théo nor the horseman can understand the blindness and refusal on the part of some teachers and equerries to consider the new method in the training of horse and rider. Jealousy, vanity, or ignorance are most likely to blame.

Not only is the horseman pleased with the new method of teaching, but the horse is equally pleased. Above all, he has been given freedom of movement. Furthermore, frequent recourse to legs and hands gives the horseman's aids the desirable flexibility and a well-directed action which causes the horse no constraint. The good seat of the horseman makes him appear lighter and his daily progress makes the horse's task easier. He now obeys his commands with pleasure.

The teachers of the new method, says the horseman, have asked themselves

whether it is reasonable to assume that the strong pressure to make the horse obey is felt only on one part of his body, and whether it is reasonable to assume that this part alone is responsible for the execution of our commands. A close examination of the mechanism of the horse shows that all the parts of his body are a harmonious whole and that their convergence is essential to all the horse's movements. From this it follows that constraint of one part of the body will be felt on the entire body and hamper his movements.[25]

For the horseman (as for Baucher) the cause of a horse's resistances is his poor conformation. And, concludes the horseman,

the resistances that the horse makes to the bit are due to the difficulty he experiences in executing the required movement, which is the result of a disharmony in his organism. By re-establishing a general unity in the neck, the back, the hocks — the entire body, so to speak — one destroys the resistance and the horse, who a short while earlier seemed insensitive to the extreme pressure of the bit, now gives in at the first invitation of the hand. Experience proves this every day. It is established that this sensitivity, more or less, of the mouth has nothing to do with the horse's resistances, and that this hard mouth which has condemned so many horses is nothing but a chimera.[26]

Hippo-Théo agrees with the conclusions arrived at by the horseman and his teachers and explains that a membrane which covers the bones called the periosteum is solely responsible for the sensitivity of the bars. And while poor conformation of the horse affects his behaviour, only vanity prevents man from accepting the main responsibility in the appearance of these disorders. Hippo-Théo then discusses once more the progressive decline and degeneration of the equine species, and the

---

[23] Ibid., p. 363.   [24] Ibid., p. 364.   [25] Ibid., p. 367.   [26] Ibid., p. 367.

apathy in breeding practices which is the reason why there are so many horses with poor conformation.

Hippo-Théo then asks the horse to verify the equine problems of the past and compare them with those of the new method. The horse is only too willing to discuss the physical and moral weaknesses of the past, how his mouth was always bloody, his bars in shreds, how he had continually to use his defences to prevent himself from being crippled, and how he was always in a state of exhaustion. Now, with the new method, he can, in a short time, execute those movements which those of his brothers more favoured by nature are able to do.

All our principles are based on reasoning and experience, says the horseman.

We begin by appreciating and coordinating the strength of the horse. And by means of this well-directed power, we obtain the transference of the necessary weight. Coordination of strength and weight brings about the balance of the horse and lightness in the hand. Later, balance of the mass gives harmony to his movements. Once lightness has been achieved, we rapidly reach our goal: the horseman sets the position and the horse executes the movement.[27]

In conclusion, as god of the horse and his benefactor, Hippo-Théo wants to know how the horseman utilizes the resources 'of this precious creature that I placed under your control'.[28] The analogy and analysis Baucher gives through his intermediary the horseman is the same one he was to use later in his 1842 work, namely, that the head and neck are the compass and the helm of the horse and that the horseman attempts to place them under his direction. Once the jaw is flexed and made mellow and mobile, the head may be placed vertically and the neck, once suppled, acquires the flexibility that is necessary. Work conducted on foot, then astride, will balance the forehand and the hindquarters and connect the rest of the body to the neck. 'Each part of the horse has its own role; the hindquarters are the impulsive force, the forehand the guiding force. While with his legs the horseman provokes impulsion, his hand guides the movement of the horse. This perfect unity established between legs and hands results in an accord between weight and strength, that is, lightness.'[29] And, adds the horse, not to be outdone by the horseman,

the new system is one which combines the education of my master as well as of myself . . . My instinct is in continuous contact with the intelligence of my master and uses him as model. It thus follows that the progress of one carries with it the progress of the other. The horseman becomes proud of his mount and the horse, recognizing the benefits of the education acquired, devotes to his master an obedience that is all the greater in that it has become easier.[30]

With these wise words Hippo-Théo recognizes that the horseman no longer needs his advice, and that he is following the sound path. He has, at last, understood the nature and destiny of the horse. And, addressing himself to the horseman, he says: 'Horseman, remember that *intelligence obliges*, and that you have to make the future forget mankind's past errors, far too prolonged, with respect to your noble steed.'[31]

Critics have neglected this aspect of Baucher's work. If it was mentioned at all, it was done obliquely, in that it was considered of marginal value. While his *Méthode d'Equitation* is, unquestionably, of greater importance to the horseman, *Dialogues sur l'Equitation* and *Système pénitentiaire* appeal to the individual who is equally interested in Baucher the man. The same points made in *Dialogues sur l'Equitation* are made in his later manual dealing with his *nouvelle méthode*; but here they have been rendered more dramatic. By giving the horse an intelligence, a personality and the ability to speak, he has brought this quadruped closer to the human species.

While Baucher's affection and respect for

---

[27] Ibid., pp. 369–70. [28] Ibid., p. 370. [31] Ibid., p. 372. *Intelligence obliges* is a parody of *nobility obliges* (*noblesse oblige*).
[29] Ibid., p. 371. [30] Ibid., p. 371.

the noble quadruped are evident throughout his writings, it is in the *Dialogues sur l'Equitation* that they are most evident. Despite the date of the early publication of the work, one has the impression that as the years went by, and the more he felt betrayed by society and some of his friends and disciples, the closer a bond developed between him and the horse. Much has been said of Baucher's reticence, his awkwardness, his morose behaviour with those who, he felt, had slighted him or betrayed him, and that he was a complex and solitary being. L'Hotte tells us that when schooling a horse, especially a problem horse, he would rise early in the morning and insist on being alone in the ring with his horse. He was also a man who was very sensitive about his background and social status. While often defending his status as a circus performer, or, as he put it, of being a *saltimbanque* (a circus showman),[32] his ego, nevertheless, was affected by the fact that he was forced to perform before an audience not only to make a living, but also to put his method into practice. When the army finally rejected him and his method, he was greatly and irretrievably hurt and did not forget this rejection for the rest of his life. He saw himself as a man with a mission, who, due to jealousy, intrigue and narrow-mindedness, was scorned by society because of his background.

It is very likely that his sensitivity, his sense of social inferiority and of being an underdog, made it easy for him to understand the sensitivity of the horse, especially the problem horse. They undoubtedly also gave him a feeling for the problems of society and its disorders. This concern for society's flotsam is revealed in his essay dealing with society's attitude towards the criminal and the penal system. His own isolation and loneliness is perhaps reflected in his concern for the individual who has to spend long days in isolation, surrounded by four walls and excluded from society. The question that Baucher asks is whether punishment and isolation are really the only remedies that society has to cure the problems that afflict it. For isolating an individual is really to mitigate his offences rather than to cure them. It is obvious that Baucher is rejecting society's concept of incarceration and punishment as a deterrent. In opting for rehabilitation rather than merely punishment and deterrence, he is ahead of his time.

Society, says Baucher, has two ways of incarcerating an offender. He either lives isolated in a cell or he lives in a dormitory, sometimes containing more than a hundred men. Both are bad. But the second type is more pernicious in that the detainee receives the advice and counsel of others who are more experienced than he is. For he will find in this very prison 'all the subversive passions of the social order; the veterans of shame who, so to speak, are always the victims of injustice, and who soon convey to him that society alone is to blame'.[33] And very soon whatever regret, sorrow or intimidation he may have shown earlier will dissipate. This is not rehabilitation, believes Baucher. And if, perchance, the prisoner is intelligent or moral enough to resist these suggestions, discouragement will take over, for he knows that once out again further difficulties will arise. He will ask himself what will he do once he is out? Indeed, asks Baucher, what *will* he do once he is released? He is without money, without papers, without a job, without a home to go to, for who would want to have a criminal under his roof? And if his moral energy has not been sapped and he is released, what will he do with his new freedom? He has become a real pariah, sometimes even in the eyes of his own family. All these factors may contribute to his backsliding. In fact, adds Baucher, he may even look forward to returning to prison, with its hard bed and its black bread, for at least

---

[32] To L'Hotte he once said that he was 'living as a circus showman. I have lived with clowns and I show myself for ten sous' (L'Hotte, *Un Officier de Cavalerie: Souvenirs* (Paris, Plon, 1906), p. 99).

[33] Baucher, 'Système pénitentiaire', *O.C.*, 1859, p. 720.

there he had security and tranquillity. And, continues Baucher, while imprisonment and harsh treatment punishes the individual, they do not rehabilitate, much less improve, an individual.

Let us consider, says Baucher, the penal system of the past to determine whether there is a correlation between repressive treatment and rehabilitation. Since the abolishment of the various tortures and repressive treatment of the past, have the number of criminals increased? Not at all. If this is true, one is thus forced to believe that repressive treatment and corporal punishment have no value in deterring criminals. On the contrary, 'we note that with the relaxation of the penal system, crimes and misdemeanors have diminished in seriousness and number'.[34] It is not the system of repression, explains Baucher, that contributed to this decline; rather it is the

improvement of the masses through the raising of moral standards of society. As one awakened within the human heart affection for the family, one also awakened love for one's fellow-man, and soon bloodthirsty feelings lost their intensity. As soon as the child in his crib saw his father handle instruments of work rather than instruments of war and pillage, the taste for work replaced the inclination for rapine. The labourer, finding in industry daily bread for his family, became used to work and pursued his honourable career giving no thought to tribunals and codes whose names he barely knew. But this felicitous influence on the part of civilization, it is true, comes in contact with rebellious characters and its edge seems to become blunt; in others it is combated through examples taken from perverted milieux. Here is the origin of social vice which the laws wish to curb; here is the necessity of the penal code which, in turn, renders powerless, if not dangerous, the system now present in prisons.[35]

Society has condemned and expelled the guilty ones. But in doing its duty, it has only done half of its duty. By merely punishing the criminal, it has not rehabilitated him. On the contrary, it has aggravated the situation, and by not trying to find a moral cure it has failed to do its moral duty. And to this day no serious effort has been made in this direction. It has merely pushed him into the midst of others as depraved as he is.

Thus repression and detention alone do not suffice. Detention must be accompanied by the moral education or re-education of the convicted man. In some prisons where women are placed, some moral education has been introduced. That has taken the form of work. But the kind of work that they are made to do, and what is demanded of them, has little or no effect on their moral character. It does not act on their moral fibre because it gives them no personal interest or incentive. It should not be forgotten that it is the lure of gain that motivates the individual and enables him to withstand fatigue. This is especially true of manual labour. If your goal is to instil in the lazy individual a taste for work, paying nothing or practically nothing does not accomplish this. All he feels is disgust.

In an atmosphere of this sort, traits such as honour and justice become meaningless. For these traits to have some meaning for the convicted man, it is necessary that he be rehabilitated, not only in the eyes of society, but in his own eyes. He needs to find in the penitentiary an expression of interest, solicitude and encouragement for his welfare. When a man gives an indication that he wishes to reform and is, in fact, reforming, he should be praised by those in charge of the prison. And the only way they can show their satisfaction with him is to improve the conditions of the detainee in the prison. This will also serve as an example to the other detainees. The present prison system makes no provision for this sort of thing. Prisoners who have spent ten years in prison and who have behaved in an exemplary fashion find themselves in the same situation as they did upon arrival. Nothing exists to direct them towards the good path and should they follow it, it is purely chance that guided them.

---

[34] Ibid., p. 722.   [35] Ibid., p. 723.

Baucher then discusses another pernicious aspect of the current penal system, namely the releasing of an individual without any period of transition. How can a man, deprived of his freedom for a long time, when suddenly released, resist the temptations of his senses that are now no longer deprived? The answer is obvious when one considers that 30 per cent of prisoners freed are re-arrested before they even reach their destination. Unaccustomed to freedom, they live in the frenzy of the moment, trying to drown their present fears and the desperation of tomorrow. They are not armed with the means of protecting themselves. The prison system has done nothing to prepare them for the outside. Should the reader want further proof of the failure of penalty and prisons, an analysis of the police surveillance system to which some convicted men are subjected after they are free may perhaps convince him.

A convicted man, when set free, experiences immense difficulties in attempting to integrate into and cope with society. This becomes even more acute when he is under surveillance. He is forced to live in a town in which he is a stranger and where often his skill has no outlet. At times he cannot get work because the surveillance to which he is subjected is proof to many that he is dangerous to society. All these arguments should indicate that it is in the interest of society that a complete and prompt revision of the penal system be initiated.

Now that Baucher has dealt with the ills of the penal system in France, he begins to analyse the goals of the reformed penal system and presents the principles that are basic to his system:

Progressive amelioration of the detainee's inclinations;
Complete freedom when there is proof of moral improvement;
Elimination of the prejudices that afflict and censure the freed convicted man.

To achieve these goals, Baucher believes that

detention must be considered as a period of retreat during which time one withdraws the condemned man from pernicious and perverse counsel and subjects him to positive influences. This detention or exile must last as long as the condemned man has not given sufficient proof of his rehabilitation. To make the condemned man become aware that his freedom depends upon his rehabilitation, the judge, after indicating the prison term, must also add '*and more*'.[36]

Baucher now becomes specific in setting down the prerequisites for his new penal system. Detainees will be divided into three classes. The third class will contain those who have not yet completed a third of their punishment. The second class is those who have completed a third of their punishment and who are considered worthy of better conditions. The first class will consist of those who have completed two-thirds of their punishment and have exhibited those qualities that make it possible for them to enter this class which serves as a transition between captivity and freedom.

Each class of detainees will be housed in three different buildings, each with its own courtyard and workshops. The type of lodging will correspond to the progress they have made with respect to their rehabilitation. It is important that the lodgings of those in the first class resemble as much as possible the lodgings of workers out in society.

Work will be obligatory in the three classes and remunerated accordingly. Each type of industry will have its own workshop and will be chosen in accordance with the ones in existence in the area in which the prison is located.

The meals of the detainees must be sufficient in order to maintain the necessary strength to perform the necessary work. The quality of the food will vary from class to class.

As far as dress is concerned, it should be left to those men in charge and competent to make such decisions. Nevertheless, it is important that the men belonging to the first class should

---

[36] Ibid., p. 728.

be dressed to conform with the way men dress outside and suitable for their weekly outings. The detainee of this class should perhaps be made to pay for his clothes and he should be allowed to keep them when he leaves the prison permanently.

In order to instil in the detainee a work ethic and give him sufficient earnings for the day of his liberation, his income should be proportionate to the class to which he belongs.

It will be up to the competent men in charge to determine the problems of discipline, hospitals, infirmaries, surveillance, etc. It is advisable to give the detainees instruction comparable to that of primary schools, and which is fitting for a worker. Moral education must also be included.

The procedures of passing from one class to the next depends upon certain determined conditions which will be made known to the detainees. They will pass from one class to the other only when and if they have fulfilled the required one-third or two-thirds of their punishment and have fulfilled the other necessary requirements. The detainees of the first class will be set free only if and when they have met the necessary requirements and are morally without reproach. Going backwards from one class to another will occur if and when the detainee incurs a serious punishment or punishments.

All rules pertaining to the three classes will be posted in all the rooms. Furthermore, rules pertaining to the first class will be posted in the rooms of the second class as well as in its own room.

Baucher feels that special attention must be given to the detainees of the first class. They must be prepared to enter life outside the prison and therefore should be subject to different rules, as well as different meals and dress. Discipline there should be at a minimum and the detainee should, as much as possible, lead the life of a workman.

Discipline in the workshops must be similar to that in the workshops of public life. Since it is essential that one avoids a sudden transition between captivity and freedom, it is good that the detainee of the first class be allowed to have a weekly outing. These outings will occur between the two meals. A sum of money will be put at his disposal. He will be subject to certain rules which, if broken, will incur punishment, even a return to the second class. During his outing, he must, of course, carry a permit issued by the proper authorities.

Every six months, meritorious detainees will be recommended to the authorities. Each 15 February and 15 August those in the first class will celebrate certain solemn feasts.

The prisoner, once he leaves the prison, must be issued a passport indicating his chosen destination. He must also be provided with a certificate of good conduct, issued by the warden and approved by the prefect. Special recommendations should be given to the mayor of the town to which the ex-prisoner is going.

Baucher then itemizes the amount of money a prisoner can earn who is condemned for a certain period of time and depending upon which one of the three classes he belongs to. The sum earned will be given to him upon his release from prison. At no time will a sum of money be subtracted from the total for any reason whatsoever, even for legal fines. The only amount that can be deducted is for the clothes he has been issued when he is released.

Baucher's goal for writing this essay was not so much to present a new penitentiary system, as to point out the flaws of the present system. Baucher believed, however, that by taking cognizance of some of his recommendations, the condemned man can be rehabilitated and, once released, he can be better integrated into society where he can practise his skills and once again take his honourable place in society.

The nineteenth century, in France as elsewhere, evinced a keen interest in the prison system and tried to pressure the various governments that came and went to initiate reform. The eighteenth century, the age of enlightenment, with its belief in reason and progress, believed also in the perfectibility of man and, consequently, in the belief of reform: social, moral, as well as political. Jean-Jacques Rousseau believed that man, at birth, was neither good nor bad. If he became bad, it was society that made him so. Like so many of the later Romanticists, Rousseau believed in the nobility of primitive man, more specifically the American Indian who, because he lived in a state of nature, physically as well as politically, was good. Modern civilization, that is, the civilization of the eighteenth century, with its stress on reason, philosophical materialism, material possessions, competition and power, was, according to Rousseau, the cause of man's degeneracy. The Revolution of 1789 had adopted many of the ideas of Rousseau, especially the idea and ideals of the common weal, the distribution of wealth and the general will, but was incapable of fulfilling them. Unfortunately, the revolutionaries were kept busy fighting the counter-revolution within France and the Coalitions of the various monarchies and empires from without that had formed and were threatening to invade and destroy them.

However, gradually, some of the ideas of the Revolution made themselves felt. It became obvious even to the most obtuse that reforms were necessary if only out of enlightened self-interest. Each successive government that headed France in the nineteenth century tried to cope with reform. Romanticists like George Sand and Victor Hugo put their ideas on the ills of society and the need to reform, including prison reform, in their writings. In England, Charles Dickens was already attempting to do the same. Revolution and reform were very much in the air by the mid nineteenth century. And the Revolution of February 1848, the first proletarian revolution, either gave hope to or frightened the men and women of the age. It is therefore not astonishing that Baucher, a man who exhibited many traits and had a similar background to Rousseau, would contain within him ideas that were born in the eighteenth century and which finally began to take fruition in the mid nineteenth century.

8

Conclusion: The legacy of Baucher

In the Preface to *Baucher et son Ecole* (*Baucher and his School*), General Decarpentry says that 'these pages are devoted to the memory of Baucher and to the history of his method which, one hundred years ago, seemed to replace, definitively, all that experience and tradition had legated to us in precepts for the schooling and treatment of the saddle horse'.[1] He advances the idea that from Xenophon until 1842 when Baucher published his new method, horsemen in all countries used almost identical procedures to school and guide their horses. While these precepts were coherent recopies, they never consisted of a method, properly speaking, for, continues Decarpentry, 'former equerries were never concerned with theories. In an art that is primarily execution, the "how" of their skill preoccupied them more than the "why".'[2] As has been noted in earlier chapters, this is precisely what Baucher has been saying throughout his works. In a sense one can say that the final cry of despair on the part of Baucher as indicated in 'Sin acknowledged is sin forgiven', his poor health (he was almost blind at the end of his life) compounded by his poverty (a pension he had received from Napoleon III was eventually taken away from him), was compensated for by his friend and disciple General L'Hotte and by General Decarpentry who, perhaps more than anyone else, brought the work and life of Baucher to the attention of the contemporary equestrian world. Equally instrumental in furthering the work of Baucher were General Făverot de Kerbrech and Colonel Guérin (the latter succeeded d'Aure as *écuyer-en-chef* at the *Ecole de Cavalerie* at Saumur).

Decarpentry tells us at the outset of his book that General L'Hotte met Baucher in 1849 and that he was 'Baucher's best pupil' and has 'traced an outstanding portrait of his master'.[3] Decarpentry is referring to General L'Hotte's *Un Officier de Cavalerie: Souvenirs du Général L'Hotte*. While this work deals primarily with the general's military life, it devotes several chapters to Baucher and to d'Aure. Both men were L'Hotte's teachers in the equestrian art. He admired both men. Perhaps it is possible to detect in his *Souvenirs* a greater affection and attachment for Baucher, possibly because Baucher, while reserved and solitary throughout his life, allowed a greater intimacy to develop between him and L'Hotte than did d'Aure. While busy with his own military career, L'Hotte managed to spend time with Baucher, especially during the last years of the master's life. It is thanks to L'Hotte that we have, if not a complete, at least a fairly detailed picture of Baucher's life and work. Especially sad is L'Hotte's description of the master's last days. Knowing that he only had a few days to live, in great pain and almost blind, he was nevertheless able to talk with passion about equitation.

'I will have much to say', says L'Hotte, 'with respect to this great teacher, having lived with him in complete equestrian intimacy. What

---

[1] Decarpentry, *Baucher et son Ecole*, p. 9. [2] Ibid., pp. 9–10. [3] Ibid., p. 10.

General L'Hotte, presenting the Cadre Noir at Saumur. (Musée de Saumur)

concerns him will be found in the pages that follow and will be complete when I have presented you with Count d'Aure, my other teacher.'[4] L'Hotte states that what he has to relate about Baucher is exact, not only because of his memory, but also because he took daily copious and precise notes during all his meetings and discussions with the master. L'Hotte cherishes these notes and likes to believe that 'they will afford you some interest, as well as to those men of the horse who preserved the cult of his memory or who, younger, could only penetrate his writings'.[5]

The portrait that L'Hotte gives of the master is one respect and love for a man who devoted his whole life to an art that was dear to him as well as to L'Hotte. L'Hotte presents a man of great intelligence and sound judgement, whose philosophical bent was visible in his writings as well as in his conversation. But he also paints for us a man sensitive to the attitude and judgement of others, at times even oversensitive, who was often morose, and who believed that society was against him and had treated him unjustly. But, in the final analysis, L'Hotte believes that Baucher was 'the most exceptional genius in the art of equitation that ever lived'.[6]

Comparing the achievements of Baucher with those of d'Aure, in the final analysis, Baucher is considered by many to be the greater master in that he set down his principles with a more solid methodology and in greater detail. Indeed, d'Aure's works are considerably slimmer than those of Baucher, for he was less the theoretician than the practitioner. Incontestably he was the better rider of the two with an excellent seat (which Baucher never had), and a light hand. Unlike d'Aure, Baucher was not an outdoor man. He was much more the

[4] L'Hotte, *Souvenirs*, p. 95.   [5] Ibid., p. 96.   [6] Ibid., p. 231.

meditative man who spent a great deal of time in his study, analysing and, if necessary, modifying his method. If Baucher was criticized more frequently and more vehemently than was d'Aure, this was because Baucher had claimed that he had discovered a *nouvelle méthode*, and had ignored the innovations and accomplishments of predecessors (Pluvinel, La Guérinière and others), especially when it pertained to the disposition of the horse's strength, the balance of his mass, and lateral flexion. Baucher's repeated statements to this effect throughout his work give credence to these accusations. D'Aure, in his *Traité d'Equitation*, says that Pluvinel's introduction to the pillars was already an attempt to 'bend, supple the neck of the horse, and supple his haunches'.[7] Indeed, continues d'Aure, the difference between the *nouvelle méthode* and the method of Pluvinel is that the former 'breaks and supples indiscriminately all the horses; whereas with the method of Pluvinel, *the prudent and judicious horseman can judge whereof his horse is capable*'.[8] Then, too, the use of the *volte* was one such attempt at flexing the horse. D'Aure and other opponents also objected to the fact that Baucher presented his principles in such absolute and categorical terms, especially since, they felt, he was leaning on principles that were somewhat questionable. But the most damaging criticism levelled against Baucher was that he totally ignored the morale, will and willingness of the horse by disposing so completely of his strength through the use of the *effets d'ensemble* and other means, and thus totally subjugating the horse to the will of the horseman. It was generally believed that Baucher's method, especially his *rassembler*, overbent the horse. It was also felt that the balance imparted to the horse was so forced and artificial, that serious difficulties could occur when one demanded of the horse a constant concentration of forces or when cadence, elevation and extension of the paces were desired. To remedy these difficulties, Baucher recommended *les attaques des éperons*.

It is obvious that the frequent use or misuse of the spurs on the part of the rider, especially the novice, aroused in the horse an undue sensitivity and irritability that often destroyed his posture and clarity of movement.

Due to achievements such as horizontal equilibrium, the horse's equal mobility in all directions, and other suppling methods, all designed for the total containment of the horse by the horseman, Baucher was able to invent new movements such as the backward trot and gallop. At the *passage* he made his horse swing his haunches and shoulders, as well as execute forward and backward movements on the same diagonal. Above all, he perfected the practice of repeated flying changes of lead at the canter.[9]

Despite the criticisms directed at Baucher's *nouvelle méthode*, one must acknowledge his superior ability to be in total command of his horse, especially difficult and misused horses, given the kind of horses with which Baucher had to work, such as Partisan, Géricault and others. Jules Janin, military men such as Oudinot, de Novital, the Duke d'Orléans, and others enthusiastically applauded Baucher's spectacular performances. Jules Janin's articles in *Le Journal des Débats* and *Le National* were as enthusiastic about Baucher as they were about the circus in general. It is ironic that Romanticists like Théophile Gautier, Jules Janin, Eugène Sue and Delacroix (Alexandre Dumas supported d'Aure) opted for Baucher, basically a traditionalist and Classicist, rather than for the innovator d'Aure, the real modernist and Romanticist. Like the general public, they too had become enthusiastic devotees of the circus and were affected by the *tours de force* of Baucher. They, like the general public, may have perceived this controversy more as a battle between *le haut monde* and *le menu peuple*, between an aristocrat and a *petit bourgeois*, a 'victim' of an aristocrat, and less as a battle between traditionalism and modernism, paralleling the conflict between Classicism and Romanticism that beset the age. Without re-

---

[7] D'Aure, *Traité d'Equitation*, pp. xii, xiii.   [8] Ibid., pp. xii, xiii.   [9] Decarpentry, *Academic Equitation*, p. 11.

The influence of d'Aure is shown in this French painting by Alfred de Dreux (1810–1860) of an English Thoroughbred in English tack. (Courtesy Arthur Ackermann and Sons)

alizing it, in their support of Baucher, they were actually upholding traditionalism against modernism in the equestrian conflict.[10]

To explain the temporary support given to Baucher by certain members of the army and other horsemen is more difficult. Undoubtedly their choice of Baucher to teach his *nouvelle méthode* to the officers and NCOs in the French cavalry at Saumur and Lunéville was due to the realization that their men were in need of better training in military horsemanship. Their choice of Baucher and his *nouvelle méthode* was an attempt to remedy this lacuna. Like the general public, they, too, had been swept off their feet by the brilliant performances of Baucher and his horse in the circus.

Baudelaire's definition of Romanticism cited earlier sums up d'Aure's equestrian art and temperament. Equally applicable to the schooling of d'Aure's horse and the training of his horseman is J. L. Talmon's definition of Romanticism: 'Not conscious and elaborate contrivance, but the free and irresistible flow of vital forces . . . and immensely active energy, experiencing the infinitude of reality in a manner wholly his own'.[11] D'Aure was, indeed, an innovator, an individualist and a revolutionary in his field and, as such, can be termed a modernist and Romanticist. But while d'Aure's type of equitation can be described as personal, improvisational, an equitation that often ignored routine and formulae, it was, as with Romanticism itself, not aimless and totally without rules. Both his *Traité d'Equitation* and his later *Cours d'Equitation* reveal method and regularization. Baucher, on the other hand, despite his *nouvelle méthode*, can be termed a Classicist. While introducing new movements and achieving by his method of *assouplissement* total control of the horse by the horseman, his type of equitation, nevertheless, remained within the idiom of the past. Baucher, like the Classicists of the seventeenth and much of the eighteenth centuries, was also spectator oriented, using primarily a stationary equitation. But instead of entertaining royalty and the nobility, Baucher, as circus equerry, was obliged to give the nineteenth-century general public greater thrills and bring in the cash.

While the achievements of both Baucher and d'Aure live on in their writings, it is primarily in the formation of their pupils that their achievements continued to prevail. Equerries such as Colonel Guérin, General Faverot de Kerbrech and General L'Hotte have expressed their indebtedness and gratitude to both men in their own writings and in the training of their pupils. Most important is the fact that especially in Guérin and L'Hotte we witness a synthesis of the equestrian art of Baucher and d'Aure. Their ideas are Baucher and d'Aure rethought and reshaped.

---

[10] It is interesting to note that in the controversy that also existed between Classicism and Romanticism in literature and art during the first half of the nineteenth century, the general public upheld Classicism and traditionalism against Romanticism and modernism.

[11] J. L. Talmon, *Romanticism and Revolt* (London, J. L. Talmon, 1967), p. 142.

Appendix: Le Comte d'Aure

Antoine Cartier d'Aure, first Viscount, then Count, was born in 1799 in Toulouse of a noble family from the region of Comminges. In 1815 he graduated from Saint-Cyr as a first lieutenant of the infantry. A year later he became a member of the *gardes du corps* in Versailles. He was noticed by d'Abzac who recognized his distinction as an outstanding horseman. In 1817 d'Abzac made him *élève-écuyer* in the *manège* of the *Grands Ecuries* of Versailles. He was then named *écuyer caval-cadour* to Louis XVIII and Charles X, whose protégé he became. He soon became known as a dare-devil. He left Versailles for a while to participate in the Spanish expedition of the Duke of Angoulème and for his service was made a *Chevalier de la Légion d'honneur*. He returned to Versailles and upon the death of his mentor d'Abzac he was made *de facto écuyer-en-chef*. In addition to these functions as chief equerry, he showed a keen interest in the raising of horses and wrote on the breeding of horses. He also spent time breaking in and schooling young horses. He experimented with all the innovations emanating from across the Channel: the English saddle, the use of less severe bits such as the snaffle, and the *trot enlevé* (rising trot). While the *trot enlevé* was still not tolerated at Saumur or, for that matter, elsewhere, he continued to pursue it. His association with the rising trot became legendary. D'Aure was also greatly interested in the establishment of an *Ecole Normale d'Equitation* which would form the *cadres civils* (civilian echelons) and the establishment of *haras*

(breeding centres) to further the breeding of horses in France. He wished to instil in his pupils a link between horsemanship and a sound knowledge of hippology, breeding, stable management, and so on.

When the *Ecole de Versailles* closed its doors once and for all in 1830, D'Aure went to Paris to direct in the Rue Cadet, a private fashionable *manège* where he taught the art of riding to, among his many pupils, the three sons of Louis-Philippe: the Dukes d'Orléans, de Nemours, and d'Aumale. He frequented the high society of the turf, the Jockey Club and the racing world. He opened another *manège* in the Rue Duphot. He was lucky to have assembled some of the best horses which he had acquired when the *Ecole de Versailles* closed down. His prestige was such that the *jeunesse dorée* foresook the *manège* of Pellier in order to take lessons from the former equerry of Versailles. Furthermore, his stress on exterior riding and the speed with which he taught his pupils the rudiments of horsemanship, especially the ability to ride as many different horses as possible, increased his prestige and popularity. Nevertheless, he went bankrupt. His acumen as a business manager was, evidently, not very good. He retired to Normandy for a while where he became involved with the breeding of horses.

D'Aure's concept of equitation differed considerably from the pure Classical and *savante* equitation. One of his masters, the Viscount d'Abzac, while continuing to train his pupils in the traditional, Classical and *savante* type of equitation, had already begun to modify and

Count d'Aure, *écuyer-en-chef* at Saumur from 1847 to 1855. (L'Ecole National d'Equitation, Saumur)

simplify equitation. For d'Abzac and other great equerries, the goal and talent of a horseman was to balance a horse, make him supple, and, above all, to regularize and perfect his natural paces. Equally important was the control and guidance of the horse's strength to give him the necessary elasticity of movement. In other words, d'Abzac and later his disciple d'Aure were attempting to school the horse in a manner reminiscent of the kind of schooling already occurring in the latter part of the eighteenth century, especially in Prussia, that is, military equitation. D'Aure, rather than resist this new type of equitation as so many others had done and were still doing, continued in the footsteps of his master and soon placed himself at the head of the new school. Hurdle jumping and obstacle riding began to take an important place in equitation and to replace, if not totally at least in importance, *manège* equitation, the latter becoming a means and no longer an end.

In 1847 d'Aure replaced de Novital as *écuyer-en-chef* at the *Ecole de Cavalerie* at Saumur. He was the last civilian to be granted this position. It was at that time that General L'Hotte met d'Aure and became his disciple and friend. According to L'Hotte, d'Aure resigned from his position when the February Revolution of 1848 occurred which put an end to the Orleanists. After the June Revolution of 1848, which terminated the Socialist provisional government and ushered in a more conservative Republic, d'Aure was given back his position as *écuyer-en-chef* at Saumur which he continued to hold until 1855.

In his *Souvenirs*, L'Hotte describes the grace and skill of d'Aure in the equestrian art.

His position on horseback, one of the most elegant and, usually, far removed from any pretentiousness and affectation, revealed at first glance one of the most privileged equestrian instincts. But it was primarily outside that his equestrian skill appeared in all its glory. And when one saw Count d'Aure, with his great ease, whose legs were neither too tightly held against the horse's sides nor too far out, pass by at full gallop or at a rising trot which he practised with much flexibility and grace, the stirrup totally raised, as he was in the habit of having it, one then had before one's eyes the picture of the ideal horseman of which one dreamed.[1]

While considering d'Aure as a rival, Baucher, nevertheless, admired the grace and skill of d'Aure's horsemanship and once referred to him as a centaur.

Having one's stirrups short was not yet the fashion and most of the well-known equerries kept them long, and since the toe could barely touch the stirrup, it was often lower than the heel. Many equerries who received their formation at the former *Ecole de Versailles* looked at d'Aure's short stirrups with annoyance. Nevertheless, says L'Hotte, 'although an innovator, d'Aure did not value any less the opinions of the men who belonged to the school from which he himself came'.[2] Having one's stirrups short was not necessarily a whim or a desire to be fashionable. He did so out of necessity. Obviously, when riding easy and disciplined horses on a terrain that was gentle and easy, long stirrups were adequate. In fact, as L'Hotte points out, long stirrups were merely an ornament of the foot. But when it came to training a difficult horse, when the terrain was uneven, when one had to jump hurdles, or when one practised the rising trot, short stirrups were a definite advantage. One had more control over oneself and over the horse.

Everyone refers to the tremendous seat d'Aure had. His legs never hung down the sides of the horse. Rather, they were in perfect harmony with the horse, placed in such a way that he could instantly make the right move. The use of his hands on the reins was also legendary. He could manipulate his fingers with great skill. While holding in the left hand all four reins, his crop, his snuffbox and his handkerchief, he managed to guide his horse with ease.

---

[1] L'Hotte, *Souvenirs*, p. 142.   [2] Ibid., p. 144.

PART TWO

New method of horsemanship

by François Baucher
translator unknown

Introduction to the translation

New Method of Horsemanship is a translation of François Baucher's *Méthode d'Equitation basée sur de nouveaux principes*, first published in 1842. The translator of Baucher's *nouvelle méthode* is unknown; equally missing is the date of publication. What we do know is that the translation is based on the ninth edition, that it was published in New York and that the publisher was Albert Cogswell. The first three American editions were published in Philadelphia in 1851, 1852 and 1856; so this one must be later. There is one additional and personal note to the copy we have of the translation, namely, that it bears a dedication to Katherine L. Anderson, 'from her Father', Cincinnati, O., September 28, 1889.

The translator of this American edition has added to the title the phrase 'Including the Breaking and Training of Horses, with Instructions for Obtaining a Good Seat'. The expression I find interesting is the 'breaking' of horses, a term which contradicts Baucher's method, which is to treat the horse with gentle-ness and respect. Furthermore, Baucher did later include some instructions for obtaining a good seat, but these instructions are limited to a few basic points. As Baucher himself mentions, his new method is intended for the training of horsemen who are already competent riders, and, above all, for the schooling of horses.

I have read this translation carefully and compared it to the French original. It is a good translation and denotes familiarity with the *nouvelle méthode* of François Baucher. It goes without saying that the translator is himself a horseman and, most likely, a military man. There are, however, a few expressions that are somewhat archaic. While their meanings are self-evident, I give, nevertheless, the modern terms in the list below.

The translator has been faithful in translating all of Baucher's footnotes, with one exception, namely, when Baucher talks of *l'encapuchonne-ment* of the horse, a position the horse takes when his chin is too close to his chest, as

Baucher's terms	Translator's terms	Modern terms
Rassembler	Gathering the horse	Collection
Effet d'ensemble	Combination of effect	Coordinated effect
Reculer	Backing	Rein-back
Deux pistes	Horse goes on *two lines*	Horse goes on *two tracks* or *treads*
Attaques des éperons	*Touches* with the spurs	*Attacks* with the spurs[1]
Arrière-main	Hind-parts	Hindquarters
Avant-main	Fore-parts	Forehand

---

[1] *Attacks* is stronger, which is one of the reasons why Baucher was criticized so vehemently.

though he is hooded. In this footnote, Baucher compares his concept of equilibrium (which the translator includes) with that of former times and that of d'Aure (both of which the translator omits). The full note has been reinstated here (pp. 116–17), but apart from this the translation has been reprinted as it stands with no change to American spelling and conventions, and only the correction of a handful of printing errors.

Hilda Nelson

1

New means of obtaining a good seat

It may undoubtedly be thought astonishing that, in the first editions of this work, having for its object the horse's education, I should not have commenced by speaking of the rider's seat. In fact, this, so important a part of horsemanship, has always been the basis of classical works on this subject. Nevertheless, it is not without a motive that I have deferred treating of this question until now. Had I had nothing new to say on this subject, I might very easily have managed, by consulting old authors, by transposing a sentence here and changing a word there, to have sent forth into the equestrian world another inutility. But I had other ideas; I wished to make a thorough reform. My system for giving a good seat to the rider, being also an innovation, I feared lest so many new things at one time should alarm even the best intentioned amateurs, and give a hold to my adversaries. They would not have failed to say that my means of managing a horse were impracticable, or that they could not be applied without recourse to a seat still more impracticable. But now I have proved the contrary — that, upon my plan, horses have been broken by troops without regard to the men's seat. To give more force to my method, and render it more easily comprehensible, I have divested it of all accessories, and said nothing about those new principles that concern the rider's seat. I reserved these last until after the indisputable success of the official trials. By means of these principles, added to those I have published upon the art of horse-breaking, I both shorten the man's work, and establish a system not only

precise, but complete in these two important parts of horsemanship, hitherto so confused.

By following my new instructions relating to the man's seat on horseback, we will promptly arrive at a certain result; they are as easy to understand as to demonstrate. Two sentences are sufficient to explain all to the rider, and he will get a good seat by the simple advice of the instructor.

The seat of the rider

The rider will expand his chest as much as possible, so that each part of his body rests upon that next below it, for the purpose of increasing the adhesion of his buttocks to the saddle; the arms will fall easily by the sides. The thighs and legs must, by their own strength, find as many points of contact as possible with the saddle and the horse's sides; the feet will naturally follow the motion of the legs.

You see by these few lines how simple the rider's seat is.

The means which I point out for quickly obtaining a good seat, remove all the difficulties which the plan pursued by our predecessors presented. The pupil used to understand nothing of the long catechism, recited in a loud voice by the instructor, from the first word to the last, consequently he could not execute it. Here one word replaces all those sentences; but we previously go through a course of supplings. This course will make the rider expert, and consequently intelligent. One month will not elapse without the most stupid and awkward recruit being able to seat himself properly without the aid of the word of command.

Preparatory lesson (the lesson to last an hour, two lessons a day for a month)

The horse is led upon the ground, saddled and bridled. The instructor must take two pupils; one will hold the horse by the bridle, all the while watching what the other does, that he may be able to perform in his turn. The pupil will approach the horse's shoulder and prepare to mount; for this purpose he will lay hold of and separate, with the right hand, a handful of mane, and pass it into the left hand, taking hold as near the roots as possible, without twisting them; he will seize the pommel of the saddle with the right hand, the four fingers in, and the thumb outside; then springing lightly, will raise himself upon his wrists. As soon as his middle is the height of the horse's withers, he will pass the right leg over the croup, without touching it, and place himself lightly in the saddle. This vaulting being very useful in making the man active, he should be made to repeat it eight or ten times, before letting him finally seat himself. The repetition of this will soon teach him what he is able to do, using the powers of his arms and loins.

Exercise in the saddle

(This is a stationary exercise on horseback; an old, quiet horse to be chosen in preference; the reins are knotted, and hang on his neck.) The pupil being on horseback, the instructor will examine his natural position, in order to exercise more frequently those parts which have a tendency to give way or stiffen. The lesson will commence with the chest. The instructor will make use of the flexions of the loins, which expand the chest, to straighten the upper part of the pupil's body; he whose loins are slack will be made to hold himself in this position for some time, without regard to the stiffness which

this will bring along with it the first few times. It is by the exertion of force that the pupil will become supple, and not by the *abandon* so much and so uselessly recommended. A movement at first obtained by great effort, will, after a while, not require so much, for he will then have gained skill, and skill, in this case, is but the result of exertions combined and employed properly. What is first done with twenty pounds of force, reduces itself afterwards to fourteen, to ten, to four. Skill will be the exertion reduced to four pounds. If we commenced by a less, we would not attain this result. The flexions of the loins will be often renewed, allowing the pupil often to let himself down into his natural relaxed position, in order to make him properly employ the force that quickly gives a good position to the chest. The body being well placed, the instructor will pass: (1) To the lesson of the arm, which consists in moving it in every direction, first bent, and afterwards extended; (2) To that of the head; this must be turned right and left without its motions reacting on the shoulders.

When the lessons of the chest, arms, and head give a satisfactory result, which ought to be at the end of four days (eight lessons), they will pass to that of the legs.

The pupil will remove one of his thighs as far as possible from the quarters of the saddle; and afterwards replace it with a rotatory movement from without inwards, in order to make it adhere to the saddle by as many points of contact as possible. The instructor will watch that the thigh does not fall back heavily; it should resume its position by a slowly progressive motion, and without a jerk. He ought, moreover, during the first lesson, to take hold of the pupil's leg and direct it, in order to make him understand the proper way of performing this displacement. He will thus save him fatigue, and obtain the result more quickly.

This kind of exercise, very fatiguing at first, requires frequent rests; it would be wrong to prolong the exercise beyond the powers of the pupil. The motions of drawing in (*adduction*, which makes the thigh adhere to the saddle),

François Baucher on horseback. (Paul Morand (ed.) *Anthologie de la litterature equestre* (Paris, Oliver Perrier, 1966))

and putting out (*abduction*, which separates it from the saddle), becoming more easy, the thighs will have acquired a suppleness which will admit of their adherence to the saddle in a good position. Then comes the flexion of the legs.

Flexion of the legs

The instructor will watch that the knees always preserve their perfect adherence to the saddle. The legs will be swung backward and forward like the pendulum of a clock; that is, the pupil will raise them so as to touch the cantle of the saddle with his heels. The repetition of these flexions will soon render the legs supple, pliable and independent of the thighs. The flexions of the legs and thighs will be continued for four days (eight lessons). To make each of these movements more correct and easier, eight days (or sixteen lessons), will be devoted to it. The fifteen days (thirty lessons), which remain to complete the month, will continue to be occupied by the exercise of stationary supplings;

but, in order that the pupil may learn to combine the strength of his arms, and that of his loins, he will be made to hold at arm's length, progressively, weights of from ten to forty pounds. This exercise will be commenced in the least fatiguing position, the arm being bent, and the hand near the shoulder, and this flexion will be continued to the full extent of the arm. The chest should not be affected by this exercise, but be kept steady in the same position.

Of the knees

The strength of pressure of the knees will be judged of, and even obtained, by the aid of the following method: this, which at first sight will perhaps appear of slight importance, will, nevertheless, bring about great results. The instructor will take a narrow piece of leather about twenty inches long; he will place one end of this strap between the pupil's knee and the side of the saddle. The pupil will make use of the force of his knees to prevent its slipping, while the instructor will draw it towards him slowly and progressively. This process will serve as a dynamometer to judge of the increase of power.

The strictest watch must be kept that each force which acts separately does not put other forces in action; that is to say, that the movement of the arms does not influence the shoulders; it should be the same with the thighs, with respect to the body; the legs, with respect to the thighs, etc., etc. The displacement and suppling of each part separately, being obtained, the chest and seat will be temporarily displaced, in order to teach the rider to recover his proper position without assistance. This will be done as follows: the instructor being placed on one side, will push the pupil's hip, so that his seat will be moved out of the seat of the saddle. The instructor will then allow him to get back into the saddle, being careful to watch that, in regaining his seat, he makes use of his hips and knees only, in order to make him use only those parts nearest to his seat. In fact, the aid of the shoulders would soon affect the hand, and this the horse; the assistance of the legs would have still worse results. In a word, in all the displacements, the pupil must be taught not to have recourse in order to direct the horse, to the means which keep him in his seat, and *vice versa*, not to employ, in order to keep his seat, those which direct the horse.

Here, but a month has elapsed, and these equestrian gymnastics have made a rider of a person, who at first may have appeared the most unfit for it. Having mastered the preliminary trials, he will impatiently await the first movements of the horse, to give himself up to them with the ease of an experienced rider.

Fifteen days (thirty lessons) will be devoted to the walk, trot and gallop. Here the pupil should solely endeavor to follow the movements of the horse; therefore, the instructor will oblige him to occupy himself only with his seat, and not attempt to guide the horse. He will only exact that the pupil ride, at first, straight before him, then in every direction, one rein of the snaffle in each hand. At the end of four days (eight lessons), he may be made to take the curb-rein in his left hand.

The right hand, which is now free, must be held alongside of the left, that he may early get the habit of sitting square (with his shoulders on a level); the horse will trot equally to the right and to the left. When the seat is firmly settled at all the paces, the instructor will explain simply, the connection between the wrist and the legs, as well as their separate effects.

Education of the horse

Here the rider will commence the horse's education, by following the progression I have pointed out, and which will be found farther on. The pupil will be made to understand all that there is rational in it, and what an intimate connection exists between the education of the man and that of the horse.

Recapitulation and progression

	Days	Lessons
1. Flexion of the loins to expand the chest	4	8
2. Extending and replacing of the thighs, and flexion of the legs	4	8
3. General exercise of all the parts in succession	8	16
4. Displacement of the man's body, exercise of the knees and arms with weights in the hands	15	30
5. Position of the rider, the horse being at a walk, trot and gallop, in order to fashion and settle the seat at these different paces	15	30
6. Education of the horse by the rider	75	150
Total	121	242

2

Of the forces of the horse

Of their causes and effects

The horse, like all organized beings, is possessed of a weight and a force peculiar to himself. The weight inherent to the material of which the animal is composed, renders the mass inert, and tends to fix it to the ground. The force, on the contrary, by the faculty it gives him of moving this weight, of dividing it, of transferring it from one of his parts to another, communicates movement to his whole being, determines his equilibrium, speed and direction. To make this truth more evident, let us suppose a horse in repose. His body will be in perfect equilibrium, if each of its members supports exactly that part of the weight which devolves upon it in this position. If he wishes to move forward at a walk, he must first transfer that part of the weight resting on the leg he moves first to those that will remain fixed to the ground. It will be the same thing in other paces, the transfer acting from one diagonal to the other in the trot, from the front to the rear, and reciprocally in the gallop. We must not then confound the weight with the force; the latter determines, the former is subordinate to it. It is by carrying the weight from one extremity to the other that the force puts them in motion, or makes them stationary. The slowness or quickness of the transfers fixes the different paces, which are correct or false, even or uneven, according as these transfers are executed with correctness or irregularity.

It is understood that this motive power is subdivided *ad infinitum*, since it is spread over all the muscles of the animal. When the latter

himself determines the use of them, the forces are instinctive; I call them transmitted when they emanate from the rider. In the first case, the man governed by his horse remains the plaything of his caprices; in the second, on the contrary, he makes him a docile instrument, submissive to all the impulses of his will. The horse, then, from the moment he is mounted, should only act by transmitted forces. The invariable application of this principle constitutes the true talent of the horseman.

But such a result cannot be attained instantaneously. The young horse, in freedom, having been accustomed to regulate his own movements, will, at first, submit with difficulty to the strange influence which comes to take the entire control of them. A struggle necessarily ensues between the horse and his rider, who will be overcome unless he is possessed of energy, patience, and, above all, the knowledge necessary to gain his point. The forces of the animal being the element upon which the rider must principally work, first to conquer, and finally to direct them, it is necessary he should fix his attention upon these before anything else. He will study what they are, whence they spring, the parts where they contract the most for resistance, the physical causes which occasion these contractions. When this is discovered, he will proceed with his pupil by means in accordance with his nature, and his progress will then be rapid.

Unfortunately, we search in vain in ancient or modern authors, on horsemanship, I will not say for rational principles, but even for any data in connection with the forces of the horse. All speak very prettily about resistances, oppositions, lightness and equilibrium; but none of them have known how to tell us what causes these resistances, how we can combat them, destroy them, and obtain this lightness and equilibrium they so earnestly recommend. It is this gap that has caused the great doubts and obscurity about the principles of horsemanship; it is this that has made the art stationary so long a time; it is this gap that, I think, I am able to fill up.

And first, I lay down the principle that all the resistances of young horses spring, in the first place, from a physical cause, and that this cause only becomes a moral one by the awkwardness, ignorance and brutality of the rider. In fact, besides the natural stiffness peculiar to all these animals, each of them has a peculiar conformation, the more or less of perfection in which constitutes the degree of harmony that exists between the forces and the weight. The want of this harmony occasions the ungracefulness of their paces, the difficulty of their movements; in a word, all the obstacles to a good education. In a state of freedom, whatever may be the bad structure of the horse, instinct is sufficient to enable him to make such a use of his forces as to maintain his equilibrium; but there are movements it is impossible for him to make until a preparatory exercise shall have put him in the way of supplying the defects of his organization by a better combined use of his motive power. A horse puts himself in motion only in consequence of a given position; if his forces are such as to oppose themselves to this position, they must first be annulled, in order to replace them by the only ones which can lead to it.

Now, I ask, if before overcoming these first obstacles, the rider adds to them the weight of his own body, and his unreasonable demands, will not the animal experience still greater difficulty in executing certain movements? The efforts we make to compel him to submission, being contrary to his nature, will they not find in it an insurmountable obstacle? He will

naturally resist, and with so much the more advantage, that the bad distribution of his forces will of itself be sufficient to paralyze those of the rider. The resistance then emanates, in this case, from a physical cause: which becomes a moral one from the moment when, the struggle going on with the same processes, the horse begins of his own accord to combine means of resisting the torture imposed on him, when we undertake to force into operation parts which have not previously been suppled.

When things get into this state, they can only grow worse. The rider, soon disgusted with the impotence of his efforts, will cast back upon the horse the responsibility of his own ignorance; he will brand as a jade an animal possessing the most brilliant resources, and of whom, with more discernment and tact, he could have made a hackney as docile in character, as graceful and agreeable in his paces. I have often remarked that horses considered indomitable are those which develop the most energy and vigor, when we know how to remedy those physical defects which prevent their making use of them. As to those which, in spite of their bad formation, are by a similar system made to show a semblance of obedience, we need thank nothing but the softness of their nature; if they can be made to submit to the simplest exercises, it is only on condition that we do not demand anything more of them, for they would soon find their energy again to resist any further attempts. The rider can then make them go along at different paces to be sure; but how disconnected, how stiff, how ungraceful in their movements, and how ridiculous such steeds make their unfortunate riders look, as they toss them about at will, instead of being guided by them! This state of things is all perfectly natural, unless we destroy the first cause of it: *the bad distribution of their forces, and the stiffness caused by a bad conformation.*

But, it is objected, since you allow that these difficulties are caused by the formation of the horse, how is it possible to remedy them? You do not possibly pretend to change the structure of the animal and reform the work of nature? Undoubtedly not; but while I confess that it is impossible to give more breadth to a narrow chest, to lengthen too short a neck, to lower too high a croup, to shorten and fill out long, weak, narrow loins, I do not the less insist that if I prevent the different contractions occasioned by these physical defects, if I supply the muscles, if I make myself master of the forces so as to use them at will, it will be easy for me to prevent these resistances, to give more action to the weak parts, and to moderate those that are too vigorous, and thus make up for the deficiencies of nature.

Such results, I do not hesitate to say, were and still are forever denied to the old methods. But if the science of those who follow the old beaten track finds so constant an obstacle in the great number of horses of defective formation, there are, unfortunately, some horses who, by the perfection of their organization, and the consequent facility of their education, contribute greatly to perpetuate the impotent routines that have been so unfavorable to the progress of horsemanship. A well constituted horse is one, all of whose parts being regularly harmonized, induce the perfect equilibrium of the whole. It would be as difficult for such a subject to leave this natural equilibrium, and take up an improper position for the purpose of resistance, as it is at first painful for the badly formed horse to come into that just distribution of forces, without which no regularity of movement can be hoped for.

It is then only in the education of these last that the real difficulties of horsemanship consist. With the others the breaking ought to be, so to say, instantaneous, since all the springs being in their places, there is nothing to be done but to put them in motion; this result is always obtained by my method. Yet the old principles demand two or three years to reach this point, and when by feeling your way without any certainty of success, the horseman gifted with some tact and experience, ends by accustoming the horse to obey the impressions communicated to him, he imagines that he

has surmounted great difficulties, and attributes to his skill a state so near that of nature that correct principles would have obtained it in a few days. Then as the animal continues to display in all his movements the grace and lightness natural to his beautiful formation, the rider does not scruple to take all the merit to himself, thus showing himself as presumptuous in this case as he was unjust when he would make the badly formed horse responsible for the failure of his attempts.

If we once admit these truths:

That the education of the horse consists in the complete subjection of his powers;
That we can only make use of his powers at will by annulling all resistances;
And that these resistances have their source in the contractions occasioned by physical defects;

The only thing will be to seek out the parts where these contractions operate, in order to endeavor to oppose and destroy them.

Long and conscientious observations have shown me that, whatever be the fault of formation that in the horse prevents a just distribution of his forces, it is always in the neck that the most immediate effect is felt. There is no improper movement, no resistance that is not preceded by the contraction of this part of the animal; and as the jaw is intimately connected with the neck, the stiffness of the one is instantly communicated to the other. These two points are the prop upon which the horse rests, in order to annul all the rider's efforts. We can easily conceive the immense obstacle they must present to the impulsions of the latter, since the neck and head, being the two principal levers by which we direct the animal, it is impossible to obtain anything from him until we are master of these first and indispensable means of action. Behind, the parts where the forces contract the most for resistance, are the loins and the croup (the haunches).

The contractions of these two opposite extremities are, mutually the one to the other, causes and effects, that is to say, the stiffness of the neck induces that of the haunches, and reciprocally. We can combat the one by the other; and as soon as we have succeeded in annulling them, as soon as we have re- established the equilibrium and harmony that they prevented between the fore and hind-parts, the education of the horse will be half finished. I will now point out the means of infallibly arriving at this result.

3

The supplings

This work being an exposition of a method which upsets most of the old principles of horsemanship, it is understood that I only address men already conversant with the art, and who join to an assured seat a sufficiently great familiarity with the horse, to understand all that concerns his mechanism. I will not, then, revert to the elementary processes; it is for the instructor to judge if his pupil possesses a proper degree of solidity of seat, and is sufficiently a part of the horse; for at the same time that a good seat produces this identification, it favors the easy and regular play of the rider's extremities.

My present object is to treat principally of the education of the horse; but this education is too intimately bound up in that of the rider, for him to make much progress in one without the other. In explaining the processes which should produce perfection in the animal, I will necessarily teach the horseman to apply them himself; he will only have to practise tomorrow what I teach him today. Nevertheless, there is one thing that no precept can give; that is, a fineness of touch, a delicacy of equestrian feeling that belongs only to certain privileged organizations, and without which, we seek in vain to pass certain limits. Having said this, we will return to our subject.

We now know which are the parts of the horse that contract the most in resistances, and we feel the necessity of suppling them. Shall we then seek to attack, exercise and conquer them all at once? No; this would be to fall back into the old error, of the inefficiency of which we are convinced. The animal's muscular power is infinitely superior to ours; his instinctive forces, moreover, being able to sustain themselves the one by the others, we will inevitably be conquered if we set them in motion all at once. Since the contractions have their seat in separate parts, let us profit by this division to combat them separately, as a skillful general destroys, in detail, forces which, when together, he would be unable to resist.

For the rest, whatever the age, the disposition, and the structure of my pupil, my course of proceeding at the start will be always the same. The results will only be more or less prompt and easy, according to the degree of perfection in his nature, and the influence of the hand to which he has been previously subjected. The suppling, which will have no other object in the case of a well-made horse than that of preparing his forces to yield to our impulsions, will re-establish calm and confidence in a horse that has been badly handled, and in a defective formation will make those contractions disappear, which are the causes of resistances, and the only obstacles to a perfect equilibrium. The difficulties to be surmounted will be in proportion to this complication of obstacles, and will quickly disappear with a little perseverance on our part. In the progression we are about to pursue in order to subject the different parts of the animal to suppling, we will naturally commence with the most important parts, that is to say, with the jaw and neck.

The head and neck of the horse are at once the rudder and compass of the rider. By them he directs the animal; by them, also, he can judge of the regularity and precision of his movements. The equilibrium of the whole body is perfect, its lightness complete, when the head and neck remain of themselves easy, pliable and graceful. On the contrary, there can be no elegance, no ease of the whole, when these two parts are stiff. Preceding the body of the horse in all its impulsions, they ought to give warning, and show by their attitude the positions to be taken, and the movements to be executed. The rider has no power so long as they remain contracted and rebellious; he disposes of the animal at will, when once they are flexible and easily handled. If the head and neck do not first commence the changes of direction, if in circular movements they are not inclined in a curved line, if in backing they do not bend back upon themselves, and if their lightness is not always in harmony with the different paces at which we wish to go, the horse will be free to execute these movements or not, since he will remain master of the employment of his own forces.

From the time I first noticed the powerful influence that the stiffness of the neck exercises on the whole mechanism of the horse, I attentively sought the means to remedy it. The resistances to the hand are always either sideways, upward or downward. I at first considered the neck alone as the source of these resistances, and exercised myself in suppling the animal by flexions, repeated in every direction. The result was immense; but, although, at the end of a certain time, the supplings of the neck rendered me perfectly master of the forces of the foreparts of the horse, I still felt a slight resistance which I could not at first account for. At last I discovered that it proceeded from the jaw. The flexibility I had communicated to the neck even aided this stiffness of the muscles of the lower jaw, by permitting the horse in certain cases to escape the action of the bit. I then bethought me of the means of combating these resistances in this, their last stronghold; and, from that time, it is there I always commence my work of suppling.

First exercise on foot
Means of making the horse come to the man, of making him steady to mount, etc., etc.

Before commencing the exercises of flexions, it is essential to give the horse a first lesson of subjection, and teach him to recognize the power of man. This first act of submission, which might appear unimportant, will have the effect of quickly rendering him calm, of giving him confidence, and of repressing all those movements which might distract his attention, and mar the success of the commencement of his education.

Two lessons, of a half hour each, will suffice to obtain the preparatory obedience of every horse. The pleasure we experience in thus playing with him will naturally lead the rider to continue this exercise for a few moments each day, and make it both instructive to the horse and useful to himself. The mode of proceeding is as follows: the rider will approach the horse, his whip under his arm, without roughness or timidity; he will speak to him without raising the voice too much, and will pat him on the face and neck; then with the left hand will lay hold of the curb-reins, about six or seven inches from the branches of the bit, keeping his wrist stiff, so as to present as much force as possible when the horse resists. The whip will be held firmly in the right hand, the point towards the ground, then slowly raised as high as his chest, in order to tap it at intervals of a second. The first natural movement of the horse will be to withdraw from the direction in which the pain comes; it is by backing that he will endeavor to do this. The rider will follow this backward movement without discontinuing the firm tension of the reins, nor the little taps with the whip on the breast, applying them all the time with the same degree of intensity. The rider should be perfectly self-possessed, that there may be no indication of anger or weakness in his motions or looks. Becoming tired of this constraint, the horse will soon seek by another movement to avoid the infliction, and it is by coming forward that he will arrive at it; the rider will seize this second instinctive movement to stop and caress the animal with his hand and voice. The repetition of this exercise will give the most surprising results, even in the first lesson. The horse having discovered and understood the means by which he can avoid the pain, will not wait till the whip touches him, he will anticipate it by rushing forward at the least gesture. The rider will take advantage of this to effect, by a downward force of the bridle hand, the depression of the neck, and the getting him in hand; he will thus early dispose the horse for the exercises that are to follow.

This training, besides being a great re-creation, will serve to make the horse steady to mount, will greatly abridge his education and accelerate the development of his intelligence. Should the horse, by reason of his restless or wild nature, become very unruly, we should have recourse to the cavesson, as a means of repressing his disorderly movements, and use it with little jerks. I would add that it requires great prudence and discernment to use it with tact and moderation.

Flexion of the jaw

The flexions of the jaw, as well as the two flexions of the neck which follow, are executed standing still, the man on foot. The horse will be led on the ground saddled and bridled, the reins on his neck. The man will first see that the bit is properly placed in the horse's mouth, and that the curb-chain is fastened so that he can introduce his finger between the links and the horse's chin. Then looking the animal good-naturedly in the eyes, he will place himself before him near his head, holding his body straight and firm, his feet a little apart to steady

himself, and dispose himself to struggle with advantage against all resistances.[1]

(1) In order to execute the flexion to the right, the man will take hold of the right curb-rein with the right hand, at about six inches from the branch of the bit, and the left rein with the left hand, at only three inches from the left branch. He will then draw his right hand towards his body, pushing out his left hand so as to turn the bit in the horse's mouth. The force employed ought to be entirely determined by and proportioned to the resistance of the jaw and neck only, in order not to affect the *aplomb*, which keeps his body still. If the horse backs to avoid the flexion, the opposition of the hands should still be continued. If the preceding exercise has been completely and carefully practised, it will be easy by the aid of the whip to prevent this retrograde movement, which is a great obstacle to all kinds of flexions of the jaw and neck (Fig. 1).

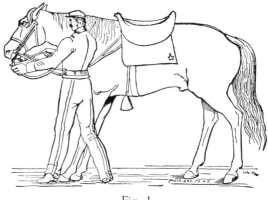

Fig. 1

(2) As soon as the flexion is obtained, the left hand will let the left rein slip to the same length as the right, then drawing the two reins equally will bring the head near to the breast, in order to hold it there oblique and perpendicular, until it sustains itself without assistance in this position. The horse by champing the bit will show his being in hand as well as his

---

[1] I have divided all the flexions into two parts, and, in order to facilitate the understanding of the text, I have added to it plates representing the position of the horse at the moment the flexion is about to commence, and at the moment it is terminated.

perfect submission. The man, to reward him, will cease drawing on the reins immediately, and after some seconds will allow him to resume his natural position (Fig. 2).

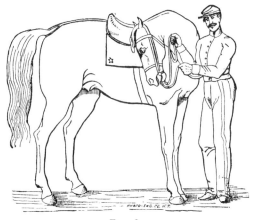

Fig. 2

The flexion of the jaw to the left is executed upon the same principles and by inverse means to the flexion to the right, the man being careful to pass alternately from one to the other.

The importance of these flexions of the jaw is easily understood. The result of them is to prepare the horse to yield instantly to the lightest pressure of the bit, and to supple directly the muscles that join the head to the neck. As the head ought to precede and determine the different attitudes of the neck, it is indispensable that the latter part be always in subjection to the other, and respond to its impulsions. That would be only partially the case with the flexibility of the neck alone, which would then make the head obey it, by drawing it along in its movements. You see, then, why at first I experienced resistances, in spite of the pliability of the neck, of which I could not imagine the cause. The followers of my method to whom I have not yet had an opportunity of making known the new means just explained, will learn with pleasure that this process not only brings the flexibility of the neck to a greater degree of perfection, but saves much time in finishing the suppling. The exercise of the jaw, while fashioning the mouth and head, brings along with it the flexion of the neck, and accelerates the getting the horse in hand.

This exercise is the first of our attempts to accustom the forces of the horse to yield to ours. It is necessary, then, to manage it very nicely, so as not to discourage him at first. To enter on the flexion roughly would be to shock the animal's intelligence, who would not have had time to comprehend what was required of him. The opposition of the hands will be commenced gently but firmly, not to cease until perfect obedience is obtained, except, indeed, the horse backs against a wall, or into a corner; but it will diminish or increase its effect in proportion to the resistance, in a way always to govern it, but not with too great violence. The horse that at first will, perhaps, submit with difficulty, will end by regarding the man's hand as an irresistible regulator, and will become so used to obeying it, that he will soon obtain, by a simple pressure of the rein, what at first required the whole strength of our arms.

At each renewal of the lateral flexions some progress will be made in the obedience of the horse. As soon as his first resistances are a little diminished, we will pass to the perpendicular flexions or depression of the neck.

Depression of the neck by the direct flexion of the jaw

(1) The man will place himself as for the lateral flexions of the jaw; he will take hold of the reins of the snaffle with the left hand, at six inches from the rings, and the curb-reins at about two inches from the bit. He will oppose the two hands by effecting the depression with the left and the proper position with the right (Fig. 3).

(2) As soon as the horse's head shall fall of its own accord and by its own weight, the man will instantly cease all kind of force, and allow the animal to resume his natural position (Fig. 4).

This exercise being often repeated, will soon bring about the suppling of the elevating muscles of the neck, which play a prominent

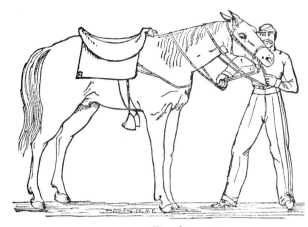

Fig. 3

Fig. 4

that the pliability and flexibility, especially necessary in the upper part of the neck, should be transmitted throughout its whole extent, so as to destroy its stiffness entirely.

The force from above downward, practised with the snaffle, acting only by the headstall on the top of the head, often takes too long to make the horse lower his head. In this case, we must cross the two snaffle-reins by taking the left rein in the right, and the right rein in the left hand, about six or seven inches from the horse's mouth, in such a way as to cause a pretty strong pressure upon the chin. This force, like all the others, must be continued until the horse yields. The flexions being repeated with this more powerful agent, will put him in a condition to respond to the means previously indicated. If the horse responded to the first flexions represented by Fig. 4, it would be unnecessary to make use of this one (Fig. 5).

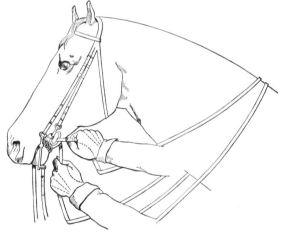

Fig. 5

part in the resistances of the horse, and will besides facilitate the direct flexions and the getting the head in position, which should follow the lateral flexions. The man can execute this, as well as the preceding exercise, by himself; yet it would be well to put a second person in the saddle, in order to accustom the horse to the exercise of the supplings with a rider. This rider should just hold the snaffle-reins, without drawing on them, in his right hand, the nails downward.

The flexions of the jaw have already communicated suppleness to the upper part of the neck, but we have obtained it by means of a powerful and direct motive power, and we must accustom the horse to yield to a less direct regulating force. Besides, it is important

We can act directly on the jaw so as to render it prompt in moving. To do this, we take the left curb-rein about six inches from the horse's mouth and draw it straight towards the left shoulder; at the same time draw the left rein of the snaffle forward, in such a way that the wrists of the person holding the two reins shall be opposite and on a level with each other. The two opposed forces will soon cause a separation of the jaws and end all resistance.

The force ought to be always proportioned to that of the horse, whether in his resistance, or in his lightness. Thus, by means of this direct force a few lessons will be sufficient to give a pliability to the part in question that could not have been obtained by any other means (Fig. 6).

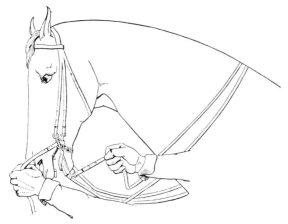

Fig. 6

Lateral flexions of the neck

(1) The man will place himself near the horse's shoulder as for the flexions of the jaw; he will take hold of the right snaffle-rein, which he will draw upon across the neck, in order to establish an intermediate point between the impulsion that comes from him and the resistance the horse presents; he will hold up the left rein with the left hand about a foot from the bit. As soon as the horse endeavors to avoid the constant tension of the right rein by inclining his head to the right, he will let the left rein slip so as to offer no opposition to the flexion of the neck. Whenever the horse endeavors to escape the constraint of the right rein by bringing his croup around, he will be brought into place again by slight pulls of the left rein (Fig. 7).

(2) When the head and neck have entirely yielded to the right, the man will draw equally on both reins to place the head perpendicularly. Suppleness and lightness will soon follow this position, and as soon as the horse evinces, by champing the bit, entire freedom from stiffness,

Fig. 7

the man will cease the tension of the reins, being careful that the head does not take advantage of this moment of freedom to displace itself suddenly. In this case, it will be sufficient to restrain it by a slight support of the right rein. After having kept the horse in this position for some seconds, he will make him resume his former position by drawing on the left rein. It is most important that the animal in all his movements should do nothing of his own accord (Fig. 8).

Fig. 8

The flexion of the neck to the left is executed after the same principles, but by inverse means. The man can repeat with the curb what he has previously done with the snaffle-reins; but the snaffle should always be employed first, its effect being less powerful and more direct.

When the horse submits without resistance to the preceding exercises, it will prove that the suppling of the neck has already made a great step. The rider can, henceforward, continue his work by operating with a less direct motive power, and without the animal's being impressed by the sight of him. He will place himself in the saddle, and commence by repeating with the full length of the reins, the lateral flexions, in which he has already exercised his horse.

Lateral flexions of the neck, the man on horseback

(1) To execute the flexion to the right, the rider will take one snaffle-rein in each hand, the left scarcely feeling the bit; the right, on the contrary, giving a moderate impression at first, but which will increase in proportion to the resistance of the horse, and in a way always to govern him. The animal, soon tired of a struggle which, being prolonged, only makes the pain proceeding from the bit more acute, will understand that the only way to avoid it is to incline the head in the direction the pressure is felt (Fig. 9).

Fig. 9

(2) As soon as the horse's head is brought round to the right, the left rein will form opposition, to prevent the nose from passing beyond the perpendicular. Great stress should be laid on the head's remaining always in this position, without which the flexion would be imperfect and the suppleness incomplete. The movement being regularly accomplished, the horse will be made to resume his natural position by a slight tension of the left rein (Fig. 10).

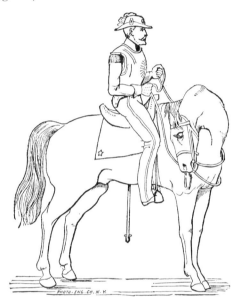

Fig. 10

The flexion to the left is executed in the same way, the rider employing alternately the snaffle and curb-reins.

I have already mentioned that it is of great importance to supple the upper part of the neck. After mounting and having obtained the lateral flexions without resistance, the rider will often content himself with executing them half-way, the head and upper part of the neck pivoting upon the lower part, which will serve as a base or axis. This exercise must be frequently repeated, even after the horse's education is completed, in order to keep up the pliability, and facilitate the getting him in hand.

It now remains for us, in order to complete the suppling of the head and neck, to combat the contractions which occasion the direct resistances, and prevent your getting the horse's head in a perpendicular position.

Direct flexions of the head and neck, or ramener[2]

(1) The rider will first use the snaffle-reins, which he will hold together in the left hand as he would the curb-reins. He will rest the outer edge of the right hand (see Fig. 11) on the reins in front of the left hand in order to increase the power of the right hand; after which he will gradually bear on the snaffle-bit. As soon as the horse yields, it would suffice to raise the right hand to diminish the tension of the reins and reward the animal. As the hand must only present a force proportioned to the resistance of the neck, it will only be necessary to hold the legs rather close to prevent backing. When the horse obeys the action of the snaffle, he will yield much more quickly to that of the curb, the effect of which is so much more powerful. The curb, of course, needs more care in the use of it than the snaffle (Fig. 11).

Fig. 11

(2) The horse will have completely yielded to the action of the hand, when his head is carried in a position perfectly perpendicular to the ground; from that time the contraction will cease, which the animal will show, as in every other case, by champing his bit. The rider must be careful not to be deceived by the feints of the horse — feints which consist in yielding one-fourth or one-third of the way, and then hesitating. If, for example, the nose of the horse having to pass over a curve of ten degrees to attain the perpendicular position (Fig. 11), should stop at the fourth or sixth and again resist, the hand should follow the movement and then remain firm and immovable, for a concession on its part would encourage resistance and increase the difficulties. When the nose shall descend to No. 10, the perpendicular position will be complete and the lightness perfect. The rider can then cease the tension of the reins, but so as to keep the head in this position, if it should offer to leave it. If he lets it return at all to its natural situation, it should be to draw it in over again, and to make the animal understand that the perpendicular position of the head is the only one allowed when under the rider's hand. He should, at the outset, accustom the horse to cease backing at the pressure of the legs, as all backward movements would enable him to avoid the effects of the hand or create new means of resistance (Fig. 12).

This is the most important flexion of all; the others tended principally to pave the way for it. As soon as it is executed with ease and promptness, as soon as a slight touch is sufficient to place and keep the head in a perpendicular position, it will prove that the suppling is complete, contraction destroyed, lightness and equilibrium established in the fore-hand. The direction of this part of the animal will, henceforward, be as easy as it is natural, since we have put it in a condition to receive all our impressions, and instantly to yield to them without effort.

[2] *Ramener* means to place the horse's head in a perpendicular position. [TRANSLATOR.]

Fig. 12

As to the functions of the legs, they must support the hind-parts of the horse, in order to obtain the *ramener*, in such a way that he may not be able to avoid the effect of the hand by a retrograde movement of his body. This complete getting in hand is necessary to drive the hind-legs under the centre. In the first case, we act upon the fore-hand; in the second, upon the hind-parts; the first serves for the *ramener*, the second for the *rassembler*, or gathering the horse.[3]

Combination of effects

I published four editions of my Method, without devoting a special article to the combination of effects. Although I myself made a very frequent use of it, I had not attached sufficient importance to the great necessity of this principle in the case of teaching; later experiments have taught me to consider it of more consequence.

The combination of effects means the continued and exactly opposed force of the hand and legs. Its object should be to bring back

again into a position of equilibrium all the parts of the horse which leave it, in order to prevent him from going ahead, without backing him, and *vice versa*; finally, it serves to stop any movement from the right to the left, or the left to the right. By this means, also, we distribute the weight of the mass equally on the four legs, and produce temporary immobility. This combination of effects ought to precede and follow each exercise within the graduated limit assigned to it. It is essential when we employ the aids (i.e. the hand and legs), in this, that the action of the legs should precede the other, in order to prevent the horse from backing against any place, for he might find, in this movement, points of support that would enable him to increase his resistance. Thus, all motion of the extremities, proceeding from the horse himself, should be stopped by a combination of effects; finally, whenever his forces get scattered, and act inharmoniously, the rider will find in this a powerful and infallible corrective.

It is by disposing all the parts of the horse in the most exact order, that we will easily transmit to him the impulsion that should cause the regular movements of his extremities; it is then also that we will address his comprehension, and that he will appreciate what we demand of him; then will follow caresses of the hand and voice as a moral effect; they should not be used, though, until after he has done what is demanded of him by the rider's hand and legs.

The horse's resting his chin on his breast

Although few horses are disposed by nature to do this, it is not the less necessary, when it does occur, to practise on them all the flexions, even the one which bends down the neck. In this position, the horse's chin comes back near the breast and rests in contact with the lower part of the neck; too high a croup, joined to

---

[3] The full meaning of the word *rassembler* will be understood after reading the chapter, further on in this work, under that head. With regard to the other word, *ramener*, to avoid the constant circumlocution of saying, 'placing the horse's head in a perpendicular position', it will be used in future wherever it occurs. [TRANSLATOR.]

a permanent contraction of the muscles that lower the neck, is generally the cause of it. These muscles must then be suppled in order to destroy their intensity, and thereby give to the muscles that raise the neck, their antagonists, the predominance which will make the neck rest in a graceful and useful position. This first accomplished, the horse will be accustomed to go forward freely at the pressure of the legs, and to respond, without abruptness or excitement, to the touch of the spurs (*attaques*); the object of these last is to bring the hind legs near the centre, and to lower the croup. The rider will then endeavor to raise the horse's head by the aid of the curb-reins; in this case, the hand will be held some distance above the saddle, and far from the body;[4] the force it transmits to the horse ought to be continued until he yields by elevating his head. As these sorts of horses have generally little action, we must take care to avoid letting the hand produce an effect from the front to the rear, in which case it would take away from the impulse necessary for movement. The pace commencing with the walk, must be kept up at the same rate, while the hand is producing an elevating effect upon the neck. This precept is applicable to all the changes of position that the hand makes in the head and neck; but is particularly essential in the case of a horse disposed to depress his neck.

It should be remembered that the horse has two ways of responding to the pressure of the bit; by one, he yields but withdraws himself at the same time by shrinking and coming back to his former position; this kind of yielding is only injurious to his education, for if the hand is held too forcibly, if he does not wait till the horse changes of his own accord the position of his head, the backward movement of his body would precede and be accompanied by a shifting of the weight backwards. In this case, the contraction of his neck remains all the while the same. The second kind of yielding, which contributes so greatly to the rapid and certain education of the horse, consists in giving a half or three-quarter tension to the reins, then to sustain the hand as forcibly as possible without bringing it near the body. In a short time the force of the hand, seconded by the continued pressure of the legs, will make the horse avoid this slight but constant pressure of the bit, but by means of his head and neck only. Then the rider will only make use of the force necessary to displace the head. It is by this means that he will be able to place the horse's body on a level, and will obtain that equilibrium,[5] the

---

[4] This position of the hand at a distance from the saddle and the body will be criticized; but let the rider be reassured, eight or ten lessons will suffice to make the horse change the position of his head, and allow the hand to resume its normal position.

[5] The word equilibrium, so often repeated in the course of this work, must be categorically explained. People have never rightly understood what it means, this true equilibrium of a horse, which serves as the basis of his education, and by which he takes instantly, at the rider's will, such a pace, or such a change of direction.

It is not here a question of the equilibrium which prevents the horse from falling down, but of that upon which depends his performance, when it is prompt, graceful and regular, and by means of which his paces are either measured or extended at will.

All the practitioners who have written about equitation are far from being in agreement on the subject of equilibrium. Former equitation (like German equitation) and up to that of M. d'Aure, defined equilibrium when a horse constantly went on his haunches, his hindlegs giving the impression that they are nailed to the ground, and his forelegs raised considerably.

It is clear to what extent a position that is perpetually reversed is unsound and dangerous, even in the hands of an expert, for it compromises the hindquarters by allowing, as I stated earlier, only a shorter trot, low behind and raised in front.

Equilibrium of former equitation

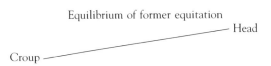

M. d'Aure, while calling to his aid the principles of his predecessors, totally destroys their method of equitation. He gives a reversed direction to the equilibrium of a horse; he does not put a horse on the haunches, he throws him on his shoulders.

perfect balance of which has not hitherto been appreciated.

Resuming what we have just explained in the case of a horse who rests his chin on his breast, we repeat that it is by producing one force from the rear to the front with the legs, and another from below upwards with the hand, that we will soon be enabled to improve the position and movements of the horse. So that whatever may be his disposition at first, it is by first causing the depression of the neck that we will quickly gain a masterly and perfect elevation of it.

I will close this chapter by some reflections on the supposed difference of sensibility in horses' mouths, and the kind of bit which ought to be used.

Of the horse's mouth and the bit

I have already treated this subject at length in my *Comprehensive Dictionary of Equitation*; but as in this work I make a complete exposition of my method, I think it necessary to repeat it in a few words.

I cannot imagine how people have been able so long to attribute to the mere difference of formation of the bars,[6] those contrary dispositions of horses which render them so light or so hard to the hand. How can we believe that, according as a horse has one or two lines of flesh, more or less, between the bit and the bone of the lower jaw, he should yield to the lightest impulse of the hand, or become unmanageable in spite of all the efforts of two vigorous arms? Nevertheless, it is from remaining in this inconceivable error, that

people have forged bits of so strange and various forms, real instruments of torture, the effect of which is to increase the difficulties they sought to remove.

Had they gone back a little further to the source of the resistances, they would have discovered that this one, like all the rest, does not proceed from the difference of formation of a feeble organ, like the bars, but from a contraction communicated to the different parts of the body, and, above all, to the neck, by some serious fault of constitution. It is, then, in vain that we attach to the reins, and place in the horse's mouth a more or less murderous instrument; he will remain insensible to our efforts as long as we do not communicate suppleness to him, which alone can enable him to yield.

In the first place, then, I lay down as a fact, that there is no difference of sensibility in the mouths of horses; that all present the same lightness when in the position called *ramener*, and the same resistances in proportion as they recede from this position. There are horses hard to the hand; but this hardness proceeds from the length or weakness of their loins, from a narrow croup, from short haunches, thin thighs, straight hocks, or (a most important point) from a croup too high or too low in proportion to the withers; such are the true causes of resistances; the contractions of the neck, the closing of the jaws are only the effects; as to the bars, they are only there to show the ignorance of self-styled equestrian theoreticians. By suppling the neck and the jaw, this hardness completely disappears. Experiments a hundred times repeated give

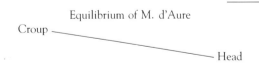

Equilibrium of M. d'Aure

This is a new way of paralysing the total potential of the horse.

Equilibrium of Baucher

Croup————————————Head

Here the weight and the forces are equally distributed. By means of this just distribution the different positions, the different paces, and the equilibriums that belong to them, are obtained without effort on the part of man or horse.

[6] The bars are the continuations of the two bones of the lower jaw between the masticating and the front teeth. It is on these that the bit rests.

me the right to advance this principle boldly; perhaps it may, at first, appear too arbitrary, but it is none the less true.

Consequently, I only allow one kind of bit, and this is the form and the dimensions I give it, to make it as simple as it is easy.

The branches straight and six inches long, measuring from the eye of the bit to the extremity of the branch; circumference of the canon,[7] two inches and a half; port, about two inches wide at the bottom, and one inch at the top. The only variation to be in the width of the bit, according to the horse's mouth.

I insist that such a bit is sufficient to render passively obedient all horses that have been prepared by supplings; and I need not add that, as I deny the utility of severe bits, I reject all means not coming directly from the rider, such as martingales, *piliers*, etc.

---

[7] The mouth-piece of the bit consists of three parts: the port, to give freedom to the tongue, and the two canons, which are the parts that come in contact with the bars. [TRANSLATOR.]

4

Continuation of supplings

The hind-parts

In order to guide the horse, the rider acts directly on two of his parts: the fore-parts and the hind-parts. To effect this, he employs two motive powers: the legs, which give the impulse by the croup; and the hand, which directs and modifies this impulse by the head and neck. A perfect harmony of forces ought then to exist always between these two motive powers; but the same harmony is equally necessary between the parts of the animal they are intended particularly to impress. In vain would be our labor to render the head and neck flexible, light, obedient to the touch of the hand; incomplete would be the results, the equilibrium of the whole imperfect, as long as the croup remained dull, contracted and rebellious to the direct governing agent.

I have just explained the simple and easy means of giving to the fore-parts the qualities indispensable to a good management thereof: it remains to tell how we will fashion, in the same way, the hind-parts, in order to complete the suppling of the horse, and bring about a uniform harmony in the development of all his moving parts. The resistances of the neck and croup mutually aiding one another, our labor will be more easy, as we have already destroyed the former.

The flexions of the croup, and making it movable

(1) The rider will hold the curb-reins in the left hand, and those of the snaffle, crossed, in the right, the nails of the right hand held downward; he will first bring the horse's head into a perpendicular position, by drawing lightly on the bit; after that, if he wishes to execute the movement to the right, he will carry the left leg back behind the girths and fix it near the flanks of the animal, until the croup yields to this pressure. The rider will at the same time make the left snaffle-rein felt, proportioning the effect of the rein to the resistance which is opposed to it. Of these two forces transmitted thus by the left leg and the rein of the same side, the first is intended to combat the resistance, and the second, to determine the movement. The rider should content himself in the beginning with making the croup execute one or two steps only sideways (Fig. 13).

Fig. 13

— 119 —

(2) The croup having acquired more facility in moving, we can continue the movement so as to complete to the right and the left reversed pirouettes.[1] As soon as the haunches yield to the pressure of the leg, the rider, to cause the perfect equilibrium of the horse, will immediately draw upon the rein opposite to this leg. The motion of this, slight at first, will be progressively increased until the head is inclined to the side towards which the croup is moving, as if to look at it coming (Fig. 14).

Fig. 14

To make this movement understood, I will add some explanations, the more important as they are applicable to all the exercises of horsemanship.

The horse, in all his movements, cannot preserve a perfect and constant equilibrium, without a combination of opposite forces, skillfully managed by the rider. In the reversed pirouette, for example, if when the horse has yielded to the pressure of the leg, we continue to oppose the rein on the same side as this leg, it is evident that we will shoot beyond the mark, since we will be employing a force which has become useless. We must then establish two motive powers, the effect of which

balances, without interfering; this, the tension of the rein on the opposite side from the leg will produce in the pirouette. So, we will commence with the rein and the leg of the same side, until it is time to pass to the second part of the work, then with the curb-rein in the left hand, and finally, with the snaffle-rein opposite to the leg. The forces will then be kept in a diagonal position, and in consequence, the equilibrium natural, and the execution of the movement easy. The horse's head being turned to the side where the croup is moving, adds much to the gracefulness of the performance, and aids the rider in regulating the activity of the haunches, and keeping the shoulders in place. For the rest, tact alone will be able to show him how to use the leg and the rein, in such a way that their motions will mutually sustain, without at any time counteracting one another.

I need not remind you that during the whole of this exercise, as on all occasions, the neck should remain supple and light; the head in position (perpendicular) and the jaw movable. While the bridle hand keeps them in this proper position, the right hand, with the aid of the snaffle, is combating the lateral resistances, and determining the different inclinations, until the horse is sufficiently well broken to obey a simple pressure of the bit. If, when combating the contraction of the croup, we permitted the horse to throw its stiffness into the fore-parts, our efforts would be vain, and the fruit of our first labors lost. On the contrary, we will facilitate the subjection of the hind-parts, by preserving the advantages we have already acquired over the fore-parts, and by keeping separated those contractions we have yet to combat.

The leg of the rider opposite to that which determines the rotation of the croup, must not be kept off during the movement, but remain close to the horse and keep him in place, while giving from the rear forward an impulse which the other leg communicates from right to left,

---

[1] See note 3 below.

or from left to right. There will thus be one force which keeps the horse in position, and another which determines the rotation. In order that the pressure of the two legs should not counteract one another, and in order to be able to use them both together, the leg intended to move the croup will be placed farther behind the girths than the other, which will remain held with a force equal to that of the leg that determines the movement. Then the action of the legs will be distinct, the one bearing from right to left, the other from the rear forwards. It is by the aid of the latter that the hand places and fixes the fore legs.

To accelerate these results, at first, a second person may be employed who will place himself at the height of the horse's head, holding the curb-reins in the right hand, and on the side opposite to which we wish the croup to go. He will lay hold of the reins at six inches from the branches of the bit, so as to be in a good position to combat the instinctive resistances of the animal. The one in the saddle will content himself with holding lightly the snaffle-reins, acting with his legs as I have already shown. The second person is only useful when we have to deal with a horse of an intractable disposition, or to aid the inexperience of the one in the saddle; but, as much should be done without assistance as possible, in order that the practitioner may judge by himself of the progress of his horse, seeking all the while for means to increase the effects of his touch.

Even while this work is in an elementary state, he will make the horse execute easily all the figures of the *manège de deux pistes*.[2] After eight days of moderate exercise, he will have accomplished, without effort, a performance that the old school did not dare to undertake until after two or three years' studying and working at the horse.

When the rider has accustomed the croup of the horse to yield promptly to the pressure of the legs, he will be able to put it in motion, or fix it motionless at will, and can, consequently, execute ordinary pirouettes.[3] For this purpose he will take a snaffle-rein in each hand, one to direct the neck and shoulders towards the side to which we wish to wheel, the other to second the opposite leg, if it is not sufficient to keep the croup still. At the beginning, this leg should be placed as far back as possible, and not be used until the haunches bear against it. By careful and progressive management the results will soon be attained; at the start, the horse should be allowed to rest after executing two or three steps well, which will give five or six halts in the complete rotation of the shoulders around the croup.

Here the stationary exercises cease. I will now explain how the suppling of the hind-parts will be completed, by commencing to combine the play of its springs with those of the fore-parts.

Backing

The retrograde movement, otherwise called backing, is an exercise, the importance of which has not been sufficiently appreciated, and which yet ought to have a very great influence upon his education. When practised after the old erroneous methods, it would have been without success, since the thread of exercises that ought to precede it were unknown. Backing properly differs essentially from that incorrect backward movement which carries the horse to the rear with his croup contracted and his neck stiff;

[2] *La piste* is an imaginary line upon which the horse is made to walk. When the hind legs follow the same line as the fore ones, the horse is said to go *d'une piste*, or on one line. He goes *de deux pistes*, or on two lines, when his hind legs pass along a line parallel to that traced by the fore legs. Baucher, *Dictionnaire d'Equitation*.

[3] The *pirouette* is executed on the fore or hind legs, by making the horse turn round upon himself, in such a way, that the leg on the side he is going, acts as a pivot, and is the principal support around which the other three legs move. Baucher, *Dictionnaire d'Equitation*.

Pirouettes are either *ordinary* or *reversed*. In the ordinary pirouette, one of the hind legs is the pivot on which the horse moves; in the reversed, one of the fore legs. [TRANSLATOR.]

that is, backing away from and avoiding the effect of the reins. Backing correctly supples the horse, and adds grace and precision to his natural motions. The first of the conditions upon which it is to be obtained, is to keep the horse in hand; that is to say, supple, light in the mouth, steady on his legs, and perfectly balanced in all his parts. Thus disposed, the animal will be able with ease to move and elevate equally his fore and hind legs.

It is here that we will be enabled to appreciate the good effects and the indispensable necessity of suppling the neck and haunches. Backing, which at first is tolerably painful to the horse, will always lead him to combat the motions of our hand, by stiffening his neck, and those of our legs, by contracting his croup; these are the instinctive resistances. If we cannot obviate the bad disposition of them, how will we be able to obtain that shifting and re-shifting of weight, which alone ought to make the execution of this movement perfect? If the impulsion which, to back him, ought to come from the fore-parts, should pass over its proper limits, the movement would become painful, impossible in fact, and occasion, on the part of the animal, sudden, violent movements which are always injurious to his organization.

On the other hand, the displacements[4] of the croup, by destroying the harmony which should exist between the relative forces of fore and hind-parts, would also hinder the proper execution of the backing. The previous exercise to which we have subjected the croup will aid us in keeping it in a straight line with the shoulders, in order to preserve the necessary transferring of the forces and weight.

To commence the movement, the rider ought first to assure himself that the haunches are on a line with the shoulders, and the horse light in hand; then he will slowly close his legs, in order that the action they will communicate to the hind-parts of the horse may make him lift one of his hind legs, and prevent the body

from yielding before the neck. It is then that the immediate pressure of the bit, forcing the horse to regain his equilibrium behind, will produce the first part of the backing. As soon as the horse obeys, the rider will instantly give the hand to reward the animal, and not to force the play of his fore-parts. If his croup is displaced, the rider will bring it back by means of his leg, and if necessary, use for this purpose the snaffle-rein on that side.

After having defined what I call the proper backing (*reculer*), I ought to explain what I understand by backing so as to avoid the bit (*l'acculement*). This movement is too painful to the horse, too ungraceful, and too much opposed to the right development of his mechanism, not to have struck any one who has occupied himself at all with horsemanship. We force a horse backwards in this way, whenever we crowd too much his forces and weight upon his hind-parts; by so doing we destroy his equilibrium, and render grace, measure and correctness impossible. Lightness, always lightness! this is the basis, the touchstone of all beautiful execution. With this, all is easy, as much for the horse as the rider. That being the case, it is understood that the difficulty of horsemanship does not consist in the direction to give the horse, but in the position to make him assume — a position which alone can smooth all obstacles. Indeed, if the horse executes, it is the rider who makes him do so; upon him then rests the responsibility of every false movement.

It will suffice to exercise the horse for eight days (for five minutes each lesson), in backing, to make him execute it with facility. The rider will content himself the first few times with one or two steps to the rear, followed by the combined effect of the legs and hand, increasing in proportion to the progress he makes, until he finds no more difficulty in a backward than in a forward movement.

What an immense step we will then have

---

[4] These displacements of the croup mean sideway displacements, or the horse's croup not being in a line with the shoulders. [TRANSLATOR.]

made in the education of our pupil! At the start, the defective formation of the animal, his natural contractions, the resistances we encountered everywhere, seemed as if they might defy our efforts forever. Without doubt they would have been vain, had we made use of a bad course of proceeding, but the wise system of progression that we have introduced into our work, the destruction of the instinctive forces of the horse, the suppling, the separate subjection of all the rebellious parts, have soon placed in our power the whole of the mechanism to such a degree as to enable us to govern it completely, and to restore that pliability, ease, and harmony of the parts, which their bad arrangement appeared as if it would always prevent. As I shall point out hereafter in classing the general division of the labor, it will be seen that eight or ten days will be sufficient to obtain these important results.

Was I not right then in saying that if it is not in my power to change the defective formation of a horse, I can yet prevent the evil effect of his physical defects, so as to render him as fit to do everything with grace and natural ease, as the better formed horse? In suppling the parts of the animal upon which the rider acts directly, in order to govern and guide him, in accustoming them to yield without difficulty or hesitation to the different impressions which are communicated to them, I have, by so doing, destroyed their stiffness and restored the centre of gravity to its true place, namely, to the middle of the body. I have, besides, settled the greatest difficulty of horsemanship: that of subjecting, before everything else, the parts upon which the rider acts directly, in order to prepare for him infallible means of acting upon the horse.

It is only by destroying the instinctive forces, and by suppling the different parts of the horse, that we will obtain this. All the springs of the animal's body are thus yielded up to the discretion of the rider. But this first advantage will not be enough to make him a complete horse-man. The employment of these forces thus abandoned to him, demand, in order to execute the different paces, much study and skill. I will show in the subsequent chapters the rules to be observed. I will conclude this one by a rapid recapitulation of the progression to be followed in the supplings.

Stationary exercise, the rider on foot: fore-parts

1. Flexions of the jaw to the right and left, using the curb-bit
2. Direct flexions of the jaw, and depression of the neck.
3. Lateral flexions of the neck with the snaffle-reins and with the curb.

Stationary exercise, the rider on horse-back

1. Lateral flexions of the neck with the snaffle-reins, and with the curb-reins.
2. Direct flexions of the head or placing it in a perpendicular position with the snaffle, and with the curb-reins.

Hind-parts

3. Lateral flexions, and moving the croup around the shoulders.
4. Rotation of the shoulders around the haunches.
5. Combining the play of the fore and hind legs of the horse, or backing.

I have placed the rotation of the shoulders around the haunches in the nomenclature of stationary exercise. But the ordinary pivoting, or *pirouettes*, being a pretty complicated movement, and one difficult for the horse, he should not be completely exercised in it until he has acquired the measured time of the walk, and of the trot, and will easily execute the changes of direction.

5

Of the employment of the forces of the horse by the rider

When the supplings have subjected the in-stinctive forces of the horse, and given them up completely into our power, the animal will be nothing more in our hand than a passive, expectant machine, ready to act upon the impulsion we choose to communicate to him. It will be for us, then, as sovereign disposers of all his forces, to combine the employment of them in correct proportion to the movements we wish to execute.

The young horse, at first stiff and awkward in the use of his members, will need a certain degree of management in developing them. In this, as in every other case, we will follow that rational progression which tells us to commence with the simple, before passing to the com-plicated. By the preceding exercise, we have made our means of acting upon the horse sure. We must now attend to facilitating his means of execution, by exercising all his forces together. If the animal responds to the aids of the rider by the jaw, the neck and the haunches; if he yields by the general disposition of his body to the impulses communicated to him, it is by the play of his extremities that he executes the movement. The mechanism of these parts ought then to be easy, prompt and regular; their application, well directed in the different paces, will alone be able to give them these qualities, indispensable to a good education.[1]

The walk

This pace is the mother of all the other paces; by it we will obtain the cadence, the regularity, the extension of the others. But to obtain these brilliant results, the rider must display as much knowledge as tact. The preceding exercises have led the horse to bear the combined effect of hand and legs, which could not have been done previously to the destruction of the in-stinctive resistances; we have now only to act on the inert resistances which appertain to the animal's weight; upon the forces which only move when an impulse is communicated to them.

Before making the horse go forward, we should first assure ourselves of his lightness; that is to say, of his head being perpendicular, his neck flexible, his hind-part straight and plumb. The legs will then be closed lightly, to give the body the impulse necessary to move it. But we should not, in accordance with the precepts of the old method, give the bridle hand at the same time; for then the neck, being free from all restraint, would lose its lightness; would contract, and render the motion of the hand powerless. The rider will remember that his hand ought to be to the horse an insurmountable barrier, whenever he would leave the position of *ramener*. The animal will never attempt it, without pain; and only

---

[1] It must not be forgotten that the hand and legs have their vocabulary also; and a very concise one. This mute, laconic language consists of these few words. *You are doing badly; this is what you should do; you do well now.* It is sufficient for the rider to be able to translate, by his mechanism, the meaning of these three remarks, to possess all the equestrian erudition, and share his intelligence with his horse.

within this limit will he find ease and comfort. By the application of my method, the rider will be led to guide his horse all the time with the reins half tight, except when he wishes to correct a false movement, or determine a new one.

The walk, I have said, ought to precede the other paces, because the horse having three supports upon the ground, his action is less, and consequently easier to regulate than in the trot and gallop. The first exercises of the supplings will be followed by some turns in the riding-house at a walk, but only as a relaxation, the rider attending less to animating his horse than to making him keep his head, while walking in a perpendicular position. Little by little he will complicate his work, so as to join to the lightness of the horse that precision of movement indispensable to the beauty of all his paces.

He will commence light oppositions of the hand and legs to make the forces of the fore and hind-parts work together in harmony. This exercise, by accustoming the horse always to yield the use of his forces to the direction of the rider, will be also useful in forming his intelligence, as well as in developing his powers. What delights the expert horseman will experience in the progressive application of his art! His pupil at first rebellious will insensibly yield himself to his every wish; will adopt his character, and end by becoming the living personification of him. Take care, then, rider! If your horse is capricious, violent, fantastic, we will have the right to say that you yourself do not shine by the amenity of your disposition, and the propriety of your proceedings.

In order to keep the measure and quickness of the walk equal and regular, it is indispensable that the impulsive and governing forces which come from the rider, should themselves be perfectly in harmony. We will suppose, for example, that the rider to move his horse forward, should make use of a force equal to twenty pounds, fifteen for the impulse forward, and five to bring his head into position. If the legs increase their motion without the hands increasing theirs in the same proportion, it is evident that the surplus of communicated force will be thrown into the neck, cause it to contract, and destroy all lightness. If, on the contrary, it is the hand which acts with too much violence, it will be at the expense of the impulsive force necessary to move the horse forward; on this account, his forward movement will be slackened and counteracted, at the same time that his position will lose its gracefulness and power.

This short explanation will suffice to show the harmony that should exist between the legs and hands. It is understood that their motion should vary according as the formation of the horse renders it necessary to support him more or less before or behind; but the rule is the same, only the proportions are different.

As long as the horse will not keep himself supple and light in his walk, we will continue to exercise him in a straight line; but as soon as he acquires more ease and steadiness, we will commence to make him execute changes of direction to the right and left, while walking.

Changes of direction

The use of the wrists, in the changes of direction, is so simple that it is unnecessary to speak of it here. I will only call attention to the fact, that the resistances of the horse ought always to be anticipated by disposing his forces in such a manner that they all concur in putting him in the way of moving. The head will be inclined in the direction we wish to go by means of the snaffle-rein of that side, the curb will then complete the movement. General rule: the lateral resistances of the neck are always to be opposed by the aid of the snaffle, being very careful not to commence to wheel until after destroying the obstacle that opposed it. If the use of the wrists remains very nearly the same as formerly, it is not so with the legs; their motion will be diametrically opposite to that given them in the old style of horsemanship. This innovation is so natural a one, that I cannot conceive why some one never applied it before me.

It is by bearing the hand to the right, and making the right leg felt, people have told me, and I have myself at first repeated it, that the horse is made to turn to the right. With me, practice has always taken the precedence of reasoning; and this is the way I first perceived the incorrectness of this principle.

Whatever lightness my horse had in a straight line, I remarked that this lightness always lost some of its delicacy when moving in small circles, although my outside leg came to the assistance of the inside one. As soon as the hind leg put itself in motion to follow the shoulders in the circle, I immediately felt a slight resistance. I then thought of changing the use of my aids, and of pressing the leg on the side opposite to the direction of wheeling. At the same time, in place of bearing the hand immediately to the right, to determine the shoulders in that direction, I first, by the aid of this hand, made the opposition necessary to render the haunches motionless, and to dispose the forces in such a way as to maintain the equilibrium during the execution of the movement. This proceeding was completely successful; and in explaining what ought to be the function of the different extremities, I recognize this as the only rational way of using them in wheeling.

In fact, in wheeling to the right, for example, it is the right hind leg which serves as pivot and supports the whole weight of the mass, while the left hind leg and the fore legs describe a circle more or less extended. In order that the movement should be correct and free, it is necessary that this pivot upon which the whole turns be not interfered with in its action; the simultaneous action of the right hand and the right leg must necessarily produce this effect. The equilibrium is thus destroyed, and the regularity of the wheeling rendered impossible.

As soon as the horse executes easily the changes of direction at a walk, and keeps himself perfectly light, we can commence exercising at a trot.

The trot

The rider will commence this pace at a very moderate rate of speed, following exactly the same principles as for the walk. He will keep his horse perfectly light, not forgetting that the faster the pace, the more disposition there will be on the part of the animal to fall back again into his natural contractions. The hand should then be used with redoubled nicety, in order to keep the head and neck always pliable, without affecting the impulse necessary to the movement. The legs will lightly second the hands, and the horse between these two barriers, which are obstacles only to his improper movements, will soon develop all his best faculties, and with precision of movement, will acquire grace, extension, and the steadiness inherent to the lightness of the whole.

Although many persons who would not take the trouble to examine thoroughly my method, have pretended that it is opposed to great speed in trotting, it is not the less proved that the well-balanced horse can trot faster than the one destitute of this advantage. I have given proofs of this whenever they have been demanded of me; but it is in vain that I have tried to make people understand what constitutes the motions of the trot, and what are the conditions indispensable for regularity in executing it. So, I was obliged in a race of which I was judge, to make the bets void, and to prove that the pretended trotters were not trotting really, but were ambling.

The condition indispensable to a good trotter, is perfect equilibrium of the body. Equilibrium which keeps up a regular movement of the diagonal fore and hind feet, gives them an equal elevation and extension, with such lightness that the animal can easily execute all changes of direction, moderate his speed, halt, or increase his speed without effort. The fore-parts have not, then, the appearance of towing after them the hind-parts, which keep as far off as possible; everything becomes easy and graceful for the horse, because his forces being in perfect harmony, permit the rider to dispose of them in such a way that they mutually and constantly assist each other.

It would be impossible for me to count up the number of horses that have been sent me to break, and whose paces have been so spoiled that it was impossible for them to trot a single step. A few lessons have always been sufficient for me to get them back into regular paces, and these are the means I employed.

The difficulty which the horse experiences in keeping himself square in his trot, almost always proceeds from the hind-parts. Whether these be of a feeble construction, or be rendered useless by the superior vigor of the fore-parts, the motions of these parts, which receive the shock and give the bound, in each case become powerless, and in consequence, render the movement irregular.[2] There is, then, weakness in one extremity, or excess of force in the other. The remedy in each case will be the same, viz: the depression of the neck, which by diminishing the power of the fore-parts, restores the equilibrium between the two parts. We have practised this suppling on foot, it will be easy to obtain it on horseback. We here see the usefulness of this perpendicular flexion, which allows us to place on a level the forces of the two opposite extremities of the horse, in order to make them harmonious, and induce regularity in their working. The horse being thus placed, can bend and extend his fore and hind legs, before the weight of the body forces them to resume their support.

The practice of this and some other principles that I explain in this work, will place in the rank of choice horses, animals whose inferiority caused them to be considered jades, and that the old method would never have raised from their degradation. It will suffice to accustom the horse to trot well, to exercise him at this pace only five minutes in each lesson. When he acquires the necessary ease and lightness, he can be made to execute ordinary *pirouettes*, as well as the exercise on two lines, at a walk and a trot. I have said that five minutes of trotting were enough at first, because it is less the continuance of an exercise than its being properly done that perfects the execution of it. Besides, as this pace requires a considerable displacement of forces, and as the animal will have been already subjected to a rather painful exercise, it would be dangerous to prolong it beyond the time I mention. The horse will lend himself more willingly to your efforts when nicely managed, and of short duration; his intelligence, becoming familiar with this efficient progression, will hasten success. He will submit himself calmly and without repugnance to work in which there will be nothing painful to him, and we will be able thus to push his education to the farthest limits, not only without injury to his physical organization, but in restoring to their normal state organs that a forced exercise might have weakened. This regular development of all the organs of the horse will not only give him grace, but also strength and health, and will thus prolong his existence, while increasing a hundredfold the delights of the true horseman.

---

[2] I am not of the opinion of those connoisseurs who imagine that the qualities of the horse, as well as his speed in trotting, depend principally on the height of his withers. I think, that for the horse to be stylish and regular in his movements, the croup should be on a level with the withers; such was the construction of the old English horses. A certain kind of horses, very much *à la mode*, called steppers, are constructed after an entirely different fashion; they strike out with their fore legs, and drag their hind-parts after them. Horses with a low croup, or withers very high in proportion to their croup, were preferred by horsemen of the old school, and are still in favor now-a-days among amateur horsemen. The German horsemen have an equally marked predilection for this sort of formation, although it is contrary to strength of the croup, to the equilibrium of the horse, and to the regular play of his feet and legs. This fault of construction (for it is one) has been scarcely noticed till now; nevertheless, it is a great one, and really retards the horse's education. In fact, we are obliged, in order to render his movements uniform, to lower his neck, so that the kind of lever it represents, may serve to lighten his hind-parts of the weight with which they are overburdened. I ought also to say, that this change of position, or of equilibrium, is only obtained by the aid of my principles. I explain the cause and effect, and I point out the remedies. Is this not the proper way for an author to proceed?

6

Of the concentration of the forces of the horse by the rider

The rider now understands that the only means of obtaining precision and regularity of movement in the walk and trot is to keep the horse perfectly light while he is exercised at these paces. As soon as we are sure of this lightness while going in a straight line, in changes of direction, and in circular movements it will be easy to preserve it while exercising on two lines.[1]

I would here treat immediately of the gallop; but this pace, more complicated than the two others, demands an arrangement on the part of the horse, and a power on the part of the rider, that the preceding exercises have not yet been able to give. The proper placing of the horse's head spreads his forces over the whole of his body; it is necessary, in order to perform correctly the different exercises at a gallop, and to enable yourself properly to direct the forces in energetic movements, to bring them into a common focus — that is, to the centre of gravity of the animal. I am about to explain how this is to be done.

The use of the spurs

Professors of equitation and authors upon this subject have said that the spurs are to punish the horse when he does not respond to the legs, or when he refuses to approach an object that frightens him. With them, the spur is not an aid, but a means of chastisement. With me it is, on the contrary, a powerful auxiliary, with-

out which it would be impossible to break any horse perfectly. How! you exclaim, you attack with the spur, horses that are sensitive, excitable, full of fire and action — horses whose powerful make leads them to become unmanageable, in spite of the hardest bits and the most vigorous arms! Yes, and it is with the spur that I will moderate the fury of these too fiery animals, and stop them short in their most impetuous bounds. It is with the spur, aided of course by the hand, that I will make the most stubborn natures kind, and perfectly educate the most intractable animal.

Long before publishing my *Comprehensive Dictionary of Equitation*, I was aware of the excellent effects of the spur; but I abstained from developing my principles, being prevented by an expression of one of my friends, whom I had shown how to obtain results, which to him appeared miraculous. It is extraordinary! It is wonderful! he exclaimed; but it is a razor in the hands of a monkey. It is true that the use of the spurs requires prudence, tact, and gradation; but the effects of it are precious. Now that I have proved the efficacy of my method; now that I see my most violent adversaries become warm partisans of my principles, I no longer fear to develop a process that I consider one of the most beautiful results of my long researches in horsemanship.

There is no more difference in sensibility of different horses' flanks than in their sensibility of mouth — that is to say, that the direct effect

---

[1] Previously explained.

of the spur is nearly the same in them all. I have already shown that the organization of the bars of the mouth goes for nothing in the resistances to the hand. It is clear enough that if the nose being thrown up in the air gives the horse a force of resistance equal to two hundred pounds, this force will be reduced to one hundred pounds, when we bring the horse's head half-way towards a perpendicular position; to fifty pounds when brought still nearer that position, and to nothing when perfectly placed. The pretended hardness of mouth proceeds in this case from the bad position of the head caused by the stiffness of the neck and the faulty construction of the loins and haunches of the horse. If we carefully examine the causes that produce what is called sensibility of the flanks, we will discover that they have very much the same kind of source.

The innumerable conjectures to which people have devoted themselves, in attributing to the horse's flanks a local sensibility that had no existence, have necessarily injured the progress of his education, because it was based upon false data. The greater or less sensibility of the animal proceeds from his action, from his faulty formation, and bad position resulting therefrom. To a horse of natural action, but with long weak loins, and bad action behind, every motion backward is painful, and the very disposition that leads him to rush ahead, serves him to avoid the pain of the spur. He returns to this movement whenever he feels the rider's legs touch him; and far from being a spirited horse, he is only scared and crazy. The more he feels the spur, the more he plunges out of hand, and baffles the means intended to make him obedient. There is everything to fear from such a horse; he will scare at objects from the very ease he possesses of avoiding them. Now since his fright proceeds, so to say, from the bad position we allow him to take, this inconvenience will disappear from the moment we remedy the first cause of it. We must confine the forces in order to prevent displacement. We must separate the *physical* from the *moral* horse, and force these impressions to concen-

trate in the brain. He will then be a furious madman whose limbs we have bound to prevent him from carrying his frenzied thoughts into execution.

The best proof we have that the promptness of a horse in responding to the effect of the legs and spurs, is not caused by a sensibility of the flanks, but rather by great action joined to bad formation, is that the same action is not so manifest in a well-formed horse, and that the latter bears the spur much better than one whose equilibrium and organization are inferior.

But the spur is not useful only in moderating the too great energy of horses of much action; its effect being equally good in combating the dispositions which lead the animal to throw its centre of gravity too much forward, or back. I would also use it to stir up those that are wanting in ardor and vivacity. In horses of action, the forces of the hind-parts surpass those of the fore-parts. It is the opposite in dull horses. We can thus account for the quickness of the former; the slowness and sluggishness of the latter.

By the exercise of suppling, we have completely annulled the instinctive forces of the horse. We must now reunite these forces in their true centre of gravity, that is, the middle of the animal's body; it is by the properly combined opposition of the legs and hands that we will succeed in this. The advantages we possess already over the horse, will enable us to combat from their very birth, all the resistances which tend to make him leave the proper position, the only one in which we can successfully practice these oppositions. It is also of the first importance to put into our proceedings tact and gradation, so that, for example, the legs never give an impulse that the hand is not able to take hold of and govern at the same moment. I will make this principle more clear by a short explanation.

We will suppose a horse at a walk, employing a force of forty pounds, necessary to keep the pace regular till the moment of the opposition of the hands and legs which follow. By and by comes a slow and gradual pressure of the legs, which adds ten pounds to the impulse of the pace. As the horse is supposed to be perfectly in hand, the hand will immediately feel this passage of forces, and must then make itself master of them to transfer them to the centre. Meanwhile the legs will continue their pressure, to the end that these forces thus driven back may not return to the focus they had left, which would be but a useless ebbing and flowing of forces. This succession of oppositions well combined will bring together a great quantity of forces in the centre of the horse's body, and the more these are increased, the more the animal will lose its instinctive energy. When the pressure of the legs becomes insufficient to entirely collect the forces, more energetic means must be employed, viz.: the touches of the spur.

The spurring ought to be done, not violently, and with much movement of the legs, but with delicacy and management. The rider ought to close his legs so gradually, that before coming in actual contact with the horse's flanks, the spur will not be more than a hair's breadth off, if possible. The hand should ever be the echo to the light touches with which we commence; it should then be firmly held, so as to present an opposition equal to the force communicated by the spur. If by the time being badly chosen, the hand does not exactly intercept the impulse given, and the general commotion resulting therefrom, we should, before recommencing, gather the horse together, and re-establish calm in his motions. The force of the spurring will be progressively increased until the horse bears it, when as vigorously applied as possible, without presenting the least resistance to the hand, without increasing the speed of his pace, or without displacing himself as long as we operate with a firm foot.

A horse brought thus to bear spurring, is three-fourths broken, since we have the free disposition of all his forces. Besides, his centre of gravity being where his forces are all united, we have brought it to its proper place, viz.: the middle of the body. All the oscillations of the animal will then be subordinate to us, and we will be able to transfer the weight with ease, when necessary.

It is easy now to understand where the resistances have their origin; whether the horse kicks up behind, rears, or runs away, the cause is always the centre of gravity being in the wrong place. This very cause belongs to a defective formation that we cannot change, it is true, but the effects of which we can always modify. If the horse kicks up, the centre of gravity is in the shoulders; in his croup when the animal rears, and too far forward when he runs away. The principal thought of the rider, then, ought to be to keep the centre of gravity in the middle of the horse's body, since he will thereby prevent him defending himself, and bring back the forces of the badly formed horse to their true place, which they occupy in the finest organizations. It is this that makes me assert that a well-formed horse will not make resistance nor move irregularly, for to do so requires supernatural efforts on his part to destroy the harmony of his moving parts, and so greatly displace his centre of gravity. So, when I speak of the necessity of giving the horse a new equilibrium, in order to prevent his defending himself, and also to remedy the ungracefulness of his form, I allude to the combination of forces of which I have been treating, or, rather, of the removal of the centre of gravity from one place to another. This result obtained, the education of the horse is complete. When the horseman succeeds in obtaining it, his talent becomes a truth, since it transforms ugliness into grace, and gives elegance and lightness to movements which were before heavy and confused.[2]

---

[2] I have often proved that horses that were considered dull, or unable to move their shoulders freely, have not the defect that is supposed; in other words, that it is very rare that they are paralyzed in their shoulders so as to injure the regularity and speed of their paces, principally as regards trotting. The shoulders of the horse, if I may use the comparison, resemble the wings of a wind-mill; the impulse given by the hocks replaces the motive force. There undoubtedly exist some local complaints that affect the shoulders; but this is very rare; the defect, if there is

The rider's employment of force, when properly applied, has a moral effect also on the horse, that accelerates the results. If the impulse given by the leg finds in the hand the energy and *à-propos* necessary to regulate its effects, the pain the animal sustains will be always proportioned to his resistances, and his instinct will soon make him understand how he can diminish, and even avoid altogether this constraint, by promptly yielding to what we demand of him. He will hasten then to submit, and will even anticipate our desires. But, I repeat, it is only by means of tact and delicate management that we will gain this important point. If the legs give too vigorous an impulse, the horse will quickly overcome the motion of the hands, and resume with his natural position all the advantages it gives him to foil the efforts of the rider. If, on the contrary, the hand presents too great a resistance, the horse will soon overcome the legs, and find a means of defending himself by backing. Yet these difficulties must not be allowed to frighten us; they were only serious ones when no rational principle gave the means of surmounting them. The application of my method will enable ordinary horsemen to obtain results that otherwise could be obtained only by the most favored equestrian organizations.

When the animal becomes accustomed by means of the spur to such oppositions, it will become easy enough to combat with the spur all the resistances that may afterwards manifest themselves. Since the resistances are always caused by moving the croup sideways, or getting it too far back, the spur, by immediately bringing the hind legs towards the centre of the body, prevents the support of the hocks, which were able to oppose the proper harmony of forces, and prevent the right distribution of the weight.

This is the means I always employ to make the horse pass from a swift gallop to a halt, without straining his hocks, or injuring any of the joints of his hind-parts. In fact, since it is the hocks which propel the mass forward, it suffices to destroy their motion to stop the bound. The spur, by instantly bringing the hind legs under the horse's belly, destroys their power from the moment the hand comes in the nick of time to fix them in that position. Then the haunches bend, the croup is lowered; the weight and forces arrange themselves in the order most favorable to the free and combined play of each part, and the violence of the shock, infinitely decomposed, is scarce perceptible to either horse or rider.

If, on the contrary, we stop the horse by making the hand move first, the hocks remain far in the rear of the plumb-line; the shock is violent, painful for the animal, and especially injurious to his physical organization. Horses that are thus stopped, set themselves against the bit, extending their neck, and require an arm of iron and a most violent force. Such is the custom of the Arabs, for example, in halting suddenly their horses, by making use of murderous bits that break the bars of their horses' mouths. Thus, notwithstanding the wonderful powers with which nature has gifted them, are these excellent animals injured. The use of the spur must not be commenced till by gathering him we get the horse well in hand; then the first touch of the spur should be made felt. We will continue to make use of it, at long intervals, until the horse, after his bound forward, presents resistance to the hand, and avoids the pressure of the bit, by bringing in his chin towards his chest, of his own accord. This submission once obtained, we can undertake the use of the spurs with oppositions, but we must be careful to discontinue them when the horse is in hand. This means has the double advantage of acting morally and physically.

---

one, has its origin in the hind-parts. For my part, I have been able to make all such horses very free in their movements, and that after fifteen days of exercise, half an hour a day. The means, like all I employ, are very simple. They consist in suppling the neck to get the horse in hand, and then, by the aid of the legs, and afterwards slight use of the spurs, in bringing his haunches nearer the centre. Then the hocks will obtain a leverage, by which they can propel the mass forward, and give the shoulders a freedom that people would not expect.

The first attacks will be made with a single spur, and by bearing on the opposite rein; these transverse oppositions will have a better effect and give more prompt results. When the horse begins to contain himself, the two spurs being used separately, we can make them felt together and with an equal gradation.[3]

To the work, then, cavaliers! If you will follow my principles, I can promise you that your purse will be less often emptied into the hands of horse-dealers, and that you will render the meanest of your hacks agreeable. You will charm our breeders of horses, who will attribute to their efforts of regeneration that elegance and grace that your art alone could have given to your chargers.

Lowering the hand

The lowering the hand consists in confirming the horse in all his lightness — that is, in making him preserve his equilibrium without the aid of the reins. The suppleness given to all parts of the horse, the just oppositions of hands and legs, lead him to keep himself in the best possible position. To find out exactly whether we are obtaining this result, we must have recourse to frequent lowering of the hand. It is done in this way: after having slipped the right hand to the buckle, and having assured yourself that the reins are even, you will let go of them with the left hand, and lower the right slowly to the pommel of the saddle. To do this regularly, the horse must neither increase nor diminish the speed of his pace, and his head and neck continue to preserve their proper position. The first few times that the horse is thus given up to himself, he will perhaps only take a few steps while keeping in position, and

at the same rate of speed; the rider ought then to make his legs felt first, and the hand afterwards, to bring him into his previous position. the frequent repetition of this lowering of the hand, after a complete placing of the horse's head in a perpendicular position, will give him a most exquisite mouth, and the rider a still greater delicacy of touch. The means of guiding employed by the latter will immediately be answered by the horse, if his forces have been previously disposed in a perfectly harmonious state.

The lowerings of the hand ought to be practised first at a walk, then at a trot, afterwards at a gallop. This semblance of liberty gives such confidence to the horse that he gives up without knowing it; he becomes our submissive slave, while supposing that he is preserving an entire independence.

Of gathering the horse, or rassembler

The preceding exercise will render easy to the rider that important part of horsemanship called *rassembler*. This has been a great deal talked about by people, as they have talked about Providence, and all the mysteries that are impenetrable to human perception. If it were allowable for us to compare small things to great, we might say that the more or less absurd theories that have been put forward upon the subject of divine power have not, fortunately, hindered in any way the unchangeable march of nature; but with regard to the progress of horsemanship, the case is not the same as to what has been said and written on the subject of the *rassembler*. The false principles propagated on this subject have made the horse the plaything and the victim of the rider's ignorance.

---

[3] I would never have thought that this means, which serves as a corrective to the processes used by all horsemen, would have aroused the sensibility of some amateurs. These latter have preferred to be affected by exaggerated or erroneous reports, rather than satisfy themselves by observation, that this pretended cruelty is in fact the most innocent thing in the world. Must we not teach the horse to respond to the spur as well as to the legs and the hand? Is it not by this spurring, judiciously applied, that we bring in at will the hind legs more or less near the centre of gravity? Is not this the only way of increasing or diminishing the leverage of the hocks, whether for extending or raising them in motion, or for the purpose of halting?

I proclaim it, the gathering a horse has never been understood or defined before me, for it cannot be perfectly executed without the regular application of the principles that I have developed for the first time. You will be convinced of this truth when you know that the *rassembler* demands:

1. The suppling, partial and general, of the neck and haunches.
2. The perfect position that results from this suppling.
3. The entire absorption of the forces of the horse by the rider.

Now, as the means of obtaining these different results have never been pointed out in any treatise on horsemanship, am I not justified in saying that the true *rassembler* has never been practised until now? It is, nevertheless, one of the indispensable conditions of the horse's education; consequently I think I am right in saying that before my method, horses of defective formation have never been properly broken.

How is the *rassembler* defined in the schools of horsemanship? *You gather your horse by raising the hand and closing the legs.* I ask, what good can this movement of the rider do upon an animal badly formed, contracted, and that remains under the influence of all the evil propensities of its nature? This mechanical support of the hands and legs, far from preparing the horse for obedience, will only make him redouble his means of resistance, since, while giving him notice that we are about to demand a movement on his part, we remain unable to dispose his forces in such a way as to force him to it.

The real *rassembler* consists in collecting the forces of the horse in his centre in order to ease his extremities, and give them up completely to the disposition of the rider. The animal thus finds himself transformed into a kind of balance, of which the rider is the centre-piece. The least touch upon one or other of the extremities, which represent the scales, will immediately send them in the direction we wish. The rider will know that his horse is completely gathered when he feels him ready, as it were, to rise from all four of his legs. The proper position first, and then the use of the spurs, will make this beautiful execution of the gathering easy to both horse and rider; and what splendor, grace and majesty it gives the animal! If we have been obliged at first to use the spurs in pushing this concentration of forces to its farthest limits, the legs will afterwards be sufficient to obtain the gathering necessary for the precision and elevation required in all complicated movements.

Need I recommend discretion in your demands? I think not. If the rider, having reached this stage of his horse's education, cannot comprehend and seize that fineness of touch, that delicacy of process indispensable to the right application of my principles, it will prove him devoid of every feeling of a horseman; nothing I can say can remedy this imperfection of his nature.

7

Of the employment of the forces of the horse by the rider

(continuation)

Of the gallop

I have said that, until now, the greater part of the resources of horsemanship have not been understood, and had I need of another proof to support my opinion, I would draw it from the error, the suppositions, the innumerable contradictions that have been heaped together in order to explain so simple a movement as the gallop. What contrary opinions upon the means to employ to make the horse go off with his right foot? It is the support of the rider's right leg which determines the movement, one pretends; it is that of the left leg, says another; it is the equal touch of the two legs, affirms a third; no, some others remark, very seriously, you must let the horse act naturally.

How can the truth be made out in the midst of this conflict of such contrary principles? Besides, they come from such respectable sources; the most of their authors were possessed of titles and dignities which are generally only granted to merit. Have they all been deceived for a hundred and fifty years?. This is not possible; for many of them joined to long practice a perfect knowledge of physics, anatomy, mathematics, etc., etc. To doubt such authorities would be as presumptuous as imprudent; it would have been considered a crime of high treason against horsemanship. So the riders kept their ignorance and the horses their bad equilibrium; and if any one succeeded, after two or three years of routine labor, in making certain horses of a privileged organization start with the desired foot, and in making them

change feet finally, at a fixed point, the difficulty then was to prevent them from always repeating this movement at the same place.

Thus it is that the most palpable errors gain credit, and often are perpetuated, until there comes a practical mind, gifted with some amount of common sense, who contradicts by practice all the learned theories of its predecessors. They try hard at first to deny the knowledge of the innovator; but the masses who instinctively know the true, and judge from what they see, soon range themselves on his side, turn their backs upon his detractors, and leave them to their solitude and vain pretensions.

To the mass of horsemen I address myself, when I say, either the horse is under the influence of your forces, and entirely submissive to your power, or you are struggling with him. If he gallops off with you, without your being able to modify or direct with certainty his course, it proves that, although subject to a certain extent to your power in thus consenting to carry you about, he, nevertheless, uses his instinctive forces. In this case, there is a perpetual fight going on between you and him, the chances of which depend on the temperament and caprice of the animal, upon the good or bad state of his digestion. Changes of foot, in such a state, can only be obtained by inclining the horse very much to one side, which makes the movement both difficult and ungraceful.

If, on the contrary, the animal is made submissive to a degree that he cannot contract any one of his parts without the intervention and aid of the rider, the latter can direct at his pleasure the whole of his moving parts, and, consequently, can easily and promptly execute changes of feet.

We know the contraction of any one part of the horse reacts on the neck, and that the stiffness of this part prevents the proper execution of every movement. If then, at the moment of setting off on a gallop, the horse stiffens one of his extremities, and consequently his neck, of what use in determining him in starting with the right foot can be the support of one or the other leg of the rider, or even of that of both at once? These means will evidently be ineffectual until we go back to the source of the resistance, for the purpose of combating and destroying it. Here, as in every other case, we see that suppleness and lightness alone can make the execution of the work easy.

If, when we wish to make the horse start with the right foot, a slight contraction of one part of the animal disposes him to start with the left foot, and we persist in inducing the pace, we must employ two forces on the same side, viz.: the left leg and the left hand; the first to determine the movement, the second to combat the contrary disposition of the horse.

But when the horse, perfectly supple and gathered, only brings his parts into play after the impression given them by the rider, the latter, in order to start with the right foot, ought to combine an opposition of forces proper for keeping the horse in equilibrium, while placing him in the position required for the movement. He will then bear the hand to the left, and press his right leg. Here we see that the means mentioned above, necessary when the horse is not properly placed, would be wrong when the animal is properly placed, since it would destroy the harmony then existing between his forces.

This short explanation will, I hope, suffice to make it understood that things should be studied thoroughly before laying down any principles of action. Let us have no more systems, then, upon the exclusive use of such or such leg to determine the gallop; but a settled

conviction that the first condition of this or any other performance is to keep the horse supple and light — that is *rassemblé*; then, after this, to make use of one or the other motive power, according as the animal, at the start, preserves a proper position, or seeks to leave it. It must also be understood that, while it is the force that gives the position to the horse, it is position alone upon which the regularity of movement depends.

Passing frequently from the gallop with the right foot to that with the left, in a straight line, and with halts, will soon bring the horse to make these changes of feet by the touch without halting. Violent effects of force should be avoided, which would bewilder the horse and destroy his lightness. We must remember that this lightness which should precede all changes of pace and direction, and make every movement easy, graceful and inevitable, is the important condition we should seek before everything else.

It is because they have not understood this principle, and have not felt that the first condition to dispose a horse for the gallop is to destroy all the instinctive forces of the animal (forces that oppose the position the movement demands), that horsemen have laid down so many erroneous principles, and have all remained unable to show us the proper means to be employed.

Of leaping the ditch and the bar

Although the combinations of equestrian science alone cannot give to every horse the energy and vigor necessary to clear a ditch or a bar, there are, nevertheless, principles by the aid of which we will succeed in partly supplying the deficiencies in the natural formation of the animal. By giving a good direction to the forces, we will facilitate the rise and freedom of the bound. I do not pretend by this, to say, that a horse of ordinary capabilities will attain the same height and elegance in this movement as one that is well constituted, but he will, at least, be able to display in it all the resources of

General Decarpentry, a twentieth-century disciple of Baucher, illustrates the piaffe on Professeur. (General Decarpentry, *Piaffer and Passage* (J. A. Allen, 1964), photograph by Blanchaud)

his organization to more purpose.

The great thing is to bring the horse to attempt this performance with good will. If all the processes prescribed by me for mastering the instinctive forces of the animal, and putting him under the influence of ours, have been punctually followed, the utility of this progression will be recognized by the facility we have of making the horse clear all the objects that are encountered in his way. For the rest, recourse must never be had, in case of a contest, to violent means, such as a whip in the hands of a second person; nor should we seek to excite the animal by cries; this could only produce a moral effect calculated to frighten him. It is by physical means that we should before all bring him to obedience, since they alone will enable him to understand and execute. We should then carry on the contest calmly, and seek to surmount the forces that lead him to refuse, by acting directly on them. To make the horse leap, we will wait till he responds freely to the legs and spur, in order to have always a sure means of government.

The bar will remain on the ground until the horse goes over it without hesitation; it will then be raised some inches, progressively increasing the height until the animal will be just able to clear it without too violent an effort. To exceed this proper limit would be to risk causing a disgust on the part of the horse that should be most carefully avoided. The bar having been thus gradually raised, ought to be made fast, in order that the horse, disposed to be indolent, should not make sport of an obstacle which would be no longer serious, when the touch of his feet sufficed to overturn it. The bar ought not to be wrapped in any covering that would lessen its hardness; we should be severe when we demand possibilities, and avoid the abuses that always result from an ill-devised complaisance.

Before preparing to take the leap, the rider should hold himself sufficiently firm to prevent his body preceding the motion of the horse. His loins should be supple, his buttocks well fixed to the saddle, so that he may experience no shock nor violent reaction. His thighs and legs exactly enveloping the body and sides of the horse will give him a power always opportune and infallible. The hand in its natural position will feel the horse's mouth in order to judge of the effects of impulsion. It is in this position that the rider should conduct the horse towards the obstacle; if he comes up to it with the same freedom of pace, a light opposition of the legs and hand will facilitate the elevation of the fore-hand, and the bound of the posterior extremity. As soon as the horse is raised, the hand ceases its effect, to be again sustained when the fore legs touch the ground, and to prevent them giving way under the weight of the body.

We should content ourselves with executing a few leaps in accordance with the horse's powers, and, above all, avoid pushing bravado to the point of wishing to force the animal to clear obstacles that are beyond his powers. I have known very good leapers that people have succeeded in thus disgusting forever, so that no efforts could induce them to clear things only half the height of those that at first they leaped with ease.

Of the piaffer[1]

Until now, horsemen have maintained that the nature of each horse permits of only a limited number of movements, and that if there are some that can be brought to execute a *piaffer* high and elegant, or low and precipitate, there are a great number of them to whom this exercise is for ever interdicted. Their construction, they say, is opposed to it; it is then nature that has so willed it; ought we not to bow before this supreme arbiter, and respect its decrees?

---

[1] 'The *piaffer* is the horse's raising his legs diagonally, as in the trot, but without advancing or receding.' Baucher, *Dictionnaire d'Equitation*.

This opinion is undoubtedly convenient for justifying its own ignorance, but it is none the less false. *We can bring all horses to piaffer*, and I will prove that in this particularly, without reforming the work of nature, without deranging the formation of the bones, or that of the muscles of the animal, we can remedy the consequences of its physical imperfections, and change the vicious disposition occasioned by faulty construction. There is no doubt that the horse whose forces and weight are collected in one of his extremities will be unfit to execute the elegant cadence of the *piaffer*. But a graduated exercise, the completion of which is the *rassembler*, soon allows us to remedy such an inconvenience. We can now reunite all these forces in their true centre of gravity, and the horse that bears the *rassembler* perfectly has all the necessary qualifications for the *piaffer*.

For the *piaffer* to be regular and graceful, it is necessary that the horse's legs, moved diagonally, rise together and fall in the same way upon the ground at as long intervals as possible. The animal ought not to bear more upon the hand than upon the legs of the rider, that his equilibrium may present the perfection of that balance of which I have spoken in another place. When the centre of the forces is thus disposed in the middle of the body, and when the *rassembler* is perfect, it is sufficient, in order to induce a commencement of *piaffer*, to communicate to the horse with the legs a vibration at first slight, but often repeated. By vibration I mean an invigoration of forces, of which the rider ought always to be the agent.

After this first result, the horse will be put at a walk, and the rider's legs gradually brought close, will give the animal a slight increase of action. Then, but only then, the hand will sustain itself in time with the legs, and at the same intervals, in order that these two motive powers, acting conjointly, may keep up a succession of imperceptible movements, and produce a slight contraction which will spread itself over the whole body of the horse. This reiterated activity will give the extremities a first mobility, which at the beginning will be far from regular, since the increase of action that this new exercise makes necessary will for the moment break the harmonious uniformity of the forces. But this general action is necessary in order to obtain even an irregular mobility, for without it the movement would be disorderly, and there would be a want of harmony among the different springs. We will content ourselves, for the first few days, with a commencement of mobility of the extremities, being careful to stop each time that the horse raises or puts down his feet, without advancing them to much, in order to caress him, and speak to him, and thus calm the invigoration that a demand, the object of which he does not understand, must cause in him. Nevertheless, these caresses should be employed with discernment, and when the horse has done well, for if badly applied they would be rather injurious than useful. The fit time for ceasing with the hands and legs is more important still; it demands all the rider's attention.

The mobility of the legs once obtained, we can commence to regulate it, and fix the intervals of the cadence. Here again, I seek in vain to indicate with the pen the degree of delicacy necessary in the rider's proceedings, since his motions ought to be answered by the horse with an exactness and *à-propos* that is unequaled. It is by the alternated support of the two legs that he will succeed in prolonging the lateral balancings of the horse's body, in such way as to keep him longer on one side or the other. He will seize the moment when the horse prepares to rest his fore leg on the ground, to make the pressure of his own leg felt on the same side, and add to the inclination of the animal in the same direction. If this time is well seized, the horse will balance himself slowly, and the cadence will acquire that elevation so fit to bring out all its elegance and all its majesty. These times of the legs are difficult, and require great practice; but their results are too splendid for the rider not to strive to seize the light variations of them.

The precipitate movement of the rider's legs accelerates also the *piaffer*. It is he, then, who regulates at will the greater or less degree of quickness of the cadence. The performance of the *piaffer* is not elegant and perfect until the horse performs it without repugnance, which will always be the case when the forces are kept together, and the position is suitable to the demands of the movement. It is urgent, then, to be well acquainted with the amount of force necessary for the performance of the *piaffer*, so as not to overdo it. We should, above all, be careful to keep the horse *rassemblé*, which, of itself, will induce the movement without effort.

8

Division of the work

I have developed all the means to be employed in completing the horse's education; it remains for me to say how the horseman ought to divide his work, in order to connect the different exercises and pass by degrees from the simple to the complicated.

Two months of work, consisting of two lessons a day of a half hour each — that is to say, one hundred and twenty lessons — will be amply sufficient to bring the greenest horse to perform regularly all the preceding exercises. I hold to two short lessons a day, one in the morning, the other in the afternoon; they are necessary to obtain good results.

We disgust a young horse by keeping him too long at exercises that fatigue him, the more so as his intelligence is less prepared to understand what we wish to demand of him. On the other hand, an interval of twenty-four hours is too long, in my opinion, for the animal to remember the next day what he had comprehended the day before.

The general work will be divided into five series or lessons, distributed in the following order:

First lesson: Eight days of work

The first twenty minutes of this lesson will be devoted to the stationary exercise for the flexions of the jaw and neck; the rider first on foot, and then on horseback, will follow the progression I have previously indicated. During the last ten minutes, he will make the horse go forward at a walk without trying to animate him, but applying himself all the while to keeping his head in the position of *ramener*. He will content himself with executing a single change of hand, in order to go as well to the right hand as to the left. The fourth or fifth day, the rider, before putting his horse in motion, will make him commence some slight flexions of the croup.

Second lesson: Ten days of work

The first fifteen minutes will be occupied in the stationary supplings, comprising the flexions of the croup performed more completely than in the preceding lesson; then will begin the backing. We will devote the other half of the lesson to the moving straight ahead, once or twice taking the trot at a very moderate pace. The rider during this second part of the work, without ceasing to pay attention to the *ramener*, will yet commence light oppositions of hands and legs, in order to prepare the horse to bear the combined effects, and to give regularity to his paces. We will also commence the changes of direction at a walk, while preserving the *ramener*, and being careful to make the head and neck always go first.

Third lesson: Twelve days of work

Six or eight minutes only will at first be occupied in the stationary flexions; those of the hind-parts should be pushed to the completion of the reversed *pirouettes*. We will continue by the backing; then all the rest of the lesson will be devoted to perfecting the walk and the trot, commencing at this latter pace the changes of direction. The rider will often stop the horse, and continue to watch attentively the *ramener* during the changes of pace or direction. He will also commence the exercise *de deux pistes* at a walk, as well as the rotation of the shoulders around the haunches.

Fourth lesson: Fifteen days of work

After five minutes being devoted to the stationary supplings, the rider will first repeat all the work of the preceding lessons; he will commence, with a steady foot, the *attaques*,[1] in order to confirm the *ramener* and prepare the *rassembler*. He will renew the *attaques* while in motion, and when the horse bears them patiently, he will commence the gallop. He will content himself in the commencement with executing four or five lopes only before resuming the walk, and then start again with a different foot, unless the horse requires being exercised more often on one foot than the other. In passing from the gallop to the walk, we should watch with care that the horse resumes this latter pace as quickly as possible without taking short steps on a trot, all the while keeping the head and neck light. He will only be exercised at the gallop at the end of each lesson.

Fifth lesson: Fifteen days of work

These last fifteen days will be occupied in assuring the perfect execution of all the preceding work, and in perfecting the pace of the gallop until we can execute easily changes of direction, changes of feet at every step, and passaging. We can then exercise the horse at leaping the bar and at the *piaffer*. Thus in two months, and upon any horse, we will have accomplished a work that formerly required years, and then often gave incomplete results.

And I repeat, however insufficient so short a space of time may appear, it will produce the effect I promise, if you follow exactly all my directions. I have demonstrated this upon a hundred different occasions, and many of my pupils are able to prove it as well as myself.

In establishing the above order of work, be it well understood that I found myself on the dispositions of horses in general. A horseman of any tact will soon understand the modifications that he ought to make in their application, according to the particular nature of his pupil. Such a horse, for example, will require more or less persistence in the flexions; another one in the backing; this one, dull and apathetic, will require the use of the spurs before the time I have indicated. All this is an affair of intelligence; it would be to insult my readers not to suppose them capable of supplying to the details what it is elsewhere impossible to particularize. You can readily understand that there are irritable, ill-disposed horses, whose defective dispositions have been made worse by previous bad management. With such subjects it is necessary to put more persistence into the supplings and the walk. In every case, whatever the slight modifications that the difference in the dispositions of the subjects render necessary, I persist in saying that there are no horses whose education ought not to be completed by my method in the space I designate. I mean here, that this time is sufficient to give the forces of the horse the fitness necessary for executing all the movements; the finish of education depends finally on the nicety of touch of the rider. In fact, my method has the advantages of recognizing no limits to the progress of equitation, and there is no performance *equestrianly* possible that a horseman who understands properly applying my principles cannot make his horse execute. I am about to give a convincing proof in support of this assertion, by explaining the sixteen new figures of the *manège* that I have added to the collection of the old masters.

---

[1] The use of the spurs.

9

Application of the preceding principles to the performance of the horses, Partisan, Capitaine, Neptune and Buridan

Baucher mounted on Partisan. Frontispiece by Giraud used
in the American translation published by Albert Cogswell.

The persons who systematically denied the efficacy of my method ought, necessarily, also to deny the results shown to them. They were forced to acknowledge that my performance at the *Cirque-Olympique* was new and extraordinary, but attributed it to causes, some more strange than others; all the while insisting that the equestrian talent of the rider did not go for nothing in the expertness of the horse.

According to some, I was a second Carter, accustoming my horses to obedience by depriving them of sleep and food; according to others, I bound their legs with cords, and thus held them suspended to prepare them for a kind of puppet-show; some were not far from believing that I fascinated them by the power of my looks. Finally, a certain portion of the public, seeing these animals perform in time to the sound of the charming music of one of my friends, M. Paul Cuzent, insisted seriously that they undoubtedly possessed, in a very great degree, the instinct of melody, and that they would stop short with the clarionets and trombones. So, the sound of the music was more powerful over my horse than I was myself! The animal obeyed a *do* or a *sol* nicely touched; but my legs and hands went for nothing in their effects. Would it be believed that such nonsense was uttered by people that passed for riders? I can comprehend their not having understood my means at first, since my method was new; but before judging it in so strange a manner, they ought, at least, it seems to me, to have sought to understand it.

I had found the round of ordinary feats of horsemanship too limited, since it was sufficient to execute one movement well to immediately practise the others with the same facility. So, it was proved to me that the rider who passed with precision along a straight line sideways (*de deux pistes*) at a walk, trot and gallop, could go in the same way with the head or the croup to the wall, with the shoulder in, perform the ordinary or reversed volts, the changes and counterchanges of hands, etc., etc. As to the *piaffer*, it was, as I have said, nature alone that settled this. This long and fastidious performance had no other variations than the different titles of the movements, since it was sufficient to vanquish one difficulty to be able to surmount all the others. I then created new figures of the *manège*, the execution of which rendered necessary more suppleness, more *ensemble*, more finish in the education of the horse. This was easy to me with my system; and to convince my adversaries that there was neither magic nor mystery in my performance at the *Cirque*, I am going to explain by what processes purely equestrian, and even without having recourse to *piliers*, cavessons or horse-whips, I have brought my horses to execute the sixteen figures of the *manège* that appear so extraordinary.

(1) Instantaneous flexion and support in the air of either one of the fore legs, while the other three legs remain fixed to the ground.

The means of making the horse raise one of his fore legs is very simple, as soon as the animal is perfectly supple and *rassemblé*. To make him raise, for example, the right leg, it is sufficient to incline his head slightly to the right, while making the weight of his body fall upon the left side. The rider's legs will be sustained firmly (the left a little more than the right), that the effect of the hand which brings the head to the right should not react upon the weight, and that the forces which serve to fasten to the ground the over-weighted part may give the horse's right leg enough action to make it rise from the ground. By a repetition of this exercise a few times, you will succeed in keeping this leg in the air as long a time as you wish.

(2) Mobility of the haunches, the horse resting on his fore legs, while his hind legs balance themselves alternately the one over the other; when the hind leg which is raised from left to right is moved, and is placed on the ground to become pivot in its turn, the other to be instantly raised and to execute the same movement.

The simple mobility of the haunches is one of the exercises that I have pointed out for the elementary education of the horse. We can complicate this performance by multiplying the alternate contact of the legs, until we succeed in easily carrying the horse's croup, one leg over the other, in such a way that the movement from left to right and from right to left cannot exceed one step. This exercise is good to give great nicety of touch to the rider, and to prepare the horse to respond to the lightest effects.

(3) Passing instantly from the slow *piaffer* to the precipitate *piaffer*, and *vice versa*.

After having brought the horse to display great mobility of the legs, we ought to regulate the movement of them. It is by the slow and alternated pressure of his legs that the rider will obtain the slow *piaffer*. He will make it precipitate by multiplying the contact. Both these *piaffers* can be obtained from all horses; but as this is among the great difficulties, perfect tact is indispensable.

(4) To back with an equal elevation of the transverse legs, which leave the ground and are placed again on it at the same time, the horse executing the movement with as much freedom and facility as if he were going forward, and without apparent aid from the rider.

Backing is not new, but it certainly is new upon the conditions that I lay down. It is only by the aid of a complete suppling and *ramener* that we succeed in so suspending the horse's body that the distribution of the weight is perfectly regular and the extremities acquire energy and activity alike. This movement then becomes as easy and graceful as it is painful and devoid of elegance when it is changed into *acculement*.[1]

(5) Simultaneous mobility of the two diagonal legs, the horse stationary. After having raised the two opposite legs, he carries them to the rear to bring them back again to the place they first occupied, and recommences the same movement with the other diagonal.

The suppling, and having got the horse in hand, make this movement easy. When he no longer presents any resistance, he appreciates the lightest effects of the rider, intended in this case to displace only the least possible quantity of forces and weight necessary to set in motion the opposite extremities. By repeating this exercise, it will in a little while be rendered familiar to the horse. The finish of the mechanism will soon give the finish of intelligence.

(6) Trot with a sustained extension; the horse, after having raised his legs, carries them forward, sustaining them an instant in the air before replacing them on the ground.

The processes that form the basis of my method reproduce themselves in each simple movement, and with still more reason in the complicated ones. If equilibrium is only obtained by lightness, in return there is no lightness without equilibrium; it is by the union of these two conditions that the horse will acquire the facility of extending his trot to the farthest possible limits, and will completely change his original gait.

(7) Serpentine trot, the horse turning to the right and to the left, to return nearly to his starting point, after having made five or six steps in each direction.

This movement will present no difficulty if we keep the horse in hand while executing the flexions of the neck at the walk and trot; you can readily see that such a performance is impossible without this condition. The leg opposite to the side towards which the neck turns ought always to be pressed.

(8) Instant halt by the aid of the spurs, the horse being at a gallop.

When the horse, being perfectly suppled, will properly bear the *attaques* and the *rassembler*, he will be fit to execute the halt upon the above conditions. In the application of this we will start with a slow gallop, in order to go on successively to the greatest speed. The legs preceding the hand, will bring the horse's hind legs under the middle of his body, then a prompt effect of the hand, by fixing them in this position, will immediately stop the bound. By this means we spare the horse's organization, which can thus be always kept free from blemish.

(9) Continued mobility or pawing, while stationary, of one of the horse's fore legs; the horse, at the rider's will, executing the movement by which he, of his own accord, often manifests his impatience.

This movement will be obtained by the same process that serves to keep the horse's leg in the air. In the latter case, the rider's legs must impress a continued support, in order that the force which holds the horse's leg raised keep up its effect; while, for the movement now in question, we must renew the action by a quantity of slight pressures, in order to cause the motion of the leg held up in the air. This extremity of the horse will soon acquire a

---

[1] *Acculement* and *reculer* have been previously explained; one is the horse backing falsely, the other backing correctly. [TRANSLATOR.]

movement subordinate to that of the rider's legs, and if the time is well seized, it will seem, so to say, that we make the animal move by the aid of mechanical means.

(10) To trot backwards, the horse preserving the same cadence and the same step as in the trot forwards.

The first condition, in order to obtain the trot backwards is to keep the horse in a perfect cadence and as *rassemblé* as possible. The second is all in the proceedings of the rider. He ought to seek insensibly by the combined effects to make the forces of the fore-hand exceed those of the hind-parts, without affecting the harmony of the movement. Thus we see that by the *rassembler* we will successively obtain the *piaffer* stationary, and the *piaffer* backwards, even without the aid of the reins.

(11) To gallop backwards, the time being the same as in the ordinary gallop; but the fore legs once raised, in place of coming to the ground, are carried backwards, that the hind-parts may execute the same backward movement as soon as the fore-feet are placed on the ground.

The principle is the same as for the preceding performance; with a perfect *rassembler*, the hind legs will find themselves so brought under the centre, that by raising the fore-hand, the movement of the hocks can only be an upward one. This performance, though easily executed with a powerful horse, ought not to be attempted with one not possessing this quality.

(12) Changing feet every step, each time of the gallop being done on a different leg.

In order to practise this difficult performance, the horse ought to be accustomed to execute perfectly, and as frequently as possible, changing feet at the touch. Before attempting these changes of feet every step, we ought to have brought him to execute this movement at every other step. Everything depends upon his aptness, and above all, on the intelligence of the rider; with this latter quality, there is no obstacle that is not to be surmounted. To execute this performance with the desirable degree of precision, the horse should remain light, and

perserve the same degree of action; the rider, on his part, should also avoid roughly inclining the horse's fore-hand to one side or the other.

(13) Ordinary *pirouettes* on three legs, the fore leg on the side towards which we are turning: remaining in the air during the whole time of the movement.

Ordinary *pirouettes* should be familiar to a horse broken after my method, and I have above shown the means to make him hold up one of his fore feet. If these two movements are well executed separately, it will be easy to connect them in a single performance. After having disposed the horse for the *pirouette*, we will prepare the mass in such a way as to raise the fore leg; this once in the air, we will throw the weight on the part opposite to the side towards which we wish to turn, by bearing upon this part with the hand and leg. The leg of the rider placed on the converging side, will only act during this time so as to carry the forces forward, in order to prevent the hand producing a retrograde effect.

(14) To back with a halt at each step, the right leg of the horse remaining in front motionless and held out at the full distance that the left leg has passed over, and *vice versa*.

This movement depends upon the nicety of touch of the rider, as it results from an effect of forces impossible to specify. Though this performance is not very graceful, the experienced rider will do well to often practise it, in order to learn to modify the effects of forces, and acquire all the niceties of his art in perfection.

(15) Regular *piaffer* with an instant halt on three legs, the fourth remaining in the air.

Here, also, as for the ordinary *pirouettes* upon three legs, it is by exercising the *piaffer* and the flexion of one leg separately, that we will succeed in uniting the two movements in one. We will interrupt the *piaffer* by arresting the contraction of three of the legs so as to leave it in one only. It is sufficient, then, in order to accustom the horse to this performance, to stop him while he is *piaffing*, by forcing him to contract one of his legs.

(16) Change of feet every time at equal

intervals, the horse remaining in the same place.

This movement is obtained by the same proceedings as are employed for changing feet every time while advancing; only it is much more complicated, since we must give an exact impulsion sufficiently strong to determine the movement of the legs without the body advancing. This movement consequently demands a great deal of tact on the rider's part, and cannot be practised except on a perfectly broken horse, but broken as I understand it.

Such is the vocabulary of the new figures of the *manège* that I have created, and so often executed before the public. As you see, this performance, which appeared so extraordinary that people would not believe it belonged to equestrianism, becomes very simple and comprehensible as soon as you have studied the principles of my method. There is not one of these movements in which is not discovered the application of the precepts I have developed in this book.

But, I repeat, if I have enriched equitation with a new and interesting work, I do not pretend to have attained the farthest limits of the art; and one may come after me, who, if he will study my system and practise it with intelligence, will be able to pass me on the course, and add something yet to the results I have obtained.

10

Succinct exposition of the method by questions and answers

Question. What do you understand by force?

Answer. The motive power which results from muscular contraction.

Q. What do you understand by *instinctive* forces?

A. Those which come from the horse — that is to say, of which he himself determines the employment.

Q. What do you understand by *transmitted* forces?

A. Those which emanate from the rider, and are immediately appreciated by the horse.

Q. What do you understand by resistances?

A. The force which the horse presents, and with which he seeks to establish a struggle to his advantage.

Q. Ought we first to set to work to annul the forces the horse presents for resistance, before demanding any other movements of him?

A. Without doubt, as then the force of the rider, which should displace the weight of the mass, finding itself absorbed by an equivalent resistance, every movement becomes impossible.

Q. By what means can we combat the resistances?

A. By the methodical and separate suppling of the jaw, the neck, the haunches, and the loins.

Q. What is the use of the flexions of the jaw?

A. As it is upon the lower jaw that the effects of the rider's hand are first felt, these will be null or incomplete if the jaw is contracted or closed against the upper one. Besides, as in this case the displacing of the horse's body is only obtained with difficulty, the movements resulting therefrom will also be painful.

Q. Is it enough that the horse *champ his bit* for the flexion of his jaw to leave nothing more to wish for?

A. No, it is also necessary that the horse *let go of the bit* — that is to say, that he should separate (at our will) his jaws as much as possible.

Q. Can all horses have this mobility of jaw?

A. All without exception, if we follow the gradation pointed out, and if the rider does not allow himself to be deceived by the flexion of the neck. Useful as this is, it would be insufficient without the play of the jaw.

Q. In the direct flexion of the jaw, ought we to give a tension to the curb-reins and those of the snaffle at the same time?

A. No, we must make the snaffle precede (the hand being placed as indicated in Fig. 3), until the head and neck are lowered; afterwards the pressure of the bit, in time with the snaffle, will promptly make the jaws open.

Q. Ought we often to repeat this exercise?

A. It should be continued until the jaws separate by a light pressure of the bit or snaffle.

Q. Why is the stiffness of the neck so powerful an obstacle to the education of the horse?

A. Because it absorbs to its profit the force which the rider seeks in vain to transmit throughout the whole mass.

Q. Can the haunches be suppled separately?

A. Certainly they can; and this exercise is comprised in what is called stationary exercise.

Q. What is its useful object?

A. To prevent the bad effects resulting from the instinctive forces of the horse, and to make him appreciate the forces transmitted by the rider without opposing them.

Q. Can the horse execute a movement without a shifting of weight?

A. It is impossible. We must first seek to make the horse take a position which causes such a variation in his equilibrium that the movement may be a natural consequence of it.

Q. What do you understand by position?

A. An arrangement of the head, neck and body, previously disposed according to the movements of the horse.

Q. In what consists the *ramener*?

A. In the perpendicular position of the head, and the lightness that accompanies it.

Q. What is the distribution of the forces and weight in the *ramener*?

A. The forces and weight are equally distributed through all the mass.

Q. How do we address the intelligence of the horse?

A. By the position, because it is that which makes the horse know the rider's intentions.

Q. Why is it necessary that in the backward movements of the horse, the legs of the rider precede the hand?

A. Because we must displace the points of support before placing upon them the mass that they must sustain.

Q. Is it the rider that determines his horse?

A. No. The rider gives action and position, which are the language; the horse answers this demand by the change of pace or direction that the rider had intended.

Q. Is it to the rider or to the horse that we ought to impute the fault of bad execution?

A. To the rider, and always to the rider. As it depends upon him to supple and place the horse in the way of the movement, and as

with these two conditions faithfully fulfilled, everything becomes regular, it is then to the rider that the merit or blame ought to belong.

Q. What kind of bit is suitable for a horse?

A. An easy bit.

Q. Why is an easy bit necessary for all horses, whatever may be their resistance?

A. Because the effect of a severe bit is to constrain and surprise a horse, while it ought to prevent him from doing wrong and enable him to do well. Now, we cannot obtain these results except by the aid of an easy bit, and above all, of a skillful hand; for the bit is the hand, and a good hand is the whole of the rider.

Q. Are there any other inconveniences connected with the instruments of torture called severe bits?

A. Certainly there are, for the horse soon learns to avoid the painful infliction of them by forcing the rider's legs, the power of which can never be equal to that of this barbarous bit. He succeeds in this by yielding with his body, and resisting with his neck and jaw, which misses altogether the aim proposed.

Q. How is it that nearly all the horsemen of renown have invented a particular kind of bit?

A. Because being wanting in personal science, they sought to replace their own insufficiency by aids or strange machines.

Q. Can the horse, perfectly in hand, defend himself?

A. No; for the just distribution of weight that this position gives supposes a great regularity of movement, and it would be necessary to overturn this in order that any act of rebellion on the part of the horse should take place.

Q. What is the use of the snaffle?

A. The snaffle serves to combat the opposing forces (lateral) of the neck, to make the head precede in all the changes of direction, while the horse is not yet familiarized with the effects of the bit; it serves also to arrange the head and neck in a perfectly straight line.

Q. In order to obtain the *ramener*, should we make the legs precede the hand or the hand the legs?

A. The hands ought to precede until they have produced the effect of giving great suppleness to the neck (this ought to be practised in the stationary exercises); then come the legs in their turn to combine the hind and foreparts in the movement. The continual lightness of the horse at all paces will be the result of it.

Q. Ought the legs and the hands to aid one another or act separately?

A. One of these extremities ought always to have the other for auxiliary.

Q. Ought we to leave the horse a long time at the same pace in order to develop his powers?

A. It is useless, since the regularity of movements results from the regularity of the positions; the horse that makes fifty steps at a trot regularly is much further advanced in his education than if he made a thousand in a bad position. We must then attend to his position, that is to say, his lightness.

Q. In what proportions ought we to use the force of the horse?

A. This cannot be defined, since these forces vary in different subjects; but we should be sparing of them, and not expend them without circumspection, particularly during the course of his education. It is on this account that we must, so to say, create for them a reservoir that the horse may not absorb them uselessly, and that the rider may make a profitable and more lasting use of them.

Q. What good will there result to the horse from this judicious employment of his forces?

A. As we will only make use of forces useful for certain movements, fatigue or exhaustion can only result from the length of time during which the animal will remain at an accelerated pace, and will not be the effect of an excessive muscular contraction which would preserve its intensity, even at a moderate pace.

Q. When should we first undertake to make the horse back?

A. After the suppling of the neck and haunches.

Q. Why should the suppling of the haunches precede that of the loins (the *reculer*)?

A. To keep the horse more easily in a straight line and to render the flowing back and forward of the weight more easy.

Q. Ought these first retrograde movements of the horse to be prolonged during the first lessons?

A. No. As their only object is to annul the instinctive forces of the horse, we must wait till he is perfectly in hand to obtain a backward movement, a true *reculer*.

Q. What constitutes a true *reculer*?

A. The lightness of the horse (head perpendicular), the exact balance of his body, and the elevation to the same height of the legs diagonally.

Q. At what distance ought the spur to be placed from the horse's flanks before the *attaque* commences?

A. The rowel should not be farther than two inches from the horse's flanks.

Q. How ought the *attaques* to be practised?

A. They ought to reach the flanks by a movement like the stroke of a lancet, and be taken away as quickly.

Q. Are there circumstances where the *attaque* ought to be practised without the aid of the hand?

A. Never; since its only object should be to give the impulsion which serves for the hand to contain (*renfermer*) the horse.

Q. Is it the *attaques* themselves that chastise the horse?

A. No. The chastisement is in the contained position that the *attaques* and the hand make the horse assume. As the latter then finds himself in a position where it is impossible to make use of any of his forces, the chastisement has all its efficiency.

Q. In what consists the difference between the *attaques* practised after the old principles, and those which the new method prescribed?

A. Our predecessors (that we should venerate) practised spurring in order to throw the horse out of himself; the new method makes use of it to contain him; that is, to give him that first position which is the mother of all the others.

Q. What are the functions of the legs during the *attaques*?

A. The legs ought to remain adherent to the horse's flanks and in no respect to partake of the movements of the feet.

Q. At what moment ought we to commence the *attaques*?

A. When the horse supports peaceably a strong pressure of the legs without getting out of hand.

Q. Why does a horse, perfectly in hand, bear the spur without becoming excited, and even without sudden movement?

A. Because the skillful hand of the rider, having prevented all displacings of the head, never lets the forces escape outwards; it concentrates them by fixing them. The equal struggle of the forces, or if you prefer it, their *ensemble*, sufficiently explains the apparent dullness of the horse in this case.

Q Is it not to be feared that the horse may become insensible to the legs and lose all that activity necessary for accelerated movements?

A. Although this is the opinion of nearly all the people who talk of this method without understanding it, there is nothing in it. Since all these means serve only to keep the horse in the most perfect equilibrium, promptness of movement ought necessarily to be the result of it, and, consequently, the horse will be disposed to respond to the progressive contact of the legs, when the hand does not oppose it.

Q. How can we judge whether an *attaque* is regular?

A. When, far from making the horse get out of hand, it makes him come into it.

Q. How ought the hand to be supported at the moments of resistance on the part of the horse?

A. The hand ought to stop, fix itself, and only be drawn sufficiently towards the body to give the reins a three-quarter tension. In the contrary case, we must wait till the horse bears upon the hand to present this insurmountable barrier to him.

Q. What would be the inconvenience of increasing the pressure of the bit by drawing the hand towards the body in order to slacken the horse in his paces by getting him in hand?

A. It would not produce an effect upon a particular part, but would act generally upon all the forces, in displacing the weight instead of annulling the force of impulsion. We should not wish to incline to one side what we cannot stop.

Q. In what case ought we to make use of the cavesson, and what is its use?

A. We should make use of it when the faulty construction of the horse leads him to defend himself, when only simple movements are demanded of him. It is also useful to use the cavesson with restive horses, as its object is to act upon the moral, while the rider acts upon the physical.

Q. How ought we to make use of the cavesson?

A. At first, the longe of the cavesson should be held at from fifteen or twenty inches from the horse's head, held out and supported with a stiff wrist. We must watch the proper times to diminish or increase the bearing of the cavesson upon the horse's nose, so as to use it as an aid. All viciousness that leads him to act badly is to be repressed by little jerks, which should be given at the very moment of defense. As soon as the rider's movements begin to be appreciated by the horse, the longe of the cavesson ought no longer to act; at the end of a few days the horse will only need the bit, to which he will respond without hesitation.

Q. In what case is the rider less intelligent than the horse?

A. When the latter subjects him to his caprices, and does what he wishes with him.

Q. Are the defenses of the horse physical or moral?

A. At first they are physical, but afterwards become moral; the rider ought then to seek out the causes that produce them, and endeavor, by a preparatory exercise, to re-establish the correct equilibrium that a bad natural formation prevented.

Q. Can the naturally well-balanced horse defend himself?

A. It would be as difficult for a subject uniting all that constitutes a good horse to give himself up to disorderly movements, as it is impossible for the one that has not received the like gifts from nature, to have regular movements, if art did not lend him its aid.

Q. What do you mean by *rassembler*?

A. The reunion of forces at the centre of gravity.

Q. Can we *rassembler* the horse that does not contain himself under the *attaques*?

A. This is altogether impossible; the legs would be insufficient to counterbalance the effects of the hand.

Q. At what time ought we to *rassembler* the horse?

A. When the *ramener* is complete.

Q. Of what service is the *rassembler*?

A. To obtain without difficulty everything of a complicated nature in horsemanship.

Q. In what does the *piaffer* consist?

A. In the graceful position of the body and the harmonized precision of movement of the legs and feet.

Q. Is there more than one kind of *piaffer*?

A. Two; the slow and the precipitate.

Q. Which is to be preferred of these two?

A. The slow *piaffer*, since it is only when this is obtained that the equilibrium is perfect.

Q. Ought we to make a horse *piaffe* who will not bear the *rassembler*?

A. No; for that would be to step out of the logical gradation that alone can give certain results. Besides, the horse that has not been brought forward by this chain of principles would only execute with trouble and ungracefully what he ought to accomplish with pleasure and nobly.

Q. Are all riders alike suited to conquer all the difficulties and seize all the effects of touch?

A. As in horsemanship, intelligence is the starting point for obtaining every result, everything is subordinate to this innate disposition; but every rider will have the power to break his horse to an extent commensurate with his own abilities to instruct.

11

Conclusion

Everybody complains nowadays of the degeneration of our breeds of horses. Apprehensive too late of a state of things which threatens even the national independence,[1] patriotic spirits are seeking to go back to the source of the evil, and are arranging divers systems for remedying it as soon as possible. Among the causes which have contributed the most to the loss of our old breeds, they forget, it seems to me, to mention the decline of horsemanship, nor do they consider that the revival of this art is indispensable in bringing about the regeneration of the horse.

The difficulties of horsemanship have long been the same, but formerly constant practice, if not taste, kept it up; these stimulants exist no longer. Fifty years ago, every man of rank was expected to be able to handle a horse with skill, and break one if necessary. This study was an indispensable part of the education of young people of family; and as it obliged them to devote two or three years to the rough exercises of the *manège*, in the end they all became horsemen, some by taste, the rest by habit. These habits once acquired were preserved throughout life; they then felt the necessity of possessing good horses, and men of fortune spared nothing in getting them. The sale of fine horses thus became easy; all gained by it, the breeder as well as the horse. It is not so now; the aristocracy of fortune, succeeding to that of birth, is very willing to possess the advantages of the latter, but would dispense with the onerous obligations which appertained to an elevated rank. The desire of showing off in public places, or motives still more frivolous, sometimes lead gentlemen of our times to commence the study of horsemanship, but, soon wearied of a work without satisfactory results, they find only a monotonous fatigue where they sought a pleasure, and are satisfied they know enough as soon as they can stick passably well in the saddle. So insufficient a knowledge of horsemanship, as dangerous as it is thoughtless, must necessarily occasion sad accidents. They then become disgusted with horsemanship and horses, and as nothing obliges them to continue the exercise, they give it up nearly altogether, and so much the more easily as they naturally care very little about the breeds of horses and their perfection. We must then, as a preliminary measure in the improvement of horses, raise up horsemanship from the low state into which it has fallen. The government can undoubtedly do much here; but it is for the masters of the art to supply, if necessary, what it leaves undone. Let them render attractive and to the purpose studies which have hitherto been too monotonous and often barren; let rational and true principles make the scholar see a real progress, that each of his efforts brings a success with it; and we will soon see young persons of fortune become passionately

---

[1] Much in this chapter, though written for France, applies with great appropriateness to our own country [i.e. the USA]. [TRANSLATOR.]

fond of an exercise which has been rendered as interesting to them as it is noble, and discover, with their love for horses, a lively solicitude for all that concerns their qualities and education.

But horsemen can aim at still more brilliant results. If they succeed in rendering easy the education of common horses, they will make the study of horsemanship popular among the masses; they will put within reach of moderate fortunes, so numerous in our land of equality, the practise of an art that has hitherto been confined to the rich. Such has been the aim of the labors of my whole life. It is in the hope of attaining this end that I give to the public the fruit of my long researches.

But I should say, however, that if I was upheld by the hope of being one day useful to my country, it was the army above all that occupied my thoughts. Though counting many skillful horsemen in its ranks, the system they are made to follow, impotent in my eyes, is the true cause of the equestrian inferiority of so many, as well as of their horses being so awkward and badly broken. I might add that to the same motive is to be attributed the little taste for horsemanship felt by the officers and soldiers. How can it be otherwise? The low price allowed by government for horses of remount, causes few horses of good shape to be met with in the army, and it is only on these that the education is easy. The officers themselves, mounted upon a very common sort of horses, strive in vain to render them docile and agreeable. After two or three years of fatiguing exercise, they end by gaining a mechanical obedience, but the same resistances and the same faults of construction are perpetually recurring. Disgusted by difficulties that appear insurmountable, they trouble themselves no more about horses and horsemanship than the demands of the service actually require.

Yet it is indispensable that a cavalry officer be always master of his horse, so much so as to be able, so to say, to communicate his own thoughts to him; the uniformity of manœuvres, the necessities of command, the perils of the battle-field, all demand it imperatively. The life of the rider, every one knows, often depends upon the good or bad disposition of his steed; in the same way the loss or the gain of a battle often hangs on the degree of precision in manœuvring a squadron. My method will give military men a taste for horsemanship, a taste which is indispensable in the profession they practise. The nature of officers' horses, considered as so defective, is exactly the one upon which the most satisfactory results may be obtained. These animals generally possess a certain degree of energy, and as soon as we know how rightly to use their powers by remedying the physical faults that paralyze them, we will be astonished at the resources they will exhibit. The rider fashioning the steed by degrees will regard him as the work of his hand, will become sincerely attached to him, and will find as much charm in horsemanship as he previously felt *ennui* and disgust. My principles are simple, easy in their application, and within the reach of every mind. They can everywhere make (what is now so rare) skillful horsemen. I am sure that if my method is adopted and well understood in the army, where the daily exercise of the horse is a necessary duty, we will see equestrian capacities spring up among the officers and sub-officers by thousands. There is not one among them who, with an hour a day of study would not soon be able to give any horse in less than three months the following qualities and education:

1. General suppling.
2. Perfect lightness.
3. Graceful position.
4. A steady walk.
5. Trot steady, measured, extended.
6. Backing as easily and freely as going forward.
7. Gallop easy with either foot, and change of foot by the touch.
8. Easy and regular movement of the haunches, comprising ordinary and reversed *pirouettes*.
9. Leaping the ditch and the bar.
10. *Piaffer*.
11. Halt from the gallop, by the aid of first,

the pressure of the legs, and then a light support of the hand.

I ask all conscientious men: have they seen many horsemen of renown obtain similar results in so short a time?

The education of the men's horses, being less complicated than that of those intended for officers, would on that account be more rapid. The principal things will be the supplings and the backing, followed by the walk, the trot and the gallop, while keeping the horse perfectly in hand. The colonels will soon appreciate the excellent results of this exercise, in consequence of the precision with which all the movements are made. The important flexions of the fore-hand can be executed without leaving the stables, each rider turning his horse around in the stall. It is not for me to point out to the colonels of regiments the exact way of putting my method in practice; it is enough for me to lay down my principles and to explain them. The instructors will themselves supply the details of application too long to enumerate here.

I must again repeat, this book is the fruit of twenty years of observation constantly verified by practice. A long and painful work without doubt, but what compensation I have found in the results I have been happy enough to obtain. In order to let the public judge of the importance of my discoveries, it is sufficient here to give their nomenclature, and I present these processes as new ones, because I can conscientiously say that they never were practised before me. I have added them successively to the manual of the horseman the following principles and innovations:

1. New means of obtaining a good seat.
2. Means of making the horse come to the man, and rendering him steady to mount.
3. Distinction between the instinctive forces of the horse and the communicated forces.
4. Explanation of the influence of a bad formation upon the horse's resistances.
5. Effect of bad formations on the neck and croup, the principal focuses of resistance.
6. Means of remedying the faults, or supplings of the two extremities, and the whole of the horse's body.
7. Annihilation of the instinctive forces of the horse, in order to substitute for them forces transmitted by the rider, and to give ease and beauty of motion to the ungraceful animal.
8. Equality of sensibility of mouth in all horses; adoption of a uniform bit.
9. Equality of sensibility of flanks in all horses; means of accustoming them all to bear the spur alike.
10. All horses can place their heads in the position of *ramener* and acquire the same lightness.
11. Means of bringing the centre of gravity in a badly-formed horse to the place it occupies in a well-formed one.
12. The rider disposes his horse for a moment, but he does not determine the movement.
13. Why sound horses often are faulty in their paces. Means of remedying this in a few lessons.
14. For changes of direction, use of the leg opposite to the side towards which we turn, so that it may precede the other one.
15. In all backward movements of the horse the rider's legs ought to precede the hands.
16. Distinction between the *reculer* and the *acculement*; the good effect of the former in the horse's education; the bad effect of the latter.
17. The use of the spurs as a means of education.
18. All horses can *piaffer*; means of rendering this movement slow or precipitate.
19. Definition of the true *rassembler*; means of obtaining it; of its usefulness to produce grace and regularity in complicated movements.
20. Means of bringing all horses to step out freely at a trot.
21. Rational means of putting a horse at a gallop.
22. Halt at a gallop, the legs or the spur preceding the hand.

23. Force continued in proportion to the forces of the horse; the rider should never yield until after having *annulled* the horse's resistances.

24. Education of the horse in parts, or means of exercising his forces separately.

25. Complete education of horses of ordinary formation in less than three months.

26. Sixteen new figures of the *manège* proper for giving the finishing touch to the horse's education, and for perfecting the rider's touch.

It is understood that all the details of application appertaining to these innovations are new also, and likewise belong to me.

PART THREE

Dialogues on equitation

by François Baucher
translated by Hilda Nelson

Translator's introduction

Dialogues sur l'Equitation (*Dialogues on Equitation*) was first published in 1835, shortly after Baucher had moved to Paris. Initially this work bore the authorship of François Baucher and his *confrère*, Jules Pellier. When it was reprinted in Baucher's *Oeuvres complètes* in 1854, the name Pellier was missing. Whether Pellier really did co-author this work is a moot ques-tion. However, Baucher did have the habit of showing Pellier his notes and asking for his comments. (This is evident in his Introduction to his *Dictionnaire raisonné d'Equitation*.) This translation is based on the eleventh edition of the complete works published in 1859.

Hilda Nelson

First dialogue

The Great Hippo-Théo, God of the Quadrupeds, a Horseman, and a Horse.

God (Hippo-Théo): Too many kicks with spurs and too many proddings with the crop have all too often been distributed without any discernment; too many buckings and kickings of all kinds were an answer to them. And all done without protocol, without any previous declaration of war. It is time that there be an end to all this; it is time that after this duel, there be an accounting. Perhaps it is a good idea to have the belligerent parties dine together? It is, indeed, true that a minor difficulty got in the way of any showdown; I am now raising the problem. Quadruped, you shall possess speech. Make use of all the means that the physical and anatomical sciences can afford you. Tell us if all these rigorous exertions put upon you by these imperious horsemen were well or poorly executed, or if your fits of ill-temper are part of your nature. By virtue of My Omnipotence, I accord you for one hour the gift of speech. And you, biped, you shall speak in turn. You will address your complaints to me and you will show the value of sound thinking. I want to know whether you are worthy of this most noble and most useful of gifts that nature has bestowed upon you in order to allay your sorrows and triple your joy. But above all, avoid all personal and crude insults, which prove nothing. Begin then. Both of you can count on my impartiality.

The Horseman: I'll start out first, as the one most ancient in the use of speech. And may Your Omnipotence judge if I am not justified in my complaints. For an entire five minutes I am unable to place my foot in the stirrup. I am unable, by 'Whoas' and jerks of the reins, to make this animal understand that he is intractable. But he pays no attention. Several times he almost broke my leg by bucking and kicking maliciously.

God *addressing the horse:* What do you have to say to this peremptory questioning?

The Horse: One of the most precious qualities I received from you, Almighty, is action. I was under the impression that I was to make use of it. The present Lord horseman, whose tastes are quite different from those of my previous master, has not made me comprehend, until now, the use of defences. My former master, who was agile and skilful, was pleased to employ his agility by getting astride me and, then, exciting me to caracole, gave me a tug of the reins to make me gallop. Although this last method was inopportune and it could have been easy for me to refuse, I complied pleasantly. However, I cannot understand that now the same methods have opposite effects. It is a fact that the pain I get from the brusque pressure of the bit is distressing. But this handsome horseman always has the reins too long. I only become aware of this after I have begun to move. Sometimes I even get rid of the reins due to the speed of my movements and give myself to my spirited inspirations under the impression that I am behaving correctly. And then I hear many 'Whoas'. But since my impatient horseman has not given himself the trouble to make me understand the value of this word, I am incapable of heeding him.

God: What was he supposed to do?

A lesson in mounting. (Vergnaud, *Manuel d'equitation*, 1834)

The Horse: Place a cavesson on my nose, place himself in front of me, lunge in hand, and look at me with a kind eye; then make me understand, while caressing me, what he wishes of me. At the same time have a groom place his foot in the stirrup, while reassuring me by means of a gentle voice and sonorous syllables. If I become subject to impatience, then a slight tug of the cavesson will serve as a reminder. This reminder needed to be repeated only two or three times before I would have become well behaved. But to succeed one must find the means of rendering intelligible that which one wishes us to learn. But, as Your Omnipotence has already seen, these gentlemen hardly give themselves the trouble of doing so. As for the kicks, it seems to me that it is usually some brutal grooms who whip my legs. And fear makes me contemptuous. *A cat that has been whitewashed fears cold water.*

God: Well! Sire horseman, what do you think of these arguments? It seems to me that they make any response difficult.

The Horseman: I was unaware that such procedures were necessary with an animal whose condition in life is servitude, and whose lack of intelligence forces him to submit to all our whims.

God: Are you so sure of the validity of what you are saying? But, admitting that the horse is less intelligent than you are, does it not behove you to use this intelligence, which you assume you possess exclusively, so as to make him understand what it is you want of him? But, before going any further, let it be said, and never forget, that the horse is endowed with intellectual faculties which your vanity alone prevents you from recognizing. In the final analysis, because a particular *cloth* is less fine than another does not prevent it from being *cloth*.

The Horseman: I admit to being guilty in this matter. However, I would like to point out to Your Omnipotence that our doctors of sciences and letters have judged this question quite differently. But I return to my quarrel. When, for better or for worse, I manage to place myself in the saddle, I become subject to further ill-tempered behaviour on the part of the horse. He performs what is called *le dos de carpe*, followed by a succession of jumps that throw me out of the saddle. Wherein have I failed? My behaviour, as you can see, has been quite inoffensive until then. He does not heed good behaviour.

The Horse: The sensitivity that Your Divinity has given us makes us feel immediately the clumsiness and the ignorance of our horseman. First, his uncertain and unsteady posture disturbs and muddles our most natural paces. What does it matter if he wants to subject us to his awkward and brusque movements? Am I wrong in wishing to make known to him that I do not like to be ill-treated and that he must learn the rules of an art before putting it into practice?

The Horseman: Fiddlesticks! Why should I, civilized man, have to learn what primitive peoples practise so well of their own accord and without following any principles? If I am rich, am I not able to buy a horse appropriate to my needs and thereby exempt myself from playing the role of artist? I state once more that the horse is shaking too much the yoke to which he is bound by the laws of nature.

God: It is up to me to respond to your arrogant outburst. First of all, you should know that when it comes to his physical strength, primitive man is superior to civilized man. And as money means nothing to him, he has to find other means of providing for himself and, in order to succeed, is forced to spend whole days mounted on his beloved companion. Since childhood, he has devoted himself to perilous journeys which make him into a sound horseman. Furthermore, the sandy ground upon which he rides in no way forces his attention upon avoiding stones and ruts which clutter and cut your narrow paths filled with carriages and obstacles of all types. Do you really believe that the gold amassed in your sumptuous palaces renders learning unnecessary? Become an artist in spite of yourself, otherwise your pleasures will be more limited than those of the creature whose abilities you so disdain. Or if, in spite of the God of the arts, you only listen to your inept vainglory, take heed that you do not fall from a saddle into a coffin. I end my justified reprimand and continue to listen to what you

have to say. Perhaps I will finally find the occasion to defer to your advice.

The Horseman: Tired of always remaining on the same spot, I want to make my horse go towards the promenades so that my gracefulness and posture can be admired. Well, after having struggled for some time and been defeated, I am forced to give in and continue on foot, against my will, the walk I had promised myself to do on horseback. What can one do to counteract an animal who is so strong and brutal? It seems to me that if he possessed the nobility that you attribute to him, he would be proud to exhibit in public his beautiful behaviour, if not as a professional, at least as an amateur.

The Horse: My answer is simple and easy. As your means of transmitting your commands to me are ambiguous, lack energy, and constrain me so painfully without making me understand your wishes, you must not hold it against me when I freely dispose of my own strength and try to avoid that which is painful to me.

The Horseman: But why, if my means of execution are always the same, are you obstinate only from time to time? Does this not denote caprice or ill-will?

The Horse: No. It is proof of my lack of spite. I promptly forget what your ignorance has produced and often return to the basic good nature of a horse. But then your movements exasperate me so much that, despite myself, I abandon a ride that would have been pleasant and useful to me. I prefer to remain pinioned in your unhealthy stable and suffer the harsh treatment of your groom; for as in other things, like master, like servant.

God: I hope, my Lord horseman, that your complaints rest on more solid foundations to win your case. Until now my expectations have been in vain. Continue.

The Horseman: Your Omnipotence has given the horse three gaits. Well, when I manage to get him to move, I first want him to walk straight ahead since he is walking on a straight path. Then a new mark of disobedience emerges on his part: either he trots, or he stops;

he throws himself either to the right or to the left, rendering me liable to falling in a ditch. Whereas my intention was that he should walk straight ahead. To what do I attribute these new whims?

The Horse: Only to yourself, Lord horseman. Only two things are possible: either I can dispose of my strength and I am free to do as I please, and can use this freedom as does any thinking being; or you contain my voluntary movement and I must submit myself. In the latter instance you have to know what my natural movements are so that they can be consistent with your directions. Thus you must activate me only lightly to make me go into the walk and maintain the same degree of pressure so that the gait does not change. The pressure of your legs must be graduated with respect to my sensibility and my previous action. You do just the opposite: legs unsteady and away from my flanks, then they are suddenly and abruptly felt, then they are immediately removed. It is impossible with this grotesque posture to make me understand that it is the walk that you want me to execute. Furthermore, contrary movements are indicated by your treacherous hand, for every sensitive creature wishes to escape pain. That is what I do when I swing my head from one side to the other in order to avoid the insupportable pressure of the bit which punishes me for a fault I never committed. As for the habit of zigzagging of which you complain, I will try to make you understand by means of a physical explanation that the disparity of the strength of your hand and leg aids brings with it a disparity of the distribution of my weight. Thus the weight of my body, sometimes carried to the right, sometimes to the left, cannot be equally distributed on my four legs; neither can they be given a mobility that is always equal. Thus, your awkward hand gives me these various inclinations or, not being guided by anything, I instinctively take these positions. From this originate the irregular movements which displease you so much. Am I a sorcerer? No. Are you? Nothing proves it until now.

The Horseman: Do you raise the same arguments for the trot, which is familiar to you, but which I can neither moderate nor accelerate as I wish? Whence come these two extremes? Do not forget to mention in your answer the reason why, despite the huge price I paid for you, you are subject to buckling at the knees. Also tell us why your shoes hit each other (what one calls over-reaching), which is most shocking to the ear of a gentleman who appreciates the horseman only by the qualities of his horse. Is it out of malice or ill-will that you succeed in making me appear pitiful in the eyes of all the amateur riders who mistake you for a hack? Answer me.

The Horse: I will answer all your questions no matter how complicated they may be; but to do so I must proceed methodically. What makes me accelerate at the trot is what makes me accelerate at the walk. And it will be likewise for all the gaits as long as your wrists and your legs do not coordinate. Not only is a correct opposition between these two forces[1] necessary to achieve the proper degree of strength to maintain the continuity of a given pace, but it gives us this balance which enables us to feel and appreciate the slightest constraints imparted by reins and legs and which makes us respond. You must give us this position with great exactness. Admit (and you are fully prepared to do so) that we are without any intelligence whatsoever and explain to me, you who are much weaker than we are, how you manage to move our mass and make it take the one or other direction, if you ignore the laws of balance. Since my body is carried on four columns, must one not either weigh them down or lighten them alternately, either to fix them or raise them? And is it not through certain positions of the body that you can succeed? If this is admitted, and being provided with intelligence and will-power, am I wrong in refusing

---

[1] He will later develop this idea of 'opposition between two forces', that is between hands and legs, in his discourse on the new method, first published in 1842. It is then that he will begin to talk about the *effet d'ensemble*.

to execute movements which were not preceded by a correct position? Your reproach with respect to the price I cost Your Lordship does not fall within my province. It is a question of pure swindle and we are strangers to these sorts of niceties that involve only the civilized species. Learn to distinguish the qualities that comprise a good horse and recognize if it is not a remnant of the savagery of previous masters that is the cause of his opposition and the poor service that he renders. The buckling at the knee and the over-reaching of shoes may be caused either by certain vices that I have just mentioned, or your poor way of directing us. The poor positions that you force us to take obviously bring with them an irregularity of movements which exposes us, as well as you, to all sorts of awkward and even dangerous positions. Your pride is hurt, you say; but if we should also have some pride, how much more is it due to your clumsiness which prevents us from displaying all the grace and litheness of our movements!

God: What do you conclude from this discourse, Sire horseman? Remember that to admit not to know something is knowing something. We are here to give each other advice and therefore one must do justice to the right person. Retracting a false notion and yielding to evidence is the sign of a man of honour. What must my opinion of you be?

The Horseman: I believe Your Divinity would think it ill of me, if, without being convinced, I were to adhere to the reasonings of others. I have seen so many learned men support doctrines so different from each other and based on such good reasoning and so subtle a logic, that they all seem correct to me. The matter in question is, indeed, not similar, but your quadruped has a formidable adversary to combat, namely pride. Until now I wanted to place all blame on the horse, but now I am

satisfied in believing that he was not entirely to blame.[2] You see that you are in part winning the case. Be patient and let me continue my questionings. It seems to me that I have enough arguments to justify myself and soon the balance will dip in my direction.

God: I wish it, indeed, since you hold so dearly to it. But I doubt it, for the horse seems well up in the subject.[3]

The Horseman: Admitting that I may be to blame for the irregularity of your speed, but am I also to blame for the resistances you manifest so stubbornly when I want to turn you to the right or to the left? I imitate, nevertheless, several excellent horsemen who are friends of mine. I saw what means they used to change their horse's direction, and I saw the latter respond quickly. Why is it that with the same procedure I do not have the same result?

The Horse: I will, in turn, Sire horseman, make some concessions to you. You are aware that the Most Powerful One present here created us with as many shapes as there are subjects, that is to say, that, as is the case with the human species where one does not encounter two beings endowed with the same physical traits and the same proportions, so it is that no two horses are built alike. This variety of shapes results in the fact that certain types of conformation present difficulties. On the other hand, it is due to a horse's beautiful proportions, in addition to his innate action, that some horsemen, even ignorant ones, are obeyed. In this instance, the credit that a horseman gives himself is totally due to the natural disposition of the horse. Those horses who are less well distributed by nature have, until now, awaited in vain to be compensated by good horsemen.[4]

The Horseman: Why is it, quadruped logician, that you do not admit that there are horses who have a bad disposition, but blame

---

[2] The French text reads as follows: 'now I am satisfied that I am not to blame', which, in view of the preceding lines, seems like a contradiction. I have therefore taken the liberty of translating the sentence to fit the context. I have done this in a number of other instances.

[3] This is a play on words. *Ferré* means *shod* as well as to be at home in a given subject.

[4] Baucher is obviously referring to his own expertise as a horseman and a teacher.

all their defences on their conformation and the manner they are treated? This requires a greater explanation. Explain to me also about the resistances of those horses with poor conformation and indicate the ways one can make the best of it. You see that my grandeur is not without some kindness since it condescends to ask your advice.

The Horse: I repeat, Honoured Master, horses with good conformation who are vicious (with a very few exceptions) do not exist. Horses have nothing in them to engender vice. They know neither vanity, nor pride, nor greed, nor hypocrisy, nor meanness, nor avarice, nor ambition, nor egoism, etc. On what would they base their viciousness, which would not exist even among humans were it not for these vices, which are products of civilization? For what reason would the horse, stronger and possessing a construction superior to yours for walking, not carry you with pride, even joy, for your weight, well distributed, would cost him no more than it would cost you to follow our movements. We cannot be naturally evil, since everything that gives rise to evil is unknown to us; only your poor methods, your ignorance, can give us this defect. I have already said that a horse of action, with good conformation, is less subject to vice. I will explain to you the reason for this. You do concede that a horse who is well united in his articulations, free of any defects and whose body is so well constructed that he could, so to speak, very well do without his extremities, would be all that one could wish for physically and morally, if, with this good construction, he possessed what one calls this sacred fire, or this action that renews itself constantly. Such are the good horses of English breed. For, although I was sold as originating from that country, I am a native of Mellerault.[5] And although the breed of this area produces some good horses, we are, unfortunately, forced to recognize the superiority of our brothers from across the sea. If your Lord-

ship wishes to question our Divine Creator, He will undoubtedly give him the reason for the difference between the various breeds. As far as I am concerned, I come back to the good horse, no matter from what country he originates. Balance being the basis of all our movements, the more the regularity of our proportions is brought together, the less the horseman will have to concern himself with us. This primary position being indispensable in order to obtain easily the one which tells us to change direction or gait, you will understand that we are naturally disposed to respond with promptitude and ease, as none of these movements cause either effort or confusion in our mind. It is now easier for me to explain why horses with defects, weak, who have poor conformation, are more difficult to handle and become stubborn, which are imperfections I have received to some extent from birth. To these imperfections others were soon added. I can speak from experience, not from tradition. First of all, I was ridden much too soon, at the age of four. Growth is rapid in our land; we also remain weak for quite a while. At the age of seven we have much more vigour than at six. That is why we are not asked to do long and exacting tasks until we reach at least seven years of age. Furthermore, until we have reached the age of four, we must not be abandoned in a pasture at the mercy of a brutal guardian who instils in us disgust and antipathy for all that man represents. As a result, if sold before the age of four we become wild and suspicious, having no idea of what we are supposed to do. Thus saddle, bridle, etc., everything is for us subject to fear and terror and we seek quite naturally to avoid them. When, in order to familiarize us with these objects, we are mistreated for no reason at all and without pity, do you think that it is wrong for us to make use of all the means of defence at our disposal, such as bucking and biting, that is, all that can banish the ignoramus who

[5] Mellerault is most likely Le Merlerault in Normandy, close to the famous Haras du Pin (stud-farm) where Count d'Aure served as director for a short period.

makes us the victims of his brutalities? Why are we not already made sociable in a stable at the age of three by putting us in the care of a person who is gentle and patient? Why not let us harrow a field for a few hours, a task that could be augmented as our strength increased and which would also familiarize us with the habits and ways of man who, soon, would become our best friend? Far from doing that, we are made ill-tempered and ridden too early. As I have already stated, a good conformation can compensate for these two wrongs, if the horse falls into the hands of a knowledgeable and patient equerry. But if, as in my case, his back is too long, his croup too narrow and his thighs too thin, and if with these natural defects he falls into the hands of an inexperienced man, which is what happened to me several times, is it then astonishing that he is recalcitrant? The unsoundness of my hindquarters quite naturally makes me heavy on the forehand; from this emerges the difficulty of controlling me. However, with the help of my high and large hocks, there is, indeed, a way of bringing about the disappearance of the contraction that is due to the poor conformation of my hindquarters, and a lightness of head. But to achieve this, one needs the necessary discernment, knowledge, even experience, and equerries possessing these qualities are rare. Furthermore, the poor position given us by the horseman, and which remains unchanged, forces us to use the appropriate strength to combat successfully the one with which the horseman opposes us. This will remain so for as long as our position is not changed. Unable to achieve this transference of strength and weight, the requested movement, which is merely the result, is a physical impossibility. It is then that we are not spared imprecations. In turn the crop and the spurs, the jerking of the reins, are introduced. And since mechanical punishments cannot bring about the correct position for the movements asked, we sometimes allow ourselves to be thrashed without understanding or learning any more. Sometimes pushed to despair, we punish the horseman for

his inept brutality by attempting to rid ourselves of the inhuman yoke imposed upon us. This is what you call viciousness! Think about this and you will soon change your mind and your way of acting.

The Horseman: On the basis of what I have just heard, I believe I have sometimes made use of inopportune means. However, I allow myself the right to ask you several more questions and the exactitude of your answers will, undoubtedly, call forth my conviction. Get ready for new attacks while I ask the Great Hippo-Théo why it is that good horses abound in some nations, whereas in others they are much more rare. And without going any further, I will mention France and England.

God: The fact that you ask this question, Sire horseman, does not speak favourably with respect to your knowledge in equine matters. Do you ignore the fact that your country was once the best endowed with good breeds, and that your lack of interest in these animals, and your lack of national pride, are responsible for allowing these breeds to degenerate? Instead of having recourse to well-matched cross-breedings, which would have perfected them, you allowed them to degenerate. Oh! how many times did I not reproach myself for having made a mistake in the choice of countries that I favoured! On the other hand, this is perhaps an advantage, for you would never have resigned yourself to the sacrifices which the need to perfect the breed demanded of you. What French sovereign would have dared employ, as did Henry VIII, the most violent means, going as far as having all those mares killed who were not judged adequate for suitable reproduction. When did you consent to make great sacrifices, as did the English, to buy Arab stallions and have them brought over at great expense to your country? Not caring much for horses, you do not give yourself the trouble of finding out what is right for them, such as dressings, hygienic care, walks, etc. It is true that those noble lords sometimes put their lively steeds to harsh trials; but, on the other hand, there is not a single mistress lavished with greater care than are these steeds when they enter their beautiful and healthy stables. The groom devotes himself totally to his horse, serving him exclusively. To see to it that the horse's perspiration does not cease too rapidly, he wisps down the sweat vigorously with a cloth, and continues to rub the horse until he is completely dry and his coat has become as smooth and shiny as silk. Then the nostrils and mouth are washed with a mixture of water and vinegar. The legs are wrapped with strips of flannel to prevent them from becoming fatigued and thereby obstructing the cellular tissues. Food is given only with great caution. In the final analysis, everything is taken care of, even the amount of heat in the stable which is regulated by means of a thermometer so that it compensates for the outside temperature. The French, on the other hand, are forced to demand less of their horses due to their lack of vigour; and the fact that very little interest is devoted to them contributes to rendering them quickly incapable of service. The horse enters his stall sweating and out of breath. His master does not bother about him. A light blanket is placed on his back and the groom, a sort of Jack-of-all-trades, occupied in the kitchen or any other indoor task, leaves the miserable quadruped face to face with his flake of hay, happy not to have to wash the horse's belly to remove the mud which covers it. Thus the perspiration ceases and the result is inflammation of the lungs, which reduces the poor creature to the point of death. And you believe, Sire horseman, that this unconcern on your part does not destroy the qualities of the best horse? Don't believe it! This unconcern is more detrimental to his well-being than the plague and famine. I believe I have explained sufficiently how the breeds can be improved or degenerated. But heed once more the word of a connoisseur who became blind. He heard someone beside him say that a certain horse was superb. 'Then he must be quite fat', he answered, 'for the French rate a horse as though he were a pig, namely the best one is the fattest one.' This criticism is biting but accurate, at least for most Frenchmen

who have horses.

The Horseman: Despite all the respect I bear for Your Omnipotence, I cannot stop from saying that He treats us harshly. However, I can affirm that even if His advice is not followed literally by others, as far as I am concerned, it will bring about considerable progress in the essential cares I will give to this worthy friend of man. Our stud-farms are beginning to improve with respect to the amelioration of the breeds and there is good reason to believe that soon we shall be able to rival wholeheartedly our neighbours from across the Channel. Even if we do not achieve the same perfection, we will at least come within reach of it. For this reason, Your Divinity must at times cast an eye of commiseration on our actions. The Italian says that with patience, all is possible; if You deign to believe in this maxim, our progress will be unfailing.

God: Count on me, Sire horseman. My all-seeing eye will allow none of your good attempts to go unencouraged and unrewarded.

The Horseman: I come back to you, noble creature, and beg you, as one last question, to explain to me why, when I ask you to gallop on a given leg or make you walk sideways, you refuse to do so; tell me, how can I get you to execute these movements without constraint either on your part or on mine? You see now that I want to manage you according to the rules taken from nature. Do not refuse this ability to the one who will soon have no better friend than you.

The Horse: Whosoever takes the trouble of looking for me will always find me. You know well, Lord horseman, that I am too greatly interested in the success of your endeavours to neglect telling you everything you must know with the honesty of a horse and without any flowered rhetoric. Truth is one. It is simply that it must be told. I will follow this course, regardless of the barrenness it could give to my words. When you succeed in making me take the gallop, it is either by chance that you do so, or it is by destroying the balance of a gait that you obtain another one. Thus the trot pushed to excess brings forth the gallop and it is by forcing and corrupting all the positions of this first gait that you obtain the second one. When this is the case, a good horse is quickly lost. You ask me how you can make a horse get into the gallop without forcing him painfully to do so and without exposing oneself to any danger — Pardon my honesty, Lord horseman, but it seems to me that you would not be able to understand me. Even admitting this, you would not be able to execute what you understood. To do so, you lack two things: first of all, a firm seat which identifies you, so to speak, by the whole circumference of our body; furthermore, you need a firm action of the wrists and legs in order to bring about the desired movement. Once these two conditions are fulfilled, nothing is easier for you to transmit to us instantly what you wish us to do and make us obey. How do you manage this? First by flexing us, then by placing our head correctly. And since at the gallop our forelegs are the first to depart, it is necessary to lighten them before anything else. This way, this gait will be graceful without any effort. What I say about the gallop is also applicable to all our movements, be they simple or complex. Always take into consideration the state of mobility or fixity in which our extremities must find themselves whenever you ask something of us. Then dispose of our body in such a way as to obtain the right result. Then you will possess all the secrets pertaining to equitation. Work on the haunches, existing less in nature, is even more complicated and difficult to execute well. It is not possible for me to explain to you what sort of strength is required, which is more or less considerable, since this depends on the strength with which the horse opposes you. Furthermore, in order to obtain these exact movements, one must have tact and, above all, an equestrian sensitivity. Accept to learn the principles of this art and soon your intelligence will give you its scientific aspect. Thus all the difficulties that arise on account of the specific conformations of the horse will be overcome by you. Soon you will obtain real successes and

the joys they will give to you will be incalculable. You will then admit that the horseman is always wrong when the horse executes a movement poorly. For, if he is properly suppled so that his head is well placed, and if he is then given the correct position, the execution will be prompt and precise; or else the horse does not have an adequate degree of suppleness and the proper position cannot be achieved. Then simply be prudent and ask nothing of him, for you will have no luck in achieving anything.

Inscribe well into your memory these two expressions which encompass all the principles of equitation: *suppling* and *position*, and your wishes will become mine. This makes clear to you that, once these conditions have been complied with, we are gentle and cease to be recalcitrant.

The Horseman: I finally give in, and will uphold the idea against one and all, not believing, as Boileau did, that the most stupid animal is man, but that his inexperience can make him commit all sorts of blunders, and that he often finds himself to be inferior to the animal he is handling. Indeed, Hippo-Théo, I will right away take a course in the principles of equitation and will then ask for a second audition with Your Divinity, so that You deign to initiate me into all these mysteries and strengthen me in this noble science. And I will not ride my most obliging steed until I have become worthy of him. Thank you a thousand times for this lesson. I will keep it for ever in my mind.

God: Goodbye, Sire horseman. I will return, have no doubt. But meanwhile, while waiting for this second voyage, put some perseverance and some zeal into your work. Listen patiently to the advice of your teacher and be discreet in your questionings, without, nonetheless, sparing him those questions that appear useful in enlightening your doubts. Once you have recognized in him the necessary qualities to instil in you his principles, submit yourself totally to his decisions; for if his precepts have been drawn from nature, if he is enlightened by all that physics embraces as positive and undeniable, he can never err in the progressive march that he makes you take. However, to make you aware of certain old routines that would slow down the progress of your instruction, the following is what the gradual process must be. Fifteen days suffice to limber your thighs and your back and to give them that good position which will give the proper direction to your strength; the purely mechanical mobility of arms and legs will follow this first task. The means of guiding will follow and they will serve to flex, place and finally coordinate the strength and movements of the horse. Thus, fifteen days to supple the section which constitutes the seat (holding the horse by the snaffle bridle, the reins separated), eight days (with the bit reins) to exercise the arms and legs, then the spurs.

A few days later comes the gallop. Thus at the end of a month, you can make your horse understand you, since already, by this preliminary exercise, you will be able to use your strength either together or separately.

You will be far from being a horseman, but none of the principles that you will have received will have been given in a haphazard manner, and all will be set on a rational basis. You will only make your horse do simple things, it is true, but you will ask them of him with the full knowledge of the facts, since there will be a beginning of coordination between your wrists and your legs. The rational exercise of your strength will eventually give you the tact which constitutes a real horseman. Once you have achieved brilliant results, far from being content with the pleasure that these more or less accelerated movements, produced by this beautiful creature, have given you, you will try to find the means of talking with him and making yourself *heard*. You will then understand that the horse is much more alert in his intelli-

gence when he is ridden by a horseman who, aside from being knowledgeable in the art of equitation, also has a share of the gift of gentleness and patience, because he will be able to transmit more easily and aptly all that he possesses of science and experience. If, on the other hand, you are brusque, if you are impatient, your movements, no matter how practised they are, will be felt, and the horse, ready to imitate you, will become violent and brusque. If you are brutal, the horse will respond to your unjust corrections by bucking and kicking, or by any other violent unsteadiness, for it is in this manner that most horses defend themselves. On the contrary, be calm, and the horse, even the most stubborn one, will become docile. If you have tact and finesse in your judgement, the horse will feel this felicitous frame of mind and will soon become saturated with your good qualities as he would have done with your defects. It is thus obvious that whosoever wishes to take on with care the education of a horse must make of this study a veritable course in morality, all the more effective since he must perforce subjugate his bad inclinations and put into practice the precept belonging to a former philosopher: *Know yourself first!* Thus the horse is able to offer man the possibility of acquiring the most useful knowledge and the one most difficult for him, for, as a profound moralist said: *How many defects do we not attribute to others that really belong to us!* How many vices, must I in turn say, do we not attribute to these interesting creatures, which are really the result of the ineptness or brusqueness on the part of the horseman?

Courage, Lord horseman! and to recompense your praiseworthy efforts, I will ask My Brother, the God of men, that you remain in His holy and worthy keeping.

Second dialogue

The Great Hippo-Théo, God of the Quadrupeds, a Horseman, and a Horse.

God: Faithful to my promise, I have come to inform myself, Lord horseman, of the results obtained by your steadfast attitude in your study of equitation. Tell me about your work, your success. This constant struggle between man and horse, has it finally been allayed? This perfect understanding, so desirable to the one as to the other, has it been achieved? All this interests me to the highest degree, So speak, Lord equerry.[1]

The Horseman: Since Your Divinity deigns to lower Himself to these details, permit me first, Great Hippo-Théo, to testify that the errors a horseman makes towards his horse are, in the main, due to the ineptness of his teachers. Their systems, founded on principles taken haphazardly, instil errors in their pupils, whose effect is always to the detriment of the mount. But before giving greater details, allow my steed, Great Judge, to express verbally his opinion.

The Horse: I have the gift of speech only in the presence of my Creator. This is to my regret and to yours. What mistakes could I have avoided! My advice, to our common interest, would have signalled the uselessness, even the danger, of certain principles instilled by your initial teachers. Always desirous to help and even anticipate your intentions, I deplored a thousand times your forced and unnatural movements. While cursing your incompetent teachers, I forgave you your involuntary mistakes, and my indulgence to you, based on your perseverance to learn equitation in all its verity, was not in vain. You finally discovered the teacher you needed; the soundness of his principles and his practical methods can be easily analysed. Explain them to the Great Hippo-Théo, since it is from you that He wishes to learn the truth. If necessary, I will aid your memory.

The Horseman: Amenable to the advice of Your Divinity, I applied to the most famous teachers of equitation. Diligent in my lessons, religiously attentive to their practical and oral demonstrations, I made use of everything. However, no progress crowned my efforts. My ideas remained confused, my movements awkward, without a determined goal. Two months of useless work aroused disgust in me. I would certainly have abandoned teachers, horses and equitation had I not remembered your last words, which pulled me out of this moral torpor. You suggested that I proceed from the simple to

---

[1] He now refers to the horseman as *écuyer* (equerry), stressing the fact that the horseman has improved his horsemanship, if not become an accomplished horseman. It should be noted that the term *écuyer* was used (and is still used) in France to denote someone who teaches equitation, who is an accomplished rider, and who managed the stables of royalty, of a member of the nobility, or of the bourgeoisie when in the nineteenth century they began to be seriously involved and the horse became a pleasure horse.

In his *Dictionnaire raisonné* Baucher defines *écuyer* as follows: 'The term *écuyer* is used to designate a man who is able to school a horse, manage and ride him with precision, and be aware of the means which brought about these results.'

the complex. My teachers, on the contrary, without any preamble, made me do *doublés*,[2] changes of lead, and other airs of *manège*, etc.

God: I was aware that the art of riding had fallen into decadence; but I was far from believing that the art of teaching had fallen into such disregard. What annoyances for the horseman! and what torments for the horse! How is the poor creature supposed to function, subject to a horseman himself ignorant of what he is supposed to do? But do continue, for pity's sake, horseman.

The Horseman: Strongly influenced by your advice, Lord, I realized that my first lessons had nothing rational in them. I wandered through all the *manèges* of various countries and discovered the same inadequacy of training! Certain aspects of the art were cultivated, but the most important ones were neglected. Everywhere I found ignorance, repetition and contradiction. Occasionally some rays of light shone through, though too few to reveal the truth. Then, in this blind world, they constantly came up against contradictions. The principles of one were condemned by another, and this was done without a justifying motive, simply out of a systematic contradiction. What can one do in such an inextricable labyrinth? Give up? No! Go on! Go on! cried an imperious voice within me. Seek the thread of Ariadne, lost by your precursors, and you will emerge triumphant.

God: Undoubtedly, your perseverance has been repaid. You have found conscientious equerries who, through their profound studies, have discovered the true principles of their art! What country gave you these new teachers?

The Horseman: These able equerries are French. Their first lessons, in agreement with the kindly advice Your Divinity gave me, allowed me to recognize at the very beginning the superiority of my teachers. Exercises well devised to supple my limbs inclined my body to place itself naturally on the horse. From then on there was no awkwardness in my de-

portment; I sat upright and balanced in the saddle and, thus, was easy and regular in my movements.

The Horse: Permit me, my Divine Master, to verify the rapidity with which my horseman obtained the results, the advantages of which affect me to a large extent.

The Horseman: I am delighted, Great Hippo-Théo, that my steed also appreciated these first attempts which were the result of the clear and precise presentation of the new method. The principles and the aim of equestrian science were explained to me. Instilled with old ideas, I could have easily confused them with the new ones. But able teachers guarded against this danger and substituted the old principles with their new ones. For example, they said to me: 'Everything depends upon the position the horseman gives to his mount. The horse executes the movements only if his head has been placed properly.'

God: Lord horseman, this principle is true and will rapidly become an axiom. I approve of it all the more because it obviously denotes that the horse is intelligent. At the beginning of your instruction you demanded from your mount movements which could not be performed due to your ignorance; by executing them, your horse's intelligence made up for your sparse scientific knowledge, because it found the means of understanding your intention. Better instructed today, you are familiar with the position that will determine a given movement of the horse. Instead of employing excessive strength, you indicate your intention by placing your horse's head properly, and you are obeyed. Thus the creature has understood you, since he executes the desired movement of his own accord and without any further request on your part. Besides, this principle has the advantage of forestalling the horse. It gives him the time to understand the effects of the strength employed by the equerry. This preliminary warning avoids pushing the horse, so to speak, into a mode of action which, without

---

[2] This expression used by Baucher probably refers to work at the half-pass on the diagonals of the arena.

mentioning the dangers it entails, bears a certain inconvenience in that it casts uncertainty and irregularity in its execution. Give us your advice, quadruped.

The Horse: What Your Divinity has just stated is certainly the truth; however, as an interested party, I venture to add this proof in support. Were we not intelligent, how could we know that we have to move forward when an unskilled and awkward horseman jerks the bridle sharply when he wants to get us to move? How could we finish the movements begun when the legs and the hands of our horseman are in flagrant contradiction to his commands? I certify that my master, since these new teachers put him on the right path, has now observed that all my hesitations have ceased. Without any difficulty, I execute all that he wishes, for I know that all his demands always conform to those laws which govern my organism.

The Horseman: The easy and regular movements of my steed had already persuaded me that I had succeeded in speaking clearly to his intelligence. His verbal approbation now makes my conviction solid. To what do I owe these happy results? To three months of hardworking lessons. To repeat, my teacher first applied himself to the task of placing me properly and naturally on the horse. I acquired a steady seat and the combination of various movements so limbered my nervous system, that all the positions of my body necessary to determine those of my horse became, so to speak, natural to me. A magnetic relationship of some sort was established between my organism and that of my mount. Thus no muscular contraction was imparted from one to the other. It followed that I would right away reason out and coordinate the action by means of my aids, and their correct use enabled me later to resolve the most difficult problems in equitation.

God: Sire horseman, your success is evident. Why is it that the excellent teaching methods that brought this about are not followed everywhere? I still see numerous horsemen who neglect your practical methods. They employ their strength and that of their horses without worrying about the combination of these two forces, nor about the relationship which must be established for the indispensable identification of these two organisms. From this derive these countless difficulties which hamper progress. One horseman becomes disheartened because his efforts are sterile; another cries out success because chance favoured him. Fated disgust! Ephemeral success! One wants to terminate, the other neglects the means. But let us hope that enlightenment will shine in this chaotic situation and dissipate the darkness of routine. Continue your exposition, good horseman; I await the rest with interest.

The Horseman: Up to now, Lord, my teachers developed only my mechanism; now they will devote themselves to my intelligence. Their lucid explanations and their ready answers to my opportune questions will make my role easier. Former treatises tell us: 'Movements determine the horse. Some horses have hard mouths.' The meaning of these sentences was always incomprehensible to me, or else their literal sense was for me a cause for error and discouragement. My movements, such as they were, never brought about those of my mount in the desired sense; and these words '*hard mouth*' betrayed to me a natural defect whose elimination seemed impossible to me.

My teachers made my uncertainties dissipate by expressing themselves clearly and rationally. They said to me: 'The actions of the horseman determine that the horse take the position appropriate to the movement. Some horses are heavy in the hand.'

This slight modification of the sentence seems infantile: however, it has a far-reaching implication. As a matter of fact, the horseman has no more doubts; he knows the aim of his movements and gives the correct position to his horse; there ensues no discouragement and the natural and localized defect of the horse becomes quite simply a poor distribution of weight that can be modified. The means of achieving this double goal are clearly indicated, as you shall see later. As to the universal

Baucher's lateral flexions. (Paul Morand (ed.) *Anthologie de la litterature equestre* (Paris, Oliver Perrier, 1966))

adoption of this new method, it tests the obstacles that all innovations naturally encounter. Some reject this new method because they do not understand it, lacking the appropriate education; others reject it out of vanity. Ignorance and jealousy shake hands in order to hinder the advance of art, which, first at a standstill, soon retrogresses.

God: I cannot understand the blindness of some equerries who are fond of denigrating the useful innovations of everyone else, instead of applying their undeniable talent to the triumph of correct principles. Would their scientific knowledge, their reputation be diminished because they applauded the felicitous discoveries of another? Such a false rationalization could only be inspired by a mistaken vanity; but the result is not less opposed to the general interest. Furthermore, you are right, Lord horseman, to deplore a similar state of things. Be it as it may, let us return to your new system of learning and ask your steed what advantages he derives from it.

The Horse: I was easily able, My Lords, to appreciate this method, since it gave back to me my liberty of movement. My master, compelled to retain exactly a stipulated distance between me and the horse preceding me, must frequently have recourse to his legs and wrists. This constant exercise gives his aids the desirable pliability; their well-directed action in no way constrains me. The natural position of my horseman makes me appear lighter and his daily progress, by increasing his scientific knowledge, diminishes my own tasks. It is with pleasure that I obey his commands now clearly given.

The Horseman: I proceed with the analyses of my new teachers, Divine Hippo-Théo. They attack and reduce to nothing this pernicious error that has been so long perpetuated: 'There are horses that have hard mouths.' Going back to the cause by studying the effect, one discovers the error of this sentence. By what does one recognize the apparent hardness of the mouth? By the resistance of the horse to the action of the bit. This is what makes superficial

observers believe that the insensitivity of the bars is the cause of this resistance. They then fabricated all sorts of devices, each one more cruel than the other, in order to triumph over the bars. The result was zero. And disgust once born, the disheartened equerry casts aside his horses without trying to find out if the lack of success of his attempts were not due to the false direction he took. My teachers, in order to find the truth, abandoned the general path and asked themselves whether it is reasonable to assume that the strong pressure to make the horse obey is felt only on one part of his body, and whether it is reasonable to assume that this part alone is responsible for the execution of our commands. A close examination of the mechanism of the horse shows that all the parts of his body are a harmonious whole and that their convergence is essential to all the horse's movements. From this it follows that constraint of one part of the body will be felt on the entire body and hamper his movements. If this is the case, then there exists the problem of poor conformation and the only way to combat the resistance which ensues is to rectify this vicious structure.

God: This assumption, which is perfectly logical, must have led your teacher to a correct conclusion.

The Horseman: And the conclusion, Lord is this: the resistances that the horse makes to the bit are due to the difficulty he experiences in executing the required movement, which is the result of a disharmony in his organism. By re-establishing a general unity in the neck, the back, the hocks — the entire body, so to speak — one destroys the resistance and the horse, who a short while earlier seemed insensitive to the extreme pressure of the bit, now gives in at the first invitation of the hand. Experience proves this every day. It is established that this sensitivity, more or less, of the mouth has nothing to do with the horse's resistances, and that this hard mouth that has condemned so many horses is nothing but a chimera.

God: This conclusion is exact, Lord horseman. To strengthen this opinion, I will point out that the membrane that is called periosteum and which covers the bones alone gives to the bars their sensitivity. Since this membrane plays the same role in all horses, one cannot admit any differences in the consequences. Let us go on to the condemnation of the hardness of the mouth. You wisely attribute the difficulty of handling a horse to his poor conformation, but your human vanity prevents you from attributing the initial responsibility of these disorders to man. Who else but man permitted the degeneration of the equine species that I created so perfectly? Your negligence allowed chance to decide the direction of breeding; and from there developed progressive degeneration and your horses with poor conformation. I note with pleasure that there can be found, among men, a judicious observer who put his finger on the wound and found its remedy. Tell us, quadruped, if you have already felt the benefits of this innovation?

The Horse: Let Your Divinity Himself be the judge. The former system, instead of helping my weak points, demanded from me blindly an impossible obedience. My physical handicap, set up as a moral vice, irritated my horseman who, going beyond measure, constantly tortured me. My mouth, alleged to be insensitive, was made bloody, my bars in shreds, under the action of a murderous bit. My efforts against nature exhausted me to the point of putting me in the position of either defending myself or letting myself be crippled. Everything has changed with the new method: my master asks of me only the correct use of my strength and directs it wisely. This physical well-being affects my moral well-being, and my imperfections yield little by little to this felicitous influence. I am sure that in no time I will be able to do what my brothers, more favoured by nature, are able to do.

God: I am delighted by these happy results. They must, Lord horseman, be a powerful spur in the termination of the schooling of your steed. Explain to me quickly your method of execution.

The Horseman: All our principles are based on reasoning and experience. Equitation, like all the other arts, can expect progress only if it stays within the truth. The slightest deviation can, in the long run, lead it astray to the point where the sound path disappears and the equerry seeks his goal in vain.

We sought a point of departure that is exact and fundamental, and a sure goal. We begin by appreciating and coordinating the strength of the horse. And by means of this well-directed power, we obtain the transference of the necessary weight. Coordination of strength and weight brings about the balance of the horse and lightness in the hand. Later, balance of the mass gives harmony to his movements. Once lightness has been achieved, we rapidly reach our goal: the horseman sets the position and the horse executes the movement.

God: A method that is so rational must lead you to triumph over the difficulties involving *haute école*, as they are in inverse ratio to the schooling of the horse.

The Horseman: My initiation to the method, Great Hippo-Théo, is still too recent for all equestrian problems to have become familiar to me. But I have seen my teachers obtain results which astonish all the equerries and would delight Your Divinity. I fear to abuse your kindness by prolonging our discussion if I give You the description of these exercises. Barring contrary orders, I will pass over them in silence.

God: As God of horses, Lord horseman, nothing that touches upon the interest of this species is indifferent to me. But my intimate knowledge of the qualities with which I endowed them tell me what they can do. Impart to me only the methods by which you utilize the resources of this precious creature that I placed under your control.

The Horseman: Since the head and the neck are the natural compass and the helm of the horse, we apply ourselves to making them our only guide. By means of various flexions, the jaw, having become softly mobile, allows the head to be placed vertically; the suppled neck secures the flexibility it needs. Work first on foot, then on horseback, unites and harmonizes the forehand and the hindquarters, and attaches the rest of the body to the neck.

Each part of the horse has its own role; the hindquarters are the impulsive force, the forehand the guiding force.

While with his legs the horseman provokes impulsion, his hand guides the movement of the horse.

This perfect unity established between legs and hand results in an accord between weight and strength, that is, lightness, mother of every easy execution. This is, Great Hippo-Théo, a quick resumé of our method. Permit my faithful steed to add his own reflection.

The Horse: Among other advantages, the new system is one which combines the education of my master as well as of myself. Initiated by the same lessons, we adopt the same principles. My instinct is in continuous contact with the intelligence of my master and uses him as model. It thus follows that the progress of one carries with it the progress of the other. The horseman becomes proud of his mount and the horse, recognizing the benefits of the education acquired, devotes to his master an obedience that is all the greater in that it has become easier.

God: I leave you now, Sire horseman. My advice is from now on useless to you. You have taken the good course. Your intelligence is a sure guarantee of your perseverance. You have understood the nature and the destiny of the horse. Routine disappears and your method will banish the disorders which had made necessary my intervention between man and horse. Let each one take up his role once more. Horseman, remember that *intelligence obliges*,[3] and that you have to make the future forget mankind's past errors, far too prolonged, with respect to your noble steed.

---

[3] This is a parody of *noblesse oblige*.

Postscript

In the final chapter of *Baucher et son Ecole* (1948), entitled 'And Today?', Decarpentry maintained that *bauchérisme* (as the term is used in France to denote disciples of Baucher or modified Baucher) was still in evidence in France after World War II. It is still used today. *Bauchéristes* can be found among many army officers. One name especially comes to mind, namely that of Etienne Beudant who spent much of his life in Algeria as a soldier and horseman. It is through General Faverot de Kerbrech that Beudant was initiated into *bauchérisme*. His two books, *Extérieur et Haute Ecole* (1921) and *Main sans jambes . . .* (1929, reprinted by Jean-Michel Place in 1987), reveal his devotion to many of Baucher's tenets. As was the case with his two masters, Baucher and Kerbrech, Beudant's primary goal was to render the horse light and pleasant to ride, especially in preparation for outdoor riding. While this might appear as a contradiction when one remembers that Baucher's riding was executed in the *manège* and that he performed *haute école* riding in the circus, it does not mitigate the fact that in the final analysis Baucher's concern in the training of horses was to flex them and render them light, well-balanced, and pleasant to ride, which is precisely what many of his contemporaries did and those succeeding him still do. One criticism which could be levelled against Baucher is for his insistence that no equerry before him had succeeded in explaining in precise terms *how* one goes about flexing the horse. It goes without saying that horsemen throughout the ages wanted a light, well-balanced, and pleasant horse to ride and used various flexing exercises to accomplish this. The difference between Baucher and many of his successors is one of degree and centres around the uses to which the horse is put.

Civilian horsemen as well, both professionals and skilled amateurs, continue to make use of *bauchérisme*. Many, according to Decarpentry, are not always aware that they are pursuing *bauchérisme*; while others, who think that they are disciples of Baucher, are in fact totally unaware of many of his methods. For example, says Decarpentry, 'the horses of these so-called *bauchéristes* remain more often than not outside of the realm of the *mise en main* [the *ramener*]'.

The instructor who coached me and my horse for a while, an Argentinian ex-cavalryman, in many respects belongs to the category of *bauchéristes* who are unaware of Baucher and his method. This instructor's constant 'attacks' with the spur, the severe use of the *ramener*, the neutralization of the strength of the horse between hands and legs, are, indeed, reminiscent of the Baucher of the *nouvelle méthode*.

While Baucher is still regarded in France as an important figure in equitation and printings of his final or modified teachings are in great demand, much of the training of today's French horsemen and horsewomen for competitive dressage is more in the idiom of d'Aure and l'Hotte. While the aim is competition, be it in steeplechasing, three-day events, or dressage, the underlying pursuit is akin to l'Hotte's motto: 'Calme, en avant et droit' (calm, forwards and straight). [1] Thus, with d'Aure, these modern-day horsemen and horsewomen realize that *manège* riding is a means rather than an end.

In the English-speaking world, men such as Henry Wynmalen dismiss some of Baucher's techniques of flexion, especially his 'flexion in hand', that is, when the horse's jaw is flexed by means of the bridle rein while the trainer is on foot. Like many of Baucher's contemporaries, Wynmalen condemns the notion of making the horse too much of a prisoner between legs and hands. He also condemns Baucher's excessive attacks by means of the spur. Thus for Wynmalen, as it had been for d'Aure, *manège* riding is a means to an end; it is a preparation for outdoor riding.

Jean Froissard, in the US edition of his *Equitation*, states: 'Dressage of a young horse means giving him education combined with good manners, helping him develop his physical and moral qualities, hence rendering him easy to use and pleasant to ride.' This recommendation is no different from that of Baucher. Froissard criticizes the use or misuse of the term 'dressage' on the part of Americans in particular, who use it almost exclusively to refer to competitive dressage tests. According to Froissard, 'dressage' is training and schooling of the horse, ending with a 'dressage test' (*épreuve de dressage*), which is 'just exactly what it says: a test of the accomplishments of the horse's dressage' — Baucher's ultimate goal.

---

[1] L'Hotte's precept has become the title of François Nourissier's novel published by Grasset in 1988.

Bibliography

Aubert, P.A. *Quelques Observations sur le système de M. Baucher pour dresser les chevaux*, Paris, Leneveu, 1842.

D'Aure, Antoine Cartier, *Cours d'Equitation*, Paris, Bureau du Journal des Haras et des Chasses, 1853.

D'Aure, Antoine Cartier, *Cours d'Equitation*, Paris, Emile Hazan, 1962.

D'Aure, Antoine Cartier, *Observations sur la nouvelle méthode*, Paris, Leneveu, 1842.

D'Aure, Antoine Cartier, *Traité d'Equitation*, Paris, Leclère, 1834.

Baucher, François, *Oeuvres complètes*, Paris, Dumaine, 1854.

Baucher, François, *Oeuvres complètes*, Paris, Dumaine, 1859.

Beudant, Etienne, *Extérieure et Haute Ecole*, Paris, Jean-Michel Place, 1987.

Beudant, Etienne, *Mains sans jambes . . . suivi de Dressage du Cheval de selle*, Paris, Jean-Michel Place, 1987.

Decarpentry, Albert, *Academic Equitation*, London, J.A. Allen, 1987.

Decarpentry, Albert, *Baucher et son école*, Paris, Lamarre, 1948.

Decarpentry, Albert, *Equitation académique*, Paris, Henri Neveu, 1949.

Decarpentry, Albert, *Maîtres Ecuyers du Manège de Saumur*, Paris, Emile Hazan, 1954.

Faverot de Kerbrech, *Dressage méthodique du cheval de selle, d'après les derniers enseignements de F. Baucher*, Paris, J. Rothchild, 1891.

Faverot de Kerbrech, *Dressage mèthodique*, Paris, Emile Hazan, 1958.

Felton, Sidney, *Masters of Equitation*, London, J.A. Allen, 1962.

Fillis, James, *Journal de dressage*, Paris, Flammarion, 1903.

Froissard, Jean, *Equitation*, Hollywood, Wilshire Book, 1972.

Gerhardt, Adolphe, *Manuel d'Equitation analyse raisonnée du bauchérisme*, Paris, Jean-Michel Place, 1987.

Harris, Charles, *Riding and Dressage*, London, Harris, 1981.

Henriquet, Michel, *Les Maîtres de l'équitation classique*, Paris, André Gérard, 1974.

L'Hotte, Alexis, *Questions équestres*, Paris, Plon, 1906.

L'Hotte, Alexis, *Questions équestres*, Paris, Emile Hazan, 1960.

L'Hotte, Alexis, *Un Officier de cavalerie – Souvenirs*, Paris, Plon, 1906.

L'Hotte, Alexis, *Officier de cavalerie*, Paris, Emile Hazan, 1958.

Joussaume, André, *Dressage*, Paris, Editions du fer à cheval, 1951.

Joussaume, André, *Progressive Dressage*, London, J.A. Allen, 1978.

Licart, Jean, *Basic Equitation*, London, J.A. Allen, 1968.

Monteilhet, André, *Les Maîtres de l'oeuvre équestre*, Paris, Odège, 1979.

Oliveira, Nuño, *Classical Principles of the Art of Riding*, London, Howley & Russell.

Oliveira, Nuño, *Haute Ecole*, London, J.A. Allen, 1965.

Oliveira, Nuño, *Réflexions sur l'art équestre*, Paris, Crépin-Leblond, 1965.

Oliveira, Nuño, *Reflections on Equestrian Art*, London, J.A. Allen, 1976.

Podhajsky, Alois, *Die Klassische Reitkunst*, Munich, Nymphenburger, 1965.

Podhajsky, Alois, *Die Spanische Hofreitschule*, Vienna, Hans Hammer, 1948.

Salins, Jean de, *Epaule en dedans*, Paris, Emile

Hazan, 1957.

Saurel, Etienne, *Histoire de l'equitation*, Paris, Stock, 1971.

Saurel, Etienne, *Pratique de l'équitation d'après les Maîtres français*, Paris, Flammarion, 1964.

Seunig, Waldemar, *Horsemanship*, New York, Doubleday, 1956.

Seunig, Waldemar, *Meister der Reitkunst*, Heidenheim, Erich Hoffmann, 1960.

Steinbrecht, Gustav, *Le Gymnase du cheval*, Paris, Epiac, 1963.

Thomas, Jacques-Léonard Clément, *De l'Equitation militaire de l'ancienne et de la nouvelle école*, Paris, Pagnerre, 1846. (First published in *Le National*, 6, 10, 16, and 23 September 1845.)

Weyrother, Max Ritter von, *Hinterlassene Schriften*, Hildesheim, Olms Presse, 1977.

Wynmalen, Henry, *Equitation*, London, Country Life, 1938.

Wynmalen, Henry, *Dressage*, Hollywood, Wilshire, 1972.

General index

Index to the translations